Moral Consciousness and Communicative Action

Moral Consciousness and Communicative Action

Jürgen Habermas

translated by Christian Lenhardt and
Shierry Weber Nicholsen
introduction by Thomas McCarthy

The MIT Press, Cambridge, Massachusetts

This translation © 1990 Massachusetts Institute of Technology
This work originally appeared in German under the title *Moralbewusstsein und kommunikatives Handeln*, © 1983 by Suhrkamp Verlag, Frankfurt am Main, Federal Republic of Germany. The author has added the essay "Morality and Ethical Life" for the English-language edition of this book.

This book was set in Baskerville by DEKR Corporation and printed and bound in the United States of America.

Library of Congress Cataloging-in-Publication Data

Habermas, Jürgen.
  [Moralbewusstein und kommunikatives Handeln. English]
  Moral consciousness and communicative action / Jürgen Habermas;
  translated by Christian Lenhardt and Shierry Weber Nicholsen;
  introduction by Thomas McCarthy.

    p. cm.—(Studies in contemporary German social thought)
  Translation of: Moralbewusstein und kommunikatives Handeln.
  Includes bibliographical references.
  ISBN 0-262-08192-X (hb) 0-262-58118-3 (pb)
   1. Ethics. 2. Communication—Moral and ethical aspects. 3. Act
(Philosophy) I. Title. II. Series.
  B3258.H323M6713   1990
  170—dc20   89-29746
                                     CIP

10 9 8

Contents

Introduction

Thomas McCarthy

In his approach to moral theory Habermas is closest to the Kantian tradition.[1] Like Kant, he distinguishes the types of practical reasoning and corresponding types of "ought" proper to questions about what is practically expedient, ethically prudent, and morally right.[2] Calculations of rational choice generate recommendations relevant to the pursuit of contingent purposes in the light of given preferences. When serious questions of value arise, deliberation on who one is, and who one wants to be, yields ethical advice concerning the good life. If questions of justice are involved, fair and impartial consideration of conflicting interests results in judgments concerning what is right or just. And like Kant, Habermas regards questions of the last type, rather than specifically ethical matters, to be the proper domain of moral theory. This is not to say that ethical deliberation is irrational or exhibits no general structures of its own.[3] But it is to say that the disappearance of value-imbued cosmologies and the disintegration of sacred canopies have opened the question "How should I (or one, or we) live?" to the irreducible pluralism of modern life. To suppose that all of the questions of the good life dealt with under the rubric of classical ethics—questions of happiness and virtue, character and ethos, community and tradition—could be answered once and for all, and by philosophers, is no longer plausible. Matters of individual or group self-understanding and self-realization, rooted as they are in particular life histories and traditions, do not admit of general theory; and pru-

maybe it does

dential deliberation on the good life, moving as it does within the horizons of particular lifeworlds and forms of life, does not yield universal prescriptions. In fact, without its metaphysical underpinnings, phronesis can be difficult to distinguish from the commonsense of a given way of life—with its built-in bias for the way things are and distrust of individuals who morally criticize the accepted way of doing things.[4]

what is that?

If taking modern pluralism seriously means giving up the idea that philosophy can single out a privileged way of life, or provide an answer to the question "How should I (we) live?" that is valid for everyone, it does not, in Habermas's view, preclude a general theory of a much narrower sort, namely a theory of justice. The aim of the latter is to reconstruct the moral point of view as the perspective from which competing normative claims can be fairly and impartially adjudicated. Like Kant, Habermas understands this type of practical reasoning as universal in import: it is geared to what everyone could rationally will to be a norm binding on everyone alike. His "discourse ethics," however, replaces Kant's categorical imperative with a procedure of moral argumentation: normative justification is tied to reasoned agreement among those subject to the norm in question.[5] The central principle is that for a norm to be valid, its consequences for the satisfaction of everyone's interests must be acceptable to all as participants in a practical discourse. This shifts the frame of reference from Kant's solitary, reflecting moral consciousness to the community of moral subjects in dialogue. Whether a norm is justifiable cannot be determined monologically, but only through discursively testing its claim to fairness. Unlike Rawls's original position, however, practical discourse does not feature rational egoists prudently contracting behind a veil of ignorance[6]—a procedure that can itself be carried out monologically—but moral agents trying to put themselves in each other's shoes. While models of ideal role-taking do, then, capture an aspect of Kant's fundamental intuition usually neglected in contract models, they tend to be insufficiently cognitive. Habermas's discourse model, by requiring that perspective-taking be general and reciprocal, builds the moment of empathy *into* the procedure of coming to a reasoned agreement: each must put him-

phronesis vs. sophia in Nicom. Ethics ;
practical wisdom, knowing how to apply
principles to concrete situations, takes time +
experience .

or herself into the place of everyone else in discussing whether a proposed norm is fair to all. And this must be done publicly; arguments played out in the individual consciousness or in the theoretician's mind are no substitute for real discourse.[7]

While these remarks may serve roughly to locate Habermas on the map of contemporary moral philosophy, they do not reflect the breadth of the project outlined in this volume. Persistent misinterpretations to the contrary notwithstanding, Habermas is not trying to renew transcendental philosophy.[8] In fact, there are few moral philosophers writing today who take as seriously the relation of conceptual issues to empirical research. The form this takes in the present work is an attempt to connect discourse ethics to the theory of social action via an examination of research in the social psychology of moral and interpersonal development. Starting with Kohlberg's account of the development of moral judgment, Habermas argues that the model of natural stages is plausible up to the point of the postconventional break at which the social world loses its quasi-natural validity. From that point we are dealing with stages of reflection, which have to be assessed and ordered primarily on the basis of moral-philosophical, rather than empirical-psychological, considerations. Focusing then on the preconventional and conventional stages of moral judgment whose psychological "reality" is supported by the available evidence, Habermas attempts to anchor them in his theory of communicative action.[9] The connecting links are provided by Selman's account of sociocognitive development in relation to stages of social perspective taking, which Habermas reformulates in terms of structures of social interaction. The point of this chain of argument is to connect structures of moral judgment to structures of social interaction in such a way that their developmental-logical features stand out more clearly.[10]

As the trajectory of argument around Rawls's notion of reflective equilibrium illustrates, the burden of proof on any moral theorist who hopes to ground a conception of justice in anything more universal than the "settled convictions" of our political cultures is enormous.[11] Because Habermas wants to do just that, the links he forges to action theory are crucial; they are meant to show that our basic moral intuitions spring from something deeper and more universal than contingent features of our tradition. In his view, the task of moral theory is reflectively to articulate, refine, and elaborate the intuitive grasp of the normative presuppositions of social interaction that belongs to the repertoire of competent social actors in any society. The basic moral intuitions the theorist reconstructs are, as Aristotle noted, acquired in the process of socialization, but they include an "abstract core" that is more than culture-specific. Members of our species become individuals in and through being socialized into networks of reciprocal social relations, so that personal identity is from the start interwoven with relations of mutual recognition. This interdependence brings with it a reciprocal vulnerability that calls for guarantees of mutual consideration to preserve both the integrity of individuals and the web of interpersonal relations in which they form and maintain their identities. Both of these concerns—with the inviolability of the person and the welfare of the community—have been at the heart of traditional moralities.

In the Kantian tradition, respect for the integrity and dignity of the individual has been tied to the freedom of moral subjects to act upon norms they themselves accept as binding on the basis of their own insight, and concern for the common good has been linked to the impartiality of laws that can be accepted by everyone on that basis. In Habermas's discourse ethics, which bases the justification of norms on the uncoerced, rational agreement of those subject to them, equal respect for individuals is reflected in the right of each participant to respond with a "yes" or "no" to the reasons offered by way of justification. Concern for the common good is reflected in the requirement of general and reciprocal perspective taking: in seeking mutual agreement, each attempts to get beyond an egocentric viewpoint by taking into account the interests of others and giving them equal weight to his or her own.[12] It is true that *general* norms, justified from the standpoint of impartiality, will of necessity abstract from the specific circumstances of concrete cases. They are not meant to answer questions of the type "What should I do here and now?" But, Habermas argues, this does not result in the yawning gap between form and content that neo-Aristotelians rush to fill with phronesis. For the moral point of view in the form of considerations of impartiality and fairness can guide the context-sensitive application of general norms as well. And this will require at least a partial reversal of the abstractions required in justifying them—for example, through attention to all of the relevant features of a case when determining which general norm is appropriate to it.[13]

This does not mean that Habermas ignores the neo-Aristotelian challenges to Kantian reconstructivism, the objections that have been raised against the abstraction it fosters from everything that gives content to our ethical life. These objections confront us with the choice of either returning to some version of Aristotelianism or modifying the Kantian approach so as to give them, as far as possible, their due. Discourse ethics takes the latter tack. On the one hand, in contrast to ethics of the good life, it confines itself to the limited task of reconstructing the moral point of view, leaving *all* concrete moral and ethical judgments to participants themselves.[14] On the other hand, locating the common core of morality in the normative presuppositions of communicative interaction, it develops a thoroughly intersubjectivist interpretation of the moral point of view: practical discourse as a reflective continuation of communicative interaction preserves that common core. Rather than contractual agreements among "unencumbered" individuals with arbitrarily chosen ends, it involves processes of reflective argumentation among previously socialized subjects whose needs and interests are themselves open to discussion and transformation. The egocentric perspective is treated not as primary but as derivative; autonomy is conceptualized in relation to embeddedness in shared forms of life. In this way, practical discourse presupposes and draws upon the normative structures of social interaction; it does not cut the bonds of social integration as do social contract models.

On the strength of this reconceptualization of what is involved in coming to a reasoned agreement about moral issues, communicative ethics, though Kantian in inspiration, attempts to capture at least the structural aspects of the common good. In Habermas's account, solidarity is the other side of justice, a complementary perspective to that of equal treatment. But this is not the notion of solidarity that figures in traditionalistic models: "As a component of universalistic morality, solidarity loses its merely particular meaning, in which it is limited to the internal relationships of a collectivity ethnocentrically isolated from other groups—the character of forced willingness to sacrifice oneself for a collective system that is always present in premodern forms of solidarity . . . [where] fellowship is entwined with followership. . . . Justice conceived in postconventional terms can converge with solidarity, as its other side, only when solidarity has been transformed in the light of the idea of a general, discursive formation of will."[15]

Notes

1. In addition to the essays collected in this volume, relevant materials include "Wahrheitstheorien," in J. Habermas, *Vorstudien und Ergänzungen zur Theorie des kommunikativen Handelns* (Frankfurt, 1984), pp. 127–183; "Moral Development and Ego-Identity," in J. Habermas, *Communication and the Evolution of Society* (Boston, 1979), pp. 69–94; "Justice and Solidarity: On the Discussion Concerning Stage 6," in T. Wren, ed., *The Moral Domain* (Cambridge, Mass., 1989); "Law and Morality," in *The Tanner Lectures on Human Values*, vol. 8 (Salt Lake City and Cambridge, 1988), pp. 217–279; "Kohlberg and Neo-Aristotelianism," paper read at the Commemorative Symposium in Honor of Lawrence Kohlberg, Harvard University, spring 1988; "Individual Will-Formation in Terms of What Is Expedient, What Is Good, and What Is Just," paper read at Northwestern University, fall 1988; "Erläuterungen zur Diskursethik," unpublished manuscript.

2. See the paper "Individual Will-Formation," cited in n. 1.

3. Nor is it to say that it is any less central to practical reasoning in everyday life, which is normally concerned much more with questions of expediency and prudence than with issues of justice. Furthermore, the same action situation may be considered from more than one of these perspectives.

4. See "Kohlberg and Neo-Aristotelianism," cited in n. 1, pp. 14ff. On p. 17 Habermas writes, "Recent neo-Aristotelian approaches play quite a different role in the German and American contexts. But the conservative bias they have always had in Germany since the time of Hegel is by no means accidental."

5. In this respect, his approach is similar to that of T. M. Scanlon in "Contractualism and Utilitarianism," in A. Sen and B. Williams, eds., *Utilitarianism and Beyond* (Cambridge, 1982), pp. 103–128, but he distances himself from Scanlon's contractualist understanding of this procedure. See his remarks on this in "Justice and Solidarity," cited in n. 1.

6. Of course, Rawls's original position is intended to be a "device of [indirect] representation" and not a direct depiction of the moral reasoning of agents who have themselves adopted the moral point of view. It is precisely the latter that Habermas is after, hence his reservations regarding Rawls's approach.

7. From this standpoint, Habermas's farflung writings can be viewed as a sustained reflection on the historical, psychological, social, and cultural preconditions of institutionalizing moral-political discourse. See especially *The Structural Transformation of the Public Sphere* (Cambridge, Mass., 1989).

8. These misrepresentations often involve confusing universal claims with transcendental claims, forgetting that the latter aspire to necessity as well as universality. A glance at the natural sciences serves as a reminder that universal claims need not be based on a priori reasoning or pretend to infallibility. The shoe is actually on the other foot: on what grounds do antiuniversalists claim to know—a priori?—that there are and can be no universals of language, culture, cognition, morality, and the like? There is no obvious reason why this shouldn't be treated as an empirical-theoretical question that will have to be answered, as such questions usually are, with reference to the fate of various research programs in the human sciences. This is, at any rate, Habermas's approach.

9. The rudiments of that theory are sketched in this volume. For a fuller discussion, see J. Habermas, *The Theory of Communicative Action*, vols. 1 and 2 (Boston, 1984, 1987), especially chapters 1, 3, 5, and 6.

10. That is, Habermas wants to argue that we can and do learn to deal more adequately with moral problems, and that these learning processes can be described in genetic-structural terms.

11. See especially John Rawls, "Justice as Fairness: Political Not Metaphysical," *Philosophy and Public Affairs* 14 (1985): 223–251. To see how readily this approach lends itself to anti-Kantian interpretation, see Richard Rorty, "The Priority of Democracy to Philosophy," in M. D. Peterson and R. C. Vaughan, eds., *The Virginia Statute for Religious Freedom* (Cambridge, 1988), pp. 257–282, especially pp. 261ff.

12. Postmodernist critiques of moral universalism too often simply ignore the fact that it is precisely notions of fairness, impartiality, respect for the integrity and dignity of the individual, and the like that undergird respectful tolerance of difference by placing limits on egocentrism. Typically, such notions are simply taken for granted in antiuniversalist invocations of otherness and difference—which are, it evidently goes without saying, to be respected, not obliterated.

13. For a detailed discussion of the application of general norms from a moral point of view, see Klaus Günther, *Der Sinn für Angemessenheit: Anwendungsdiskurse in Moral und Recht* (Frankfurt, 1988).

14. Thus Habermas is critical of Rawls's derivation of two substantive principles of justice from the original position.

15. "Justice and Solidarity."

Moral Consciousness and Communicative Action

Philosophy as Stand-In and Interpreter

Master thinkers have fallen on hard times. This has been true of Hegel ever since Popper unmasked him in the forties as an enemy of the open society. It has also been intermittently true of Marx. The last to denounce Marx as a false prophet were the New Philosophers in the seventies. Today even Kant is affected by this decline. If I am correct, he is being viewed for the first time as a *maître penseur*, that is, as the magician of a false paradigm from the intellectual constraints of which we have to escape. Though among a philosophical audience there may still be a majority of scholars whose image of Kant has stayed the same, in the world outside his reputation is being eclipsed, and not for the first time, by Nietzsche.

Historically, Kantian philosophy marks the birth of a new mode of justification. Kant felt that the physics of his time and the growth of knowledge brought by it were important developments to which the philosopher had to respond. For Kant, the new science represented not some philosophically indifferent fact of life but proof of man's capacity to know. Specifically, the challenge Newtonian physics posed for philosophy was to explain how empirical knowledge is at all possible, an explanation that could not itself be empirical but had to be transcendental. What Kant calls "transcendental" is an inquiry into the a priori conditions of what makes experience possible. The specific upshot of Kant's transcendental inquiry is that those conditions are identical with the conditions of possible objects of experience. The first job for the philosopher, then, is to analyze the concepts of objects as we "always already" intuitively use them. Transcendental analysis is a nonempirical reconstruction of the a priori achievements of the cognizing subject, achievements for which there is no alternative: No experience shall be thought possible under *different* conditions. Transcendental justification has nothing to do with deduction from first principles. Rather, the hallmark of the transcendental justification is the notion that we can prove the nonsubstitutability of certain mental operations that we always already (intuitively) perform in accordance with rules.

As a master thinker, Kant fell into disfavor because he used transcendental justification to found the new discipline of epistemology. In so doing, he redefined the task, or vocation if you like, of philosophy in a more demanding way. There are two principal reasons why the Kantian view of philosophy's vocation has a dubious ring today.

The first reason has directly to do with the foundationalism of epistemology. In championing the idea of a cognition *before* cognition, Kantian philosophy sets up a domain between itself and the sciences, arrogating authority to itself. It wants to clarify the foundations of the sciences once and for all, defining the limits of what can and cannot be experienced. This is tantamount to an act of showing the sciences their proper place. I think philosophy cannot and should not try to play the role of usher.

The second reason lies in the fact that transcendental philosophy refuses to be confined to epistemology. Above and beyond analyzing the bases of cognition, the critique of pure reason is also supposed to enable us to criticize the abuses of this cognitive faculty, which is limited to phenomena. Kant replaces the substantive concept of reason found in traditional metaphysics with a concept of reason the moments of which have undergone differentiation to the point where their unity is merely formal. He sets up practical reason, judgment, and theoretical cognition in isolation from each other, giving each a foundation unto itself, with the result that philosophy is cast in the role of the highest arbiter for all matters, including culture as a whole. Kantian philosophy differentiates what Weber was to call the "value spheres of culture" (science and technology, law and morality, art and art criticism), while at the same time legitimating them within their respective limits. Thus Kant's philosophy poses as the highest court of appeal vis-à-vis the sciences and culture as a whole.[1]

There is a necessary link between the Kantian foundation-alism in epistemology, which nets philosophy the unenviable role of usher, and the ahistoricity of the conceptual system Kant superimposes on culture, which nets philosophy the equally undesirable role of a judge parceling out separate areas of jurisdiction to science, morality, and art.

Without the Kantian assumption that the philosopher can decide *questiones juris* concerning the rest of culture, this self-image collapses. . . . To drop the notion of the philosopher as knowing something about knowing which nobody else knows so well would be to drop the notion that his voice always has an overriding claim on the attention of the other participants in the conversation. It would also be to drop the notion that there is something called "philosophical method" or "philosophical technique" or "the philosophical point of view" which enables the professional philosopher, *ex officio*, to have interesting views about, say, the respectability of psychoanalysis, the legitimacy of certain dubious laws, the resolution of moral dilemmas, the soundness of schools of historiography or literary criticism, and the like.[2]

Richard Rorty's impressive critique of philosophy assembles compelling metaphilosophical arguments in support of the view that the roles Kant the master thinker had envisaged for philosophy, namely those of usher and judge, are too big for it. While I find myself in agreement with much of what Rorty says, I have trouble accepting his conclusion, which is that if philosophy forswears these two roles, it must also surrender the function of being the "guardian of rationality." If I understand Rorty, he is saying that the new modesty of philosophy involves the abandonment of any claim to reason—the very claim that has marked philosophical thought since its inception. Rorty not only argues for the demise of philosophy; he also unflinchingly accepts the end of the belief that ideas like truth or the unconditional with their transcending power are a necessary condition of humane forms of collective life.

Implied by Kant's conception of formal, differentiated reason is a theory of modernity. Modernity is characterized by a

rejection of the substantive rationality typical of religious and
metaphysical worldviews and by a belief in procedural rationality and its ability to give credence to our views in the three
areas of objective knowledge, moral-practical insight, and aesthetic judgment. What I am asking myself is this: Is it true that
this (or a similar) concept of modernity becomes untenable
when you dismiss the claims of a foundationalist theory of
knowledge?

What follows is an attempt to narrate a story that might help
put Rorty's criticism of philosophy in perspective. Granted, by
going this route I cannot settle the controversy. What I can do
is throw light on some of its presuppositions. At the outset
(section 1 below) I will look at Hegel's critique of Kantian
foundationalism and the substitution of a dialectical mode of
justification for Kant's transcendental one. Next (section 2) I
will retrace some of the lines of criticism and self-criticism that
have emerged in the Kantian and Hegelian traditions. In section 3 I will dwell on a more radical form of criticism origi-
nating in pragmatist and hermeneuticist quarters, a form of
attack that repudiates Kant and Hegel simultaneously. Section
4 deals with thinkers, respectable ones no less, who respond to
this situation by annulling philosophy's long-standing claim to
reason. In conclusion (section 5) I will argue that philosophy,
while well advised to withdraw from the problematic roles of
usher (*Platzanweiser*) and judge, can and ought to retain its
claim to reason, provided it is content to play the more modest
roles of stand-in (*Platzhalter*) and interpreter.

1

Hegel fashioned his dialectical mode of justification in delib-
erate opposition to the transcendental one of Kant. Hegel—
and I can only hint at this here—agrees with those who charge
that in the end Kant failed to justify or ground the pure
concepts of the understanding, for he merely culled them from
the table of forms of judgment, unaware of their historical
specificity. Thus he failed, in Hegel's eyes, to prove that the a
priori conditions of what makes experience possible are truly
necessary. In his *Phenomenology of Spirit* Hegel proposes to cor-

rect this flaw by taking a genetic approach. What Kant regarded as a unique (Copernican) turn to transcendental
reflection becomes in Hegel a general mechanism for turning
consciousness back upon itself. This mechanism has been
switched on and off time and time again in the development
of spirit. As the subject becomes conscious of itself, it destroys
one form of consciousness after another. This process epito-
mizes the subjective experience that what initially appears to
the subject as a being in itself can become content only in the
forms imparted to it by the subject. The transcendental philosopher's experience is thus, according to Hegel, reenacted
naively whenever an in-itself becomes a for-the-subject. What
Hegel calls "dialectical" is the reconstruction of this recurrent
experience and of its assimilation by the subject, which gives
rise to ever more complex structures. Hegel goes beyond the
particular manifestation of consciousness that Kant analyzed,
attaining in the end knowledge that has become autonomous,
that is, absolute knowledge. This highest vantage point enables
Hegel, the phenomenologist, to witness the genesis of structures of consciousness that Kant had assumed to be timeless.

Hegel, it should be noted, exposes himself to a criticism
similar to the one he levels against Kant. Reconstructing successive forms of consciousness is one thing. Proving the necessity of their succession is quite another. Hegel is not unaware
of this gap, and he tries to close it by logical means, thereby
laying the basis for a philosophical absolutism that claims an
even grander role for philosophy than did Kant. In Hegel's
Logic philosophy's role is to effect an encyclopedic conceptual
synthesis of the diffuse chunks of content thrown up by the
sciences. In addition, Hegel picks up Kant's latent theory of
modernity, making it explicit and developing it into a critique
of the diremptive, self-contradictory features of modernity. It
is this peculiar twist that gave philosophy a new world-historical
relevance in relation to culture as a whole. And this is the stuff
of which the suspect image of Hegel as a master thinker is
made.[3]

The metaphilosophical attack on the *maîtres penseurs*, whether
its target be Hegel's absolutism or Kant's foundationalism, is a
recent phenomenon. Antecedents of it can be found in the

strands of self-criticism that have run through Kantianism and Hegelianism for quite some time. I shall comment briefly on two lines of self-criticism that I think complement each other in an interesting way.

2

In reference to Kant's transcendental philosophy there are today three distinct critical positions: the analytic one of Strawson, the constructivist one of Lorenzen, and the critical-rationalist one of Popper.

Analytic philosophy appropriates Kant by jettisoning any claim to ultimate justification (*Letztbegründung*). From the very outset it drops the objective Kant had in mind when he deduced the pure concepts of the understanding from the unity of self-consciousness. The analytic reception of Kant is confined to comprehending those concepts and rules that underlie experience insofar as it can be couched in elementary propositions. The analysis focuses on general, indispensable, conceptual preconditions that make experience possible. Unable to prove the objective validity of its basic concepts and presuppositions, this analysis nevertheless makes a universalistic claim. Redeeming it involves changing Kant's transcendental strategy of justification into. a testing procedure. If the hypothetically reconstructed conceptual system underlying experience as such is valid, not a single intelligible alternative to it can possibly exist. This means any alternative proposal will be scrutinized with a view to proving its derivative character, that is, with a view to showing that the alleged alternative inevitably utilizes portions of the very hypothesis it seeks to supplant. A strategy of argumentation like this tries to prove that the concepts and presuppositions it singles out as fundamental cannot be dispensed with. Turned modest, the transcendental philosopher of the analytic variety takes on the role of the skeptic who keeps trying to find counterexamples that might invalidate his theories.[4] In short, he acts like a hypothesis-testing scientist.

The *constructivist position* tried to compensate for the justificatory shortfall that has now opened up from the perspective of transcendental philosophy in the following way. It concedes from the start that the basic conceptual organization of experience is conventional while at the same time putting a constructivist critique of language in the service of epistemology.[5] Those conventions are considered valid that are generated methodically and therefore transparently. It should be clear that this approach lays, rather than uncovers, the foundations of cognition.

On the face of it, the *critical-rationalist position* breaks completely with transcendentalism. It holds that the three horns of the "Münchhausen trilemma"—logical circularity, infinite regress, and recourse to absolute certitude—can only be avoided if one gives up any hope of grounding or justifying whatsoever.[6] Here the notion of justification is being dislodged in favor of the concept of critical testing, which becomes the critical rationalist's equivalent for justification. In this connection I would argue that criticism is itself a procedure whose employment is never presuppositionless. That is why I think that critical rationalism, by clinging to the idea of irrefutable rules of criticism, allows a weak version of the Kantian justificatory mode to sneak into its inner precincts through the back door.[7]

Popper

Self-criticism in the Hegelian tradition has developed along lines parallel to the self-criticism among Kantians. Again, three distinct positions might be said to be represented by the young Lukács and his materialist critique of epistemology, which restricts the claim to justification of dialectics to the man-made world and excludes nature; by K. Korsch's and H. Freyer's practicism, wherein the classical relation of theory and practice is stood on its head and the "interested" perspective of creating a society of the future informs the theoretical reconstruction of social development; and finally by the negativism of Adorno, who finds in comprehensive logic of development only the proof that it is impossible to break the spell of an instrumental reason gone mad.

HEGELIAN SELF-CRIT.

I cannot examine these positions here. All I shall do is to point out certain interesting parallels between the Hegelian and Kantian strands of self-criticism. The self-criticism that begins by doubting the Kantian transcendental deduction and

the self-criticism that begins by doubting Hegel's passage to
absolute knowledge have this in common: they reject the claim
that the categorial makeup and the pattern of development of
the human spirit can be proved to be necessary. With regard
to constructivism and practicism a similar convergence occurs:
both are involved in a shift from rational reconstruction to
creative praxis, which is to make possible a theoretical recapi-
tulation of this praxis. Critical rationalism and negativism, for
their part, share something too, which is that they reject transcendental and dialectical means of cognition while at the same
time using them in a paradoxical way. One may also view these
two attempts at radical negation as showing that these two
modes of justification cannot be abolished except on penalty
of self-contradiction.

My comparison between parallel self-critical strategies to restrict the justificatory claims of transcendental and dialectical
philosophies gives rise to the following question: Do these self-
limiting tendencies merely reinforce each other, encouraging
the skeptic to reject justification all the more roundly? Or does
the retrenchment on either side to a position of diminished
justificatory objectives and strategies represent a precondition
for viewing them not as opposites but as supplementing each
other? I think the second possibility deserves serious consideration. The genetic structuralism of Jean Piaget provides an
instructive model along these lines, instructive for all philosophers, I think, but particularly those who want to remain philosophers. Piaget conceives "reflective abstraction" as that
learning mechanism which explains the transition between cognitive stages in ontogenetic development. The end point of this
development is a decentered understanding of the world. Reflective abstraction is similar to transcendental reflection in that
it brings out the formal elements hidden in the cognitive content, identifies them as the schemata that underlie the knowing
subject's action, differentiates them, and reconstructs them at
the next highest stage of reflection. Seen from a different
perspective, the same learning mechanism has a function similar to Hegel's power of negation, which dialectically supersedes
self-contradictory forms of consciousness.[8]

3

The aforementioned six positions in the tradition of Kant and Hegel stick to a claim to reason, however small in scope, however cautious in formulation. It is this final intention that sets off Popper and Lakatos from a Feyerabend and Horkheimer and Adono from a Foucault. They still say *something* about the indispensable conditions of claims to the validity of those beliefs we hold to be justified, claims that transcend all restrictions of time and place. Now any attack on the master thinkers questions this residual claim to reason and thus in essence makes a plea for the abolition of philosophy. I can explain this radical turn by taking briefly about a wholly different criticism, one that has been raised against both Kant *and* Hegel.

Its proponents can be found in *pragmatism* and *hermeneutic philosophy*. Their doubts concerning the justificatory and self-justificatory potential of philosophy operate at a more profound level than do the self-criticisms within the Kantian and Hegelian traditions. They step resolutely outside the parameters set by the philosophy of consciousness and its cognitive paradigm, which stresses the perception and representation of objects. Pragmatism and hermeneutics oust the traditional notion of the solitary subject that confronts objects and becomes reflective only by turning itself into an object. In its place they put an idea of cognition that is mediated by language and linked to action. Moreover, they emphasize the web of eveyday-life and communication surrounding "our" cognitive achievements. The latter are intrinsically intersubjective and cooperative. It is unimportant just how this web is conceptualized, whether as "form of life," "lifeworld," "practice," "linguistically mediated interaction," a "language game," "convention," "cultural background," "tradition," "effective history," or what have you. The important thing is that these commonsensical ideas, though they may function quite differently, attain a status that used to be reserved for the basic concepts of epistemology. Pragmatism and hermeneutics, then, accord a higher position to acting and speaking than to knowing. But there is more to it than that. Purposive action and linguistic communication play a qualitatively different role from that of self-reflection in the philosophy of consciousness. They have no justificatory function any more save one: to expose the need for foundational knowledge as unjustified.

Charles S. Peirce doubted that radical doubt is possible. His intentions were the same as those of Dilthey, who doubted that neutrality in interpretive understanding is possible. For Peirce problems always arise in a specific situation. They come to us, as it were. We do not go to them, for we do not fully control the totality of our practical existence. In a similar vein Dilthey argues that we cannot grasp a symbolic expression unless we have an intuitive preunderstanding of its context, for we do not have unlimited freedom to convert the unproblematic background knowledge of our own culture into explicit knowledge. Every instance of problem solving and every interpretation depend on a web of myriad presuppositions. Since this web is holistic and particularistic at the same time, it can never be grasped by an abstract, general analysis. It is from this standpoint that the myth of the given—that is, the distinctions between sensibility and understanding, intuition and concept, form and content—can be debunked, along with the distinctions between analytic and synthetic judgments, between a priori and a posteriori. These Kantian dualisms are all being dissolved, a fact that is vaguely reminiscent of Hegel's metacritique. Of course, a full-fledged return to Hegel is made impossible by the contextualism and historicism to which the pragmatist and hermeneutic approaches subscribe.

There is no denying that pragmatism and hermeneutics represent a gain. Instead of focusing introspectively on consciousness, these two points of view look outside at objectifications of action and language. Gone is the fixation on the cognitive function of consciousness. Gone too is the emphasis on the representational function of language and the visual metaphor of the "mirror of nature." What takes their place is the notion of justified belief spanning the whole spectrum of what can be said—of what Wittgenstein and Austin call illocutionary force—rather than just the contents of fact-stating discourses. "Saying things is not always saying how things are."[9]

Do these considerations strengthen Rorty's interpretation of pragmatism and hermeneutics, which argues for the abnegation by philosophical thought of any claim to rationality and indeed for the abnegation of philosophy per se? Or do they mark the beginning of a new paradigm that, while discarding the mentalistic language game of the philosophy of consciousness, retains the justificatory modes of that philosophy in the modest, self-critical form in which I have presented them? I cannot answer this question directly for want of compelling and simple arguments. Once again, the answer I will give is a narrative one.

4

Marx wanted to supersede (*aufheben*) philosophy by realizing it—so convinced was he of the truth of Hegelian philosophy, whose only fault was that concept and reality cleaved unbearably, a fault that Hegel studiously overlooked. The corresponding, though fundamentally different, present-day attitude toward philosophy is the dismissive goodbye and good riddance. These farewells take many forms, three of which are currently in vogue. For simplicity's sake I will call them the therapeutic, the heroic, and the salvaging farewell.

Wittgenstein championed the notion of a *therapeutic* philosophy, therapeutic in the specific sense of self-healing, for philosophy was sick to the core. Wittgenstein's diagnosis was that philosophy had disarrayed language games that function perfectly well in everyday life. The weakness of this particular farewell to philosophy is that it leaves the world as it is. For the standards by which philosophy is being criticized are taken straight from the self-sufficient, routinized forms of life in which philosophy happens to survive for now. And what about possible successors? Field research in cultural anthropology seems to be the strongest candidate to succeed philosophy after its demise. Surely the history of philosophy will henceforth be interpreted as the unintelligible doings of some outlandish tribe that today is fortunately extinct. (Perhaps Rorty will one day be celebrated as the path-breaking Thucydides of this new approach, which incidentally could only get under way after Wittgenstein's medicine had proved effective.)

There is a sharp contrast between the soft-spoken farewell of the therapeutic philosopher and the noisy demolition undertaken by someone like Georges Bataille or Heidegger. Their goodbye is *heroic*. From their perspective too, false habits of living and thinking are concentrated in elevated forms of philosophical reflection. But instead of accusing philosophy of homely category mistakes or simple disruptions of everyday life, their deconstruction of metaphysics and objectivating thought has a more incisive, epochal quality. This more dramatic farewell to philosophy does not promise a cure. Rather, it resembles Hölderlin's pathos-laden idea of a rescue attempt *in extremis*. The devalued and discredited philosophical tradition, rather than being replaced by something even more valueless than itself, is supposed to give way to a *different* medium that makes possible a return to the immemorial—to Bataille's sovereignty or Heidegger's Being.

Least conspicuous, finally, is the *salvaging* type of farewell to philosophy. Contemporary neo-Aristotelians best exemplify this type insofar as they do exegeses that are informed by hermeneutics. Some of their work is unquestionably significant. But all too often it departs from pure interpretation in an effort to salvage some old truth or other. At any rate, this farewell to philosophy has a disingenuous ring: While the salvager keeps invoking the need to preserve philosophy, he wants to have nothing to do with its systematic claims. He does not try to make the ancients relevant to the discussion of some subject matter. Nor does he present the classics as a cultural treasure prepared by philosophy and history. What he does is to appropriate by assimilation texts that were once thought to embody knowledge, treating them instead as sources of illumination and edification.

Let us return for a moment to the critique of Kant, the master thinker, and in particular to his foundationalism in epistemology. Clearly, present-day philosophies of the sort just described wisely sidestep the Kantian trap. The last thing they think they can do is show the natural sciences to their proper place. Contemporary poststructuralist, late-pragmatist, and neohistoricist tendencies share a narrow objectivistic conception of science. Over against scientific cognition they carve out a sphere where thought can be illuminating or awakening instead of being objective. These tendencies prefer to sever all links with general, criticizable claims to validity. They would rather make do without notions like consensus, incontrovertible results, and justified beliefs. Paradoxically enough, whereas they make these (unnecessary) sacrifices, they somehow keep believing in the authority and superiority of philosophical insights: their own. In terms of their views on science, the philosophers of the definitive farewell agree with the existentialist proposal (Jaspers, Sartre, Kolakowski) for a division of labor that puts science on one side and philosophical faith, life, existential freedom, myth, cultivation, or what have you, on the other. All these juxtapositions are identical in structure. Where they differ is in their assessment of what Max Weber termed the cultural relevance of science, which may range from negative to neutral to positive. As is well known, Continental philosophy has a penchant for dramatizing the dangers of objectivism and instrumental reason, whereas Anglo-American philosophy takes a more relaxed view of them.

With his distinction between normal and abnormal discourse, Richard Rorty has come up with an interesting variation on the above theme. In times of widely acknowledged theoretical progress, normality takes hold of the established sciences. This means methods become available that make problem solving and dispute settling possible. What Rorty calls commensurable discourses are those discourses that operate with reliable criteria of consensus building. In contrast, discourses are incommensurable or abnormal when basic orientations are contested. Generally, abnormal conversations tend to pass over into normal ones, their ultimate purpose being to annul themselves and to bring about universal agreement. Occasionally, however, abnormal discourses stop short of taking this self-transcending step and are content with "interesting and fruitful disagreement." That is, they become *sufficient unto themselves*. It is at this point that abnormal discourses take on the quality that Rorty calls "edifying." According to him, philosophy as a whole verges on edifying conversation once it has sloughed off all pretensions to problem solving. Such philosophical edification enjoys the benefits of all three types of farewell: therapeutic relief, heroic overcoming, and hermeneutic reawaking. It combines the inconspicuously subversive force of leisure with an elitist notion of creative linguistic imagination and with the wisdom of the ages. The desire for edification, however, works to the detriment of the desire for truth: "Edifying philosophers can never end philosophy, but they can help prevent it from attaining the secure path of a science."[10]

I am partly sympathetic to Rorty's allocation of roles, for I agree that philosophy has no business playing the part of the highest arbiter in matters of science and culture. I find his argument unconvincing all the same. For even a philosophy that has been taught its limits by pragmatism and hermeneuticism will not be able to find a resting place in edifying conservation *outside* the sciences without immediately being drawn back into argumentation, that is, justificatory discourse.

The existentialist or, if you like, exclusive division of labor between philosophy and science is untenable. This is borne out by the particular version of discourse theory Rorty proposes. Ultimately, there is only one criterion by which beliefs can be judged valid, and that is that they are based on agreement reached by argumentation. This means that *everything* whose validity is at all disputable rests on shaky foundations. It matters little if the ground underfoot shakes a bit less for those who debate problems of physics than for those who debate problems of morals and aesthetics. The difference is a matter of degree only, as the postempiricist philosophy of science has shown. Normalization of discourse is not a sufficiently trenchant criterion for distinguishing science from edifying philosophical conversation.

5

To those who advocate a cut-and-dried division of labor, research traditions representing a blend of philosophy and science have always been particularly offensive. Marxism and psychoanalysis are cases in point. They cannot, on this view, help being pseudosciences because they straddle normal and abnormal discourse, refusing to fall on either side of the dividing line. On this point Rorty speaks the same language as

Jaspers. What I know about the history of the social sciences and psychology leads me to believe that hybrid discourses such as Marxism and psychoanalysis are by no means atypical. To the contrary, they may well stand for a type of approach that marks the beginning of new research traditions.

What holds for Freud applies to all seminal theories in these disciplines, for instance, those of Durkheim, Mead, Max Weber, Piaget, and Chomsky. Each inserted a genuinely philosophical idea like a detonator into a particular context of research. Symptom formation through repression, the creation of solidarity through the sacred, the identity-forming function of role taking, modernization as rationalization of society, decentration as an outgrowth of reflective abstraction from action, language acquisition as an activity of hypothesis testing—these key phrases stand for so many paradigms in which a philosophical idea is present in embryo while at the same time empirical, yet universal, questions are being posed. It is no coincidence that theoretical approaches of this kind are the favorite target of empiricist counterattacks. Such cyclical movements in the history of science, incidentally, do not point to a convergence of these disciplines in one unified science. It makes better sense to view them as stages on the road to the philosophization of the sciences of man (*Philosophischwerden der Humanwissenschaften*) than as stages in the triumphal march toward objectivist approaches, such as neurophysiology, that quaint favorite child of the analytic philosophers.

What I have said lies mainly in the realm of speculative conjecture. But unless I am completely mistaken, it makes sense to suggest that philosophy, instead of just dropping the usher role and being left with nothing, ought to exchange it for the part of stand-in (*Platzhalter*). Whose seat would philosophy be keeping; what would it be standing in for? Empirical theories with strong universalistic claims. As I have indicated, there have surfaced and will continue to surface in nonphilosophical disciplines fertile minds who will give such theories a try. The chance for their emergence is greatest in the reconstructive sciences. Starting primarily from the intuitive knowledge of competent subjects—competent in terms of judgment, action, and language—and secondarily from systematic knowledge handed down by culture, the reconstructive sciences explain the presumably universal bases of rational experience and judgment, as well as of action and linguistic communication. Marked down in price, the venerable transcendental and dialectical modes of justification may still come in handy. All they can fairly be expected to furnish, however, is reconstructive hypotheses for use in empirical settings. Telling examples of a successful cooperative integration of philosophy and science can be seen in the development of a theory of rationality. This is an area where philosophers work as suppliers of ideas without raising foundationalist or absolutist claims à la Kant or Hegel. Fallibilistic in orientation, they reject the dubious faith in philosophy's ability to do things single-handedly, hoping instead that the success that has for so long eluded it might come from an auspicious matching of different theoretical fragments. From the vantage point of my own research interests, I see such a cooperation taking shape between philosophy of science and history of science, between speech act theory and empirical approaches to pragmatics of language, between a theory of informal argumentation and empirical approaches to natural argumentation, between cognitivist ethics and a psychology of moral development, between philosophical theories of action and the ontogenetic study of action competences.

If it is true that philosophy has entered upon a phase of cooperation with the human sciences, does it not run the risk of losing its identity? There is some justification in Spaemann's warning "that every philosophy makes a practical and a theoretical claim to totality and that not to make such a twofold claim is to be doing something which does not qualify as philosophy."[11] In defense, one might argue that a philosophy that contributes something important to an analysis of the rational foundations of knowing, acting, and speaking does retain at least a thematic connection with the whole. But is this enough? What becomes of the theory of modernity, what of the window on the totality of culture that Kant and Hegel opened with their foundational and hypostatizing concepts of reason? Down to Husserl's *Crisis of the European Sciences*, philosophy not only usurped the part of supreme judge, it also played a directing role. Again, what happens when it surrenders the role of judge in matters of science as well as culture? Does this mean philosophy's relation to the totality is severed? Does this mean it can no longer be the guardian of rationality?

The situation of culture as a whole is no different from the situation of science as a whole. As totalities, neither needs to be grounded or justified or given a place by philosophy. Since the dawn of modernity in the eighteenth cenury, culture has generated those structures of rationality that Max Weber and Emil Lask conceptualized as cultural value spheres. Their existence calls for description and analysis, not philosophical justification.

Reason has split into three moments—modern science, positive law and posttraditional ethics, and autonomous art and institutionalized art criticism—but philosophy had precious little to do with this disjunction. Ignorant of sophisticated critiques of reason, the sons and daughters of modernity have progressively learned to differentiate their cultural tradition in terms of these three aspects of rationality such that they deal with issues of truth, justice, and taste discretely rather than simultaneously. At a different level, this shift toward differentiation produces the following phenomena: (1) The sciences disgorge more and more elements of religion, thus renouncing their former claim to being able to interpret nature and history as one whole. (2) Cognitivist moral theories disgorge issues of the good life, focusing instead strictly on deontological, generalizable aspects of ethics, so that all that remains of "the good" is the just. (3) With art it is likewise. Since the turn to autonomy, art has striven mightily to mirror one basic aesthetic experience, the increasing decentration of subjectivity. It occurs as the subject leaves the spatiotemporal structures of everyday life behind, freeing itself from the conventions of everyday perception, of purposive behavior, and of the imperatives of work and utility.

I repeat, these eminent trends toward compartmentalization, constituting as they do the hallmark of modernity, can do very well without philosophical justification. But they do pose problems of mediation. First, how can reason, once it has been thus sundered, go on being a unity on the level of culture? And second, how can expert cultures, which are being pushed more

two efforts at mediation – unifying sep. spheres of culture; transl. expertise

and more to the level of rarefied, esoteric forms, be made to stay in touch with everyday communication? To the extent to which philosophy keeps at least one eye trained on the topic of rationality, that is, to the extent to which it keeps inquiring into the conditions of the unconditional, to that extent it will not dodge the demand for these two kinds of efforts at mediation.

The first type of problem of mediation arises within the spheres of science, morals, and art. In this area we witness the rise of countermovements. For example, in human sciences nonobjectivist approaches bring moral and aesthetic criticism into play without undermining the primacy of issues of truth. Another example is the way in which the discussion of ethics of responsibility and ethics of conviction and the expanded role of utilitarian considerations within universalist ethics have brought the calculation of consequences and the interpretation of needs into play—and these are perspectives situated rather in the domains of the cognitive and the expressive. Let us finally look at postmodern art as the third example. It is characterized by a strange simultaneity of realistic, politically committed schools on the one hand and authentic followers of that classical modernism to which we owe the cystallization of the specific meaning of the aesthetic on the other. In realistic and politically committed art, elements of the cognitive and the moral-practical come into play once again, but at the level of the wealth of forms unloosed by the avant-garde. To that extent they act as agents of mediation. Counterdevelopments like these, it seems, mitigate the radical differentiation of reason and point to its unity. Everyday life, however, is a more promising medium for regaining the lost unity of reason than are today's expert cultures or yesteryear's classical philosophy of reason.

In everyday communication, cognitive interpretations, moral expectations, expressions, and evaluations cannot help overlapping and interpenetrating. Reaching understanding in the life-world requires a cultural tradition that ranges across *the whole spectrum*, not just the fruits of science and technology. As far as philosophy is concerned, it might do well to refurbish its link with the totality by taking on the role of interpreter on behalf of the lifeworld. It might then be able to help set in motion the interplay between the cognitive-instrumental, moral-practical, and aesthetic-expressive dimensions that has come to a standstill today like a tangled mobile.[12] This simile at least helps identify the issue philosophy will face when it stops playing the part of the arbiter that inspects culture and instead starts playing the part of a mediating interpreter. That issue is how to overcome the isolation of science, morals, and art and their respective expert cultures. How can they be joined to the impoverished traditions of the lifeworld, and how can this be done without detriment to their reigonal rationality? How can a new balance between the separated moments of reason be established in communicative everyday life?

The critic of the master thinkers will likely express his alarm one more time. What in the world, he will ask, gives the philosopher the right to offer his services as a translator mediating between the everyday world and cultural modernity with its autonomous sectors when he is already more than busy trying to hold open a place for ambitious theoretical strategies within the system of the sciences? I think pragmatism and hermeneutics have joined forces to answer this question by attributing epistemic authority to the community of those who cooperate and speak with one another. Everyday communication makes possible a kind of understanding that is based on claims to validity and thus furnishes the only real alternative to exerting influence on one another in more or less coercive ways. The validity claims that we raise in conversation—that is, when we say something with conviction—transcend this specific conversational context, pointing to something beyond the spatiotemporal ambit of the occasion. Every agreement, whether produced for the first time or reaffirmed, is based on (controvertible) grounds or reasons. Grounds have a special property: they force us into yes or no positions. Thus, built into the structure of action oriented toward reaching understanding is an element of unconditionality. And it is this unconditional element that makes the validity (*Gültigkeit*) that we claim for our views different from the mere de facto acceptance (*Geltung*) of habitual practices.[13] From the perspective of first persons, what we consider justified is not a function of custom but a question of justification or grounding. That is why philosophy is "rooted in the urge to see social practices of justification as more than just such practices."[14] The same urge is at work when people like me stubbornly cling to the notion that philosophy is the guardian of rationality.

Notes

1. "The critique . . . arriving at all its decisions in the light of fundamental principles of its own institution, the authority of which no one can question, secures to us the peace of a legal order, in which our disputes have to be conducted solely by the recognized methods of legal action." I. Kant, *Critique of Pure Reason*, trans. N. Kemp Smith, p. 601.

2. Richard Rorty, *Philosophy and the Mirror of Nature* (Princeton, 1979), pp. 392ff.

3. Rorty approvingly paraphrases a dictum by Eduard Zeller: "Hegelianism produced an image of philosophy as a discipline which somehow both completed and swallowed up the other disciplines, rather than *grounding* them. It also made philosophy too popular, too interesting, too important, to be properly professional; it challenged philosophy professors to embody the World-Spirit, rather than simply getting on with their *Fach*." Rorty (1979), p. 135.

4. G. Schönrich, *Kaegorien und transzendentale Argumentation* (Frankfurt, 1981), chapter 4, pp. 182ff; R. Bittner, "Transzendental," in *Handbuch philosophischer Grundbegriffe*, vol. 5 (Munich 1974), pp. 1524ff.

5. C. F. Gethmann and R. Hegselmann, "Das Problem der Begründung zwischen Dezisionismus und Fundamentalismus," *Zeitschrift für allegemeine Wissenschaftstheorie* 8 (1977): 432ff.

6. H. Albert, *Treatise on Critical Reason* (Princeton, 1985).

7. H. Lenk, "Philosophische Logikbegründung und rationaler Kritizismus," *Zeitschrift für philosophische Forschung* 24 (1970): 183ff.

8. T. Kesselring, *Entwicklung und Widerspruch—Ein Vergleich zwischen Piagets genetischer Erkenntnistheorie und Hegels Dialektik* (Frankfurt, 1981).

9. Rorty (1979), p. 371.

10. Rorty (1979), p. 372.

11. R. Spaemann, "Der Streit der Philosophen," in H. Lübbe, ed., *Wozu Philosophie?* (Berlin, 1978), p. 96.

12. J. Habermas, "Modernity versus Postmodernity," *New German Critique* 22 (1981): 3–14.

13. See J. Habermas, *Theory of Communicative Action* (Boston, 1984), vol. 1, pp. 114ff.

14. Rorty (1979), p. 390.

Reconstruction and Interpretation in the Social Sciences

Introduction

Let me begin with a personal reminiscence. When in 1967 I argued for the first time that the social sciences should not abandon the hermeneutic dimension of research and that any attempt to suppress the problem of interpretation would entail serious distortions, I was concerned with two basic types of objections.[1] The first was the insistence that hermeneutics is not a matter of methodology at all. Hans-Georg Gadamer pointed out that the problem of interpretation arises in non-scientific contexts: in everyday life, in history, art, and literature, and more generally in the way we handle what has been passed down to us in the form of traditions. The task of philosophical hermeneutics, then, according to Gadamer, is to shed light on ordinary processes of understanding, not on systematic investigations or procedures for collecting and analyzing data. Gadamer conceives of "method" as something that is opposed to "truth"; truth is attained only through the skilled and prudent practice of understanding or interpretation. On this view, hermeneutics as an activity is at best an art but never a method; as far as science is concerned, hermeneutics is a subversive force that undermines all systematic approaches.[2]

The second type of objection originated with representatives of mainstream social science, and it complemented the first type. It holds that the problem of interpretation lies in the mystification of interpretation and that there are no general problems of interpretation but only particular ones, for whose solution standard research techniques are adequate. If we operationalize our theoretical terms carefully and test for the validity and reliability of our research instruments, we can be safe from uncontrolled factors which might otherwise infiltrate our inquiry, factors stemming from the unanalyzed and unwieldy complexity of ordinary language and everyday life.

In the debate of the midsixties, hermeneutics was either inflated into a philosophical substitute for Heideggerian ontology or trivialized as a problem resulting from difficulties in measurement. This constellation has changed markedly since then. Today the main arguments of philosophical hermeneutics have been for the most part accepted, albeit not as a philosophical doctrine but rather as a research paradigm *within* the social sciences, notably anthropology, sociology, and social psychology. Paul Rabinow and William Sullivan have christened this the "interpretive turn."[3] In the seventies several tendencies inside and outside academia favored the success of the interpretive paradigm. Let me mention a few of them.

The first was the Popper-Kuhn debate and the rise of a postempiricist philosophy of science that undermined the authority of logical positivism and shattered the vision of a more or less unified nomological science. One offshoot of this change has been a shift of emphasis within the history of science from normative reconstruction to approaches that are more hermeneutically sensitive.

Second, it became apparent that the conventional social sciences were unable to make good their theoretical and practical promises. For example, sociological inquiry failed to live up to the standards set by Parsons's comprehensive theory, Keynesian economics proved ineffective at the level of practical policy, and in psychology, the claim of learning theory to provide a universal explanatory model came to nought—and it had been hailed as a textbook example of an exact behavioral science. These failures opened the door for alternative approaches based on phenomenology, the later Wittgenstein, philosophical hermeneutics, critical theory, etc. What these approaches had to recommend them was not that their superiority had been established but that they offered alternatives to the prevailing objectivism.[4]

Next, two moderately successful approaches that provided examples of an interpretive type of social science gained acceptance: structuralism in anthropology, linguistics, and less convincingly, sociology and genetic structuralism in developmental psychology—a model that seems promising for the analysis of social evolution and the development of world views, moral belief systems, and legal systems.

Another tendency that should be mentioned was the shift in the philosophical climate to neoconservatism. This shift brought with it a change in the background assumptions of social scientists. We witnessed a certain revival of biologistic approaches that had been discredited for decades on political grounds (sociobiology and genetic research on intelligence), as well as a return to relativism, historicism, existentialism, and Nietzscheanism in all their varieties; this shift in the temper of the times extended from the harder disciplines like linguistics and the philosophy of science to softer areas like the study of culture and reached as far as literary criticism and architectural ideology. Both these tendencies express the same syndrome, which is reflected in the widely held belief that the universal features of human culture owe their existence more to human nature than to the rational infrastructure of human language, cognition, and action, that is, to culture itself.

Two Modes of Language Use

Let me begin by clarifying what I mean by hermeneutics. Any meaningful expression—be it an utterance, verbal or nonverbal, or an artefact of any kind, such as a tool, an institution, or a written document—can be identified from a double perspective, both as an observable event and as an understandable objectification of meaning. We can describe, explain, or predict a noise equivalent to the sounds of a spoken sentence without having the slightest idea what this utterance means. To grasp (and state) its meaning, one has to participate in some (actual or imagined) communicative action in the course of which the sentence in question is used in such a way that it is intelligible to speakers, hearers, and bystanders belonging to the same speech community. Richard Rorty presents an extreme case: "Even if we could predict the sounds made by the community of scientific inquirers of the year 4000, we should not be in a position to join in their conversation."[5] The opposition of predicting their future speech behavior and joining in their conversation highlights the important distinction between two different modes of employing language.

In one mode of language use, *one says what is or is not the case.* In the other, *one says something to someone else in a way that allows him to understand what is being said.* Only the second mode of language use is internally or conceptually tied up with the conditions of communication. Saying how things stand does not necessarily depend on any kind of real or imagined communication; one does not need to *make* a statement, that is, perform a speech act. Instead, one may say p to oneself, or simply think that p. In contrast, understanding what is said to one requires participation in communicative action. There must be a speech situation (or at least one must be imagined) in which a speaker, in communicating *with* a hearer *about* something, gives expression to what *he* means. When we are dealing with a purely cognitive, noncommunicative use of language, only *one* fundamental relation is involved; let us call it the relationship between sentences and something in the world *about* which the sentences state something. In contrast, when language is used for coming to terms or reaching an understanding with someone else (even if it is ultimately only to agree or disagree), three relations are involved: by giving an expression *of* his belief, the speaker communicates *with* another member of the same speech community *about* something in the world. Epistemology is concerned exclusively with this last relationship, the relationship between language and reality, while hermeneutics deals simultaneously with the threefold relationship involved in an utterance, which serves as (a) an expression of the speaker's intention, (b) an expression of the establishment of an interpersonal relationship between speaker and hearer, and (c) an expression about something in the world. In addition, any attempt to clarify the meaning of a linguistic utterance reveals a fourth, linguistic relation, namely that between a given utterance and the set of all utterances possible within the same language.

Hermeneutics watches language at work, so to speak, language as it is used by participants to reach a common *understanding* or a shared *view*. The visual metaphor of an observer who *looks on*, however, should not obscure the fact that language in its performative use is embedded in relationships that are more complicated than the simple *about* relationship (and the kind of intentions correlated with it). When saying something in the context of everyday life, the speaker refers not only to something in the objective world (as the sum total of what is or could be the case) but also to something in the social world (as the sum total of legitimately ordered interpersonal relations) and to something in the speaker's own world (as the sum total of experiences that can be manifested and to which he has privileged access).

This is what the threefold nexus between utterance and world looks like when it is viewed *intentione recta*, i.e., from the perspectives of speaker and hearer. The same complex of relations can also be analyzed *intentione obliqua*, from the perspective of the lifeworld, or against the background of the shared assumptions and practices in which every communication is inconspicuously embedded from the outset. Viewed from this perspective, language serves three functions: (a) that of reproducing culture and keeping traditions alive (this is the perspective from which Gadamer developed his philosophical hermeneutics), (b) that of social integration or the coordination of the plans of different actors in social interaction (my theory of communicative action was developed from this perspective), and (c) that of socialization or the cultural interpretation of needs (this was the perspective from which G. H. Mead developed his social psychology).

The cognitive, noncommunicative use of language, then, calls for an analysis of the relationship between a sentence and a particular state of affairs that uses concepts of corresponding intentions, propositional attitudes, direction of fit, and conditions of satisfaction. The communicative use of language, in contrast, poses the problem of the connection between this *about* relation and the two other relations (being an expression

of something and sharing something *with* someone). As I have
shown elsewhere, this problem can be analyzed in terms of the
concepts of ontological and deontological worlds, claims to
validity, yes and no positions, and conditions of rationally motivated consensus.

Interpretation and the Objectivity of Understanding

If we compare the third-person attitude of someone who simply says how things stand (this is the attitude of the scientist,
for example) with the performative attitude of someone who
tries to understand what is said to him (this is the attitude of
the interpreter, for example), the implications of the hermeneutic dimension of research for methodology become clear.
Let me touch on three of the more important implications of
hermeneutic procedures.

First, interpreters relinquish the superiority that observers
have by virtue of their privileged position, in that they themselves are drawn, at least potentially, into negotiations about
the meaning and validity of utterances. By taking part in communicative action, they accept in principle the same status as
those whose utterances they are trying to understand. No
longer immune to the affirmative or negative positions taken
by experimental subjects or lay persons, interpreters give themselves over to a process of reciprocal critique. Within a process
of reaching understanding, actual or potential, it is impossible
to decide a priori who is to learn from whom.

Second, in assuming a performative attitude, the interpreter
not only relinquishes a position of superiority vis-à-vis his object
domain; he also has to grapple with the problem of the context
dependency of his interpretation. He cannot be sure in advance
that he and his experimental subjects operate on the basis of
the same background assumptions and practices. The interpreter's own global preunderstanding of the hermeneutic situation can be examined piece by piece but cannot be put into
question as a whole.

Third, just as problematic as the interpreter's disengagement
in questions of validity and the decontextualization of interpretations of such questions is the fact that everyday language

extends to nondescriptive utterances and noncognitive claims to validity. In everyday life we agree (or disagree) more frequently about the rightness of actions and norms, the appropriateness of evaluations and standards, and the authenticity or sincerity of self-presentations than about the truth of propositions. That is why the knowledge we use when we say something to someone extends beyond strictly propositional or truth-related knowledge. To understand what is said to him, the interpreter has to command knowledge that is based on *additional* claims to validity. A correct interpretation, therefore, is not true in the sense in which a proposition that reflects an existing state of affairs is true. It would be better to say that a correct interpretation fits, suits, or explicates the meaning of the *interpretandum*, that which the interpreter is to understand.

These are the three implications of the fact that understanding what is said requires *participation* and not merely *observation*. It is thus not surprising that all attempts to base science on interpretation run into difficulties. One major stumbling block is the question of how symbolic expressions can be measured as reliably as physical phenomena. In the midsixties Aaron Cicourel came up with a good analysis of the transformation of context-dependent symbolic expressions whose meanings are intuitively evident into "hard" data.[6] The difficulties are derived from the fact that what has been understood in the performative attitude has to be translated into what can be established from a third-person point of view. The performative attitude necessary for interpretation permits regular shifts between the first-, second-, and third-person attitudes, but for purposes of measurement the performative attitude must be subordinated to a single attitude, namely the objectivating attitude. A further problem is that value judgments creep into fact-stating discourse. These difficulties arise because the theoretical framework for an empirical analysis of everyday behavior has to be conceptually integrated with the frame of reference within which participants themselves interpret their everyday lives. Participants' interpretations, however, are connected with both cognitive *and* noncognitive claims to validity, whereas theoretical statements (propositions) refer only to truth. For this reason Charles Taylor and Alvin Gouldner have argued convincingly against the possibility of value-neutral languages in the interpretive social sciences.[7] This position draws support from a number of very different philosophical schools—from arguments by Wittgenstein, Quine, Gadamer, and of course Marx.

In short, every science that accepts the inclusion of objectivations of meaning in its object domain has to take into account the methodological implications of the interpreter's *participant role*. The interpreter does not have to give meaning to the things he observes; rather, he has to explicate the given meaning of objectivations that can be understood only from within the context of communication processes. These implications threaten the very context independence and value neutrality that seem necessary to the *objectivity* of theoretical knowledge.[8]

Does this mean, then, that Gadamer's position should be accepted in and for the social sciences? Does the interpretive turn sound the death knell for the strict scientific status of all nonobjectivistic approaches? Should we follow Rorty's recommendation to put the social sciences on the same footing not only with the *Geisteswissenschaften* but with literary criticism, literature, and religion, indeed, with edifying discourse in general? Should we concede that the social sciences can at best contribute to our general cultivation, presuming that they are not replaced by something more serious, like neurophysiology or biochemistry? I find three main responses to these questions among social scientists today. If we keep the claims to objectivity and to explanatory power separate, we can distinguish between a hermeneutic objectivism, a radical hermeneutics, and a hermeneutic reconstructionism.

Some social scientists play down the more dramatic implications of the problem of interpretation by returning to a version of the empathy theory of understanding meaning. This theory ultimately rests on the assumption that we can put ourselves into another person's consciousness and disengage interpretations of what he says from our hermeneutic situation as interpreters. To my mind, Gadamer's convincing critique of the empathy theory of the young Dilthey has blocked this retreat once and for all.

Other social scientists, whether they use Gadamer's or Rorty's justifications, no longer hestitate to extend the principles of a radical hermeneutics to the domain that has, unfortunately and mistakenly, as they see it, been claimed by social science as its own special preserve. Whether with misgivings or hopefully, these social scientists give up both the claim to objectivity and the claim to explanatory knowledge, This results in relativism of one kind or another, which means that different approaches and interpretations are viewed as merely reflecting differences in value orientation.

Given the problem of interpretation, still other social scientists are prepared to drop the conventional postulate of value neutrality. They dissociate themselves, moreover, from an assimilation of the social sciences to the model of a strict nomological science and at the same time endorse the desirability *and* the possibility of theoretical approaches that promise to produce knowledge that is both objective and theoretical. This position needs to be justified.

The Rationality Presupposed in Interpretation

At this point I will make reference to an argument that, if fully developed, would show that the interpreter's inevitable involvement in the process of reaching understanding does indeed deprive him of the privileged status of the objective observer or the third person but *for the same reason* also provides him with the means to maintain a position of negotiated impartiality from within. The paradigm case for hermeneutics is the interpretation of a traditional text. While the interpreter initially seems to have understood what the author is saying, he subsequently comes to the confusing realization that he has not adequately understood the text, that is, not so well that he could answer the author's questions if he had to. The interpreter takes this to be a sign that he is still putting the text in a context other than the one in which it was in fact embedded. He will have to revise his understanding. This kind of disturbance of communication marks the situation from which he proceeds. Next he tries to understand why the author—in the tacit belief that certain states of affairs obtain, that certain values and norms are valid, and that certain experiences can be attributed to certain subjects—makes the assertions he does, observes or violates the conventions he does, and expresses the intentions, dispositions, feelings, and other such things he does. But only to the extent to which the interpreter also grasps the *reasons* why the author's utterances seemed rational to the author himself does he understand what the author meant.

The interpreter, then, understands the meaning of a text only insofar as he understands *why* the author felt justified in putting forth certain propositions as being true, in recognizing certain values and norms as being right, and in expressing certain experiences (or attributing them to others) as being authentic. The interpreter has to clarify the context that the author must have presupposed as being common knowledge in the audience he was addressing if the difficulties the interpreter currently experiences with the text did not exist, or were not so difficult to resolve, at the time it was written. This step indicates the immanent rationality that interpreters expect to find in all utterances insofar as they ascribe them to a subject whose mental competence they have no reason to doubt in advance. Interpreters cannot understand the semantic content of a text if they do not make themselves aware of the reasons the author could have brought forth in his own time and place if required to do so.

For reasons to be sound and for them to be merely considered sound are not the same thing, whether we are dealing with reasons for asserting facts, for recommending norms and values, or for expressing desires and feelings. That is why the interpreter cannot simply look at and understand such reasons without at least implicitly passing judgment on them *as* reasons, that is, without taking a positive or negative position on them. The interpreter may leave some claims to validity open and may decide, unlike the author, to consider some questions unanswered, to leave them as open problems. But reasons can be *understood* only insofar as they are taken seriously as reasons and *evaluated*. This is why the interpreter can elucidate the meaning of an obscure expression only if he explains how this obscurity came to be, that is, why the reasons the author might have given in his own context are no longer immediately illuminating for us.

There is a sense in which any interpretation is a *rational* interpretation. In the act of understanding, which entails an evaluation of reasons as well, the interpreter cannot avoid appealing to standards of rationality and hence to standards that he himself considers binding on all parties, including the author and his contemporaries (to the extent to which they could and would have participated in the communication that the interpreter is now resuming). While such a (normally implicit) appeal to presumably universal standards of rationality may, to a certain extent, be inescapable for the dedicated interpreter who is bent on understanding, this by no means proves that those standards are truly rational. But the fundamental intuition of every competent speaker—that his claims to truth, normative rightness, and truthfulness should be acceptable to all, under suitable conditions—does provide grounds for taking a brief look at formal pragmatic analysis, which focuses on the general and necessary conditions for the validity of symbolic expressions and achievements. I am referring to rational reconstructions of the know-how of subjects who are capable of speech and action, who are credited with the capacity to produce valid utterances, and who consider themselves capable of distinguishing, at least intuitively, between valid and invalid expressions.

This is the domain of disciplines like logic and metamathematics, epistemology and the philosophy of science, linguistics and the philosophy of language, ethics and action theory, aesthetics, argumentation theory, and so on. Common to all these disciplines is the goal of providing an account of the pretheoretical knowledge and the intuitive command of rule systems that underlie the production and evaluation of such symbolic expressions and achievements as correct inferences; good arguments; accurate descriptions, explanations, and predications; grammatically correct sentences; successful speech acts; effective instrumental action; appropriate evaluations; authentic self-presentations; etc. Insofar as rational reconstructions explicate the conditions for the validity of utterances, they also explain deviant cases, and through this indirect legislative authority they acquire a *critical* function as well. Insofar as they extend the differentiations between individual claims to validity beyond traditional boundaries, they can even establish new analytic standards and thus assume a *constructive* role. And insofar as we succeed in analyzing very general conditions of validity, rational reconstructions can claim to be describing universals and thus to represent a *theoretical* knowledge capable of competing with other such knowledge. At this level, weak *transcendental* arguments make their appearance, arguments aimed at demonstrating that the presuppositions of relevant practices are inescapable, that is, that they cannot be cast aside.[9]

It is precisely these three characteristics (the critical substance, the constructive role, and the transcendental justification of theoretical knowledge) that have occasionally led philosophers to burden certain reconstructions with claims to ultimate justification. For this reason it is important to see that *all* rational reconstructions, like other types of knowledge, have only hypothetical status. There is always the possibility that they rest on a false choice of examples, that they are obscuring and distorting correct intuitions, or, even more frequently, that they are overgeneralizing individual cases. For these reasons, they require further corroboration. While this critique of all a priori and strong transcendental claims is certainly justified, it should not discourage attempts to put rational reconstructions of presumably basic competences to the test, subjecting them to indirect verification by using them as inputs in empirical theories.

The theories in question attempt to explain such things as the ontogenetic acquisition of cognitive, linguistic, and sociomoral capacities; the evolutionary emergence and institutional embodiment of innovative structures of consciousness in the course of history; and such systematic deviations as speech pathologies, ideologies, or the degeneration of research programs. The nonrelativistic Lakatosian type of interplay between the philosophy of science and the history of science is a case in point.

Kohlberg's Theory of Moral Development

In this final section I want to take up the case of Lawrence Kohlberg's theory with an eye to corroborating my claim that the social sciences can become aware of the hermeneutic dimension while remaining faithful to the task of generating theoretical knowledge. There are three reasons why I have chosen this example. First, the claim to objectivity that Kohlberg's theory makes seems to be jeopardized by the fact that it favors one particular philosophical theory of morality over others. Second, Kohlberg's theory is an instance of a very special division of labor between the rational reconstruction of moral intuitions (philosophy) and the empirical analysis of moral development (psychology). Third, Kohlberg's declared intentions are both daring and provocative—they represent a challenge for all those who are unwilling to suppress either the social scientist or the moral philosopher in themselves. The points I am going to make are very condensed and clearly in need of further elaboration.

1

There is an evident parallel between Piaget's theory of cognitive development (in the narrower sense of the term) and Kohlberg's theory of moral development. Both have the goal of explaining *competences,* which are defined as capacities to solve particular types of empirical-analytic or moral-practical problems. The problem solving in question is measured objectively either in terms of the truth claims of descriptive statements, including explanations and predictions, or in terms of the rightness of normative statements, including justifications of actions and the norms governing them. Piaget and Kohlberg describe the terminal competence of the young adult in the framework of rational reconstructions of formal-operational thought and postconventional moral judgment. In addition, Kohlberg shares with Piaget a *constructivist concept of learning* based on the following assumptions: first, that knowledge in general can be analyzed as a product of learning processes, second, that learning is a process of problem solving in which the learning subject is actively involved, and finally, that the learning process is guided by the insights of those who are directly involved. It has to be possible to understand the learning process from the inside, so that with the transition from one interpretation of a given problem to another interpretation of the same problem, the learner can *explain*, in the light of his second interpretation, why his first interpretation is false.[10]

Along similar lines Piaget and Kohlberg lay down a hierarchy of distinct levels or "stages" or learning, with each defined as a relative equilibrium of operations that become increasingly complex, abstract, general, and reversible. Both theorists make assumptions about the internal logic of an irreversible learning process, about learning mechanisms (i.e., about the internalization of schemata of instrumental, social, or discursive action), about the endogenous development of the organism (stronger or weaker maturationist assumptions), about stage-specific stimulus inputs and the related phenomena of displacement, retardation, acceleration, etc. Kohlberg makes some additional assumptions about the interaction between sociomoral and cognitive development.

2

In view of the delicate relationship and, more important in this context, the complementary relationship between rational reconstruction and empirical analysis, there is a danger of the naturalistic fallacy. In his later writings, particularly since *Biology and Knowledge*,[11] Piaget tends to assimilate his approach to systems theory. The concept of equilibrium, which points to a relative stability of problem-solving processes and is measured in terms of the internal criterion of the degree of reversibility, carries connotations of the successful adaptation of a self-maintaining system to a changing environment. Of course, it is possible to try to combine the structuralist model with the systems-theoretical model (as is done in social theory with the action or lifeworld model on the one hand and the systems model on the other), but combining them does not mean assimilating the one to the other. Every attempt to view the superiority of higher-level achievements, which are measured in terms of the validity of problem-solving attempts, in *strictly functional* terms places the specific achievement of cognitivist developmental theory in jeopardy. If what is true or morally right could be adequately analyzed in terms of what is necessary for the maintenance of system boundaries, we would not need rational reconstructions. Kohlberg does avoid the naturalistic fallacy, but the formulation he gives in the following sentences is at least ambiguous:

Our psychological theory of morality derives largely from Piaget, who claims that both logic and morality develop through stages and that each stage is a structure which, formally considered, is in better equilibrium than its predecessor. It assumes, that is, that each new (logical or moral) stage is a new structure which includes elements of earlier structures but transforms them in such a way as to represent a more stable and extensive equilibrium.

Kohlberg does, however, follow this with the unambiguous statement:

These "equilibration" assumptions of our psychological theory are naturally allied to the formalistic tradition in philosophic ethics from Kant to Rawls. This isomorphism of psychological and normative theory generates the claim that a psychologically more advanced stage of moral judgment is more morally adequate, by moral philosophic criteria.[12]

3

Theory formation in the domain of moral consciousness is faced with a particular difficulty that distinguishes Kohlberg's theory from that of Piaget. Both Kohlberg and Piaget explain the acquisition of presumably universal competences in terms of patterns of development that are invariant across cultures, these patterns being determined by what is conceived as an internal logic of the corresponding learning processes. Now cognitive universalism is easier to defend than moral universalism (although the former too remains controversial); there is a great deal of evidence to suggest that formal operations are used in explaining observable states and events in ways that are consistent across cultures. Kohlberg's burden as a moral theorist is more difficult, for he has to prove (a) that a univer-

salist and cognitivist position can be defended against a moral
relativism and skepticism deeply rooted in empiricist traditions
(and in bourgeois ideologies) and (b) that a formalistic ethics
along Kantian lines can be demonstrated to be superior to
utilitarian and contractarian theories. Current debates in moral
theory provide the context for the justification of these two
points. Although conclusive arguments are not readily available, my guess is that Kohlberg might well win the debate on
moral universalism. As regards the second issue (the distinction
between his stage 6, formalistic morality, and his stage 5, rule-
utilitarian and contractarian morality), Kohlberg's philosophical position is not as strong.

If one's intention is to explain ethical formalism in terms of
concepts of *procedural rationality*, a statement like the following
is unacceptable: "A morality on which universal agreement
could be based would require a different foundation. It would
require that moral obligation be directly derived from a substantive moral principle which can define the choices of any
man without conflict or inconsistency."[13] When, on the other
hand, Kohlberg points to "ideal role-taking" as an "appropriate
procedure" for moral-practical decisions, he is being guided
by genuine Kantian intuitions that have been reinterpreted
from the pragmatist point of view by Peirce and Mead to mean
participation in a "universal discourse." Kohlberg finds in
Rawls's theory as well the same basic intuition that valid norms
have to find universal assent: "A just solution to a moral dilemma is a solution acceptable to all parties, considering each
as free and equal, and assuming none of them knew which role
they would occupy in the situation."[14]

4

Let us assume that we succeed in defending moral universalism. A further difficulty remains. Taking a deontological
position, Kohlberg asserts—correctly, I believe—that postconventional moral consciousness requires the recognition that the
moral sphere is autonomous. Autonomy means that the form
of moral argumentation is distinct from all other forms of
argumentation, whether they involve stating and explaining

facts, evaluating works of art, clarifying utterances, bringing unconscious motives to light, or whatever. In practical discourse what is at issue is not whether propositions are true, evaluations appropriate, constructions well formed, or expressive utterances truthful but whether actions and the norms governing them are right. The question is, Is it morally right?[15]

It follows from this, however, that the rational reconstructions on which Kohlberg has to rely belong to a type of theory that is "normative" in two different respects. In the first place, a cognitivist moral theory is normative in the sense that it explains the conditions of a particular type of validity claim. In this respect theories of moral judgment do not differ from reconstructions of what Piaget calls formal-operational thought. But since moral cognitivism consists of more than its metaethical considerations, it is normative in a different sense as well, namely that in seeking to establish the validity of its own assertions it appeals to standards not of propositional truth but of normative rightness. In this respect Kohlberg's point of departure differs from that of Piaget.

Does it follow that a theory of moral development is somehow poisoned by the normative status of the particular kind of rational reconstruction that is built into it? Is Kohlberg's theory merely pseudoempirical, a hybrid that can neither claim the dignity of a moral theory endowed with full normative status nor meet the demands of an empirical theory whose theoretical statements must be either true or false? The answer to this question is, I believe, no.

5

Kohlberg's own position on the relationship between the philosophical reconstruction of reliable moral intuitions and the psychological explanation of how this intuitive knowledge is acquired is admittedly not without ambiguity. Let us begin by looking at the stronger thesis according to which the two undertakings are parts of one and the same theory. Kohlberg formulates this "identity thesis" in the following fashion: "[An] ultimately adequate *psychological* theory as to why a child does move from stage to stage and an ultimately adequate *philosoph-*

ical explanation as to why a higher stage is more adequate than a lower stage is one and the same theory extended in different directions."[16] This view is based on the constructivist concept of learning. A subject who moves from one stage to the next should be able to explain why his higher-stage judgments are more adequate than those at lower stages. It is this line of the natural moral reasoning of the lay person that the moral philosopher takes up reflexively. This affinity rests on the fact that both the moral philosopher and the experimental subjects whom the psychologist faces take the same performative attitude of participants in a practical discourse. In both cases the results of moral reasoning, whether they represent the expert's attempt at reconstruction or merely the lay person's moral intuition, are assessed in the light of normative validity claims. Only the psychologist takes a different attitude, and the type of validity to which his search for knowledge is oriented is also different. Granted, the psychologist too looks at the utterances of his experimental subject in terms of how the latter criticizes the moral judgments of the stage he has just advanced beyond and how he justifies the moral judgments of the higher stage. But unlike the lay person (and his reflective alter ego the moral philosopher), the psychologist describes and explains those judgments in the third person, which means that the results of his reflections can be assessed only in terms of their claim to propositional truth. Kohlberg blurs this important distinction in formulations like the following: "The scientific theory as to why people factually do move upward from stage to stage, and why they factually do prefer a higher stage to a lower, is broadly the same as a moral theory as to why people *should* prefer a higher stage to a lower."[17]

Actually, there is a complementary relationship between philosophical and psychological theory, a relationship that Kohlberg describes accurately in another passage:

While moral criteria of adequacy of moral judgment help define a standard of psychological adequacy or advance, the study of psychological advance feeds back and clarifies these criteria. Our psychological theory as to why individuals move from one stage to the next is grounded on a moral-philosophical theory which specifies that the later stage is morally better or more adequate than the earlier stage.

Our psychological theory claims that individuals prefer the highest stage of reasoning they comprehend, a claim supported by research. This claim of our psychological theory derives from a philosophical claim that a later stage is "objectively" preferable or more adequate by certain *moral* criteria. This philosophic claim, however, would be thrown into question for us if the facts of moral advance were inconsistent with its psychological implications.[18]

This complementarity thesis grasps the division of labor between moral philosophy and moral development theory better than the identity thesis does. The success of an empirical theory, which can only be true or false, may serve as a safeguard of the normative validity of a moral theory used for empirical purposes: "The fact that our conception of the moral 'works' empirically is important for its philosophical adequacy." It is in this sense that rational reconstructions can be checked or tested, where "test" means to investigate whether different pieces of theory are complementary and fit into the same pattern. Kohlberg's clearest formulation of this reads as follows: "Science, then, can test whether a philosopher's conception of morality phenomenologically fits the psychological facts. Science cannot go on to justify that conception of morality as what morality ought to be."[19]

6

This relationship of mutual fit suggests that the hermeneutic circle is closed only on the metatheoretical level. The empirical theory presupposes the validity of the normative theory it uses. Yet the validity of the normative theory is cast into doubt if the philosophical reconstructions prove to be unusable in the context of application within the empirical theory. The employment of a normative theory has, in turn, an effect on the hermeneutic dimension of research. Generating data is a more theory-laden process than normal interpretation. Compare these two versions of the same test problem:

In Europe, a woman was near death from a very bad disease, a special kind of cancer. There was one drug that the doctors thought might save her. It was a form of radium for which the druggist was charging ten times what the drug cost him to make. The sick woman's husband,

Heinz, went to everyone he knew to borrow the money, but he could only get together about half of what it cost. He told the druggist that his wife was dying, and asked him to sell it cheaper or let him pay later. But the druggist said, "No, I discovered the drug and I'm going to make money from it." So Heinz got desperate and broke into the man's store to steal the drug for his wife. Should the husband have done that? Why?

A man and wife had just migrated from the high mountain. They started to farm, but there was no rain, and no crops grew. No one had enough food. The wife got sick, and finally she was close to dying from having no food. There was only one grocery store in the village, and the storekeeper charged a very high price for the food. The husband asked the storekeeper for some food for his wife, and said he would pay for it later. The storekeeper said, "No, I won't give you any food unless you pay first." The husband went to all the people in the village to ask for food, but no one had food to spare. So he got desperate, and broke into the store to steal food for his wife. Should the husband have done that? Why?[20]

The first formulation is Kohlberg's famous "Heinz dilemma." It is a good illustration of the method used to induce American children to produce moral judgments that can be compared with one another. Their responses to a dilemma of this type are assigned to moral stages in accordance with standard stage descriptions. The second formulation is a retranslation into English from Chinese of the same dilemma, that is, of the version that Kohlberg used to test children in a Taiwanese village. I have no way of judging the extent to which Western conceptions are superimposed on this Chinese version. However weak the translation into Chinese may be, it does throw the hermeneutic problem itself into relief. If and only if the theory is correct are we in a position to find context-sensitive equivalents for the Heinz dilemma in all cultures so that we get Taiwanese responses that can be compared with American responses with respect to important dimensions of theory. It follows from the theory itself that stories relevant to it can be translated from one context to another. What is more, the theory gives us an indication of how this is to be accomplished. If it cannot be done without violence and distortion, this very failure of hermeneutic application is an indication that the dimensions postulated are being externally imposed and are not the result of a reconstruction from within.

Let me emphasize in closing that I have used Kohlberg's theory for purposes of illustration in these methodological reflections on the structure of developmental-psychological theories where reconstructions of allegedly universal competences are built into the theory, as it were. I have not touched on questions that regard the substantive portions of the theory—questions such as whether Kohlberg's description of postconventional stages of moral consciousness needs to be improved, whether the formalistic approach to ethics in particular unduly ignores contextual and interpersonal aspects, whether the notion of a logic of development, a notion derived from Piaget, is too strong, and finally, whether Kohlberg's assumptions about the relationship between moral judgment and moral action neglect psychodynamic aspects.[21]

Notes

1. Jürgen Habermas, "Zur Logik der Sozialwissenschaften: Ein Literaturbericht," special issue of *Philosophische Rundschau* (1967). Reprinted in J. Habermas, *Zur Logik der Sozialwissenschaften* (Frankfurt, 1982), pp. 89ff (English translation, *On the Logic of the Social Sciences*, [Cambridge, Mass., 1988]).

2. Hans-Georg Gadamer, "Rhetorik, Hermeneutik, und Ideologiekritik: Metakritische Erörterungen zu 'Wahrheit und Methode,'" in Karl-Otto Apel et al., *Hermeneutik und Ideologiekritik* (Frankfurt, 1971), pp. 57ff. English translation, "On the Scope and Function of Hermeneutical Reflection," in Gadamer, *Philosophical Hermeneutics* (Berkeley, 1976), pp. 18ff.

3. Paul Rabinow and William M. Sullivan, eds., *Interpretive Social Science* (Berkeley, 1979).

4. Richard J. Bernstein, *Restructuring Social and Political Theory* (New York, 1976).

5. Richard Rorty, *Philosophy and the Mirror of Nature* (Princeton, 1979), p. 355.

6. Aaron Cicourel, *Method and Measurement* (Glencoe, 1964).

7. Charles Taylor, "Interpretation and the Sciences of Man," in *Review of Metaphysics* 1971: 3–51. Alvin Gouldner, *The Coming Crisis of Western Sociology* (New York, 1970).

8. I should add that by distinguishing sciences based on hermeneutic procedures from those that are not, I am not advocating an ontological dualism between specific domains of reality (e.g., culture versus nature, values versus facts, or similar neo-Kantian dichotomies introduced chiefly by Windelband, Rickert, and Cassirer). What I do advocate is a *methodological* distinction between sciences that gain access to their object domain by understanding what is said to someone and those which do not. All sciences

have to address problems of interpretation at the *metatheoretical level* (this became the focus of postempiricist philosophy of science; see Mary Hesse, "In Defence of Objectivity," in *Proceedings of the British Academy* 58 [1972]: 275–292). Yet only those with a hermeneutic dimension of research face problems of interpretation already at the level of *data generation*. See Anthony Giddens, *New Rules of Sociological Method* (London, 1976), which discusses this problem of a "double hermeneutics." In advocating a methodological definition of sciences that proceed hermeneutically, I dissociate myself from Richard Rorty's conception of hermeneutics as an activity confined to "abnormal discourses." I agree that what most often triggers hermeneutic efforts in everyday life is the breakdown of routine communication. But the need for interpretation does not arise solely in situations where one no longer understands anything or may even feel a Nietzschean thrill in the presence of the unforeseen, the new, or the creative. This need also arises in thoroughly mundane encounters with what happens to be less familiar. Under the ethnomethodologist's microscope even the most ordinary features of everyday life become something strange. This artificially created need for interpretation is the normal case in the social sciences. Hermeneutics, then, is not reserved for what is noble and unconventional; at the very least, Rorty's aristocratic notion of hermeneutics does not hold for the methodology of the social sciences.

9. I. Watt, "Transcendental Arguments and Moral Principles," in *Philosophical Quarterly* 25 (1975): 38ff.

10. Compare the discussion between Stephen Toulmin and D. W. Hamlyn in the latter's "Epistemology and Conceptual Development," in T. Mischel, ed., *Cognitive Development and Epistemology* (New York, 1971), pp. 3–24.

11. Jean Piaget, *Biologie et connaissance* (Paris, 1967). English translation, *Biology and Knowledge* (Chicago, 1971).

12. Lawrence Kohlberg, "Justice as Reversibility: The Claim to Moral Adequacy of a Highest Stage of Moral Judgment," in his *Essays on Moral Development*, vol. 1, *The Philosophy of Moral Development* (San Francisco, 1981), p. 194.

13. Lawrence Kohlberg, "From Is to Ought: How to Commit the Naturalistic Fallacy and Get Away with It in the Study of Moral Development," in Kohlberg (1981), pp. 161–2.

14. Kohlberg (1981), p. 167.

15. Kohlberg (1981), p. 170.

16. Kohlberg (1981), p. 104.

17. Kohlberg (1981), p. 179.

18. Kohlberg, "The Claim to Moral Adequacy," in Kohlberg (1981), p. 194.

19. Kohlberg, "From Is to Ought," in Kohlberg (1981), p. 178.

20. Kohlberg (1981), pp. 12 and 115.

21. Compare the essay "Moral Consciousness and Communicative Action," in this volume.

Discourse Ethics: Notes on a Program of Philosophical Justification

In his recent book *After Virtue*, Alasdair MacIntyre argues that the Enlightenment's project of establishing a secularized morality free of metaphysical and religious assumptions has failed. He accepts as the incontestable outcome of the Enlightenment what Max Horkheimer once pointed out with critical intent, the idea that an instrumental reason restricted to purposive rationality must let its ends be determined by blind emotional attitudes and arbitrary decisions: "Reason is calculative; it can assess truths of fact and mathematical relations but nothing more. In the realm of practice it can speak only of means. About ends it must be silent."[1] Since Kant this conclusion has been opposed by cognitivist moral philosophies that maintain that in one sense or another practical questions admit of truth.

A number of significant current theoretical approaches, notably those of Kurt Baier, Marcus Singer, John Rawls, Paul Lorenzen, Ernst Tugendhat, and Karl-Otto Apel, derive from this Kantian tradition. All share the intention of analyzing the conditions for making impartial judgments of practical questions, judgments based solely on reasons.[2] Of these theories, Apel's is not the one elaborated in the most detail. Yet I consider his approach, in which an ethics of discourse is recognizable in outline form, to be the most promising at present. I would like to support my assessment of the current state of the debate in ethics by presenting my own program of philosophical justification. In so doing, I will address other cognitivist approaches only in passing and will concentrate primarily on elaborating the shared problematic that distinguishes cognitivist theories from noncognitivist approaches.

I will begin by singling out the "ought" character (*Sollgeltung*) of norms and the claims to validity raised in norm-related (or regulative) speech acts as the phenomena a philosophical ethics must be able to explain (part I, section 1). It becomes clear in section 2 that such familiar philosophical positions as metaphysical definitional theories and intuitionist value ethics on the one hand and noncognitivist theories like emotivism and decisionism on the other fail from the outset to address the phenomena in need of explanation. They assimilate normative statements to a false model, either the model of descriptive statements and evaluations or that of experiential statements and imperatives. Something similar is true of prescriptivism, which uses intentional statements as its model.[3] As I will show in part II, moral phenomena can be elucidated in terms of a formal-pragmatic analysis of communicative action, a type of action in which the actors are oriented to validity claims. It will become clear why philosophical ethics, unlike epistemology, for example, can readily assume the form of a special theory of argumentation. In part III the fundamental question of moral theory will be posed: How can we justify the principle of universalization itself, which alone enables us to reach agreement through argumentation on practical questions? This is where Apel's transcendental-pragmatic justification of ethics on the basis of general pragmatic presuppositions of argumentation as such enters the picture. We will see, however, that this "deduction" cannot claim the status of an ultimate justification (*Letztbegründung*), and I will show why such a strong claim should not even be raised. In the form proposed by Apel, the transcendental-pragmatic argument is even too weak to counter the consistent skeptic's opposition to *any* kind of rational ethics. This problem, finally, will require me to devote at least a few brief remarks to Hegel's critique of Kantian morality, in order to provide a simple interpretation of the primacy of ethical life (*Sittlichkeit*) over morality, an interpretation that is immune to neo-Aristotelian and neo-Hegelian attempts to ideologize it.

I Preliminary Remarks

1 On the phenomenology of the moral

The comments by MacIntyre cited above are reminiscent of a critique of instrumental reason directed against certain one-sided conceptions characteristic of the modern understanding of the world, notably its stubborn tendency to narrow down to the cognitive-instrumental domain the domain of questions that can be decided on the basis of reasons. Moral-practical questions of the form What ought I to do? are considered not amenable to rational debate unless they can be answered in terms of purposive rationality. This pathology of modern consciousness calls for an explanation in terms of *social theory*.[4] Since philosophical ethics is unable to provide such an explanation, it has to proceed in a therapeutic manner, invoking the self-curative powers of reflection to oppose the obscuring of basic moral phenomena. P. F. Strawson's well-known essay "Freedom and Resentment" points in this direction. It develops a linguistic phenomenology of ethical consciousness whose purpose is maieutically to open the eyes of the empiricist in his role as moral skeptic to his own everyday moral intuitions.[5]

Strawson begins by examining an emotional response which in its obtrusiveness is well suited to convince even the most diehard skeptic that moral experience has real content. That response is the indignation we feel in the face of personal insults. When there is no restitution for the initial injury, our unambiguous reaction will harden into smouldering resentment. This enduring emotion lays bare the moral dimension hidden in every insult. Unlike fright and rage, which are immediate responses to an injury as it occurs, resentment is a response to the disgraceful wrong done to one by another. Resentment is an expression, albeit a relatively powerless one, of moral condemnation.[6] Using the example of resentment as his point of departure, Strawson makes four important points.

1

When actions violate the integrity of another person, the perpetrator or a third person may produce excuses. As soon as an aggrieved party accepts an excuse, he no longer feels injured or slighted in quite the same way as before; his initial indignation will not turn into lasting resentment. Excuses are like repairs we make to disturbed interactions. To grasp the nature of these disturbances, Strawson distinguishes two types of excuses. In the one case we adduce circumstances that are meant to make it seem clear that the offending action should not be taken as a wrong: "He didn't mean it that way." "He couldn't help it." "He had no choice." "He didn't know that. . . ." These are examples of a type of excuse that tries to throw a different light on the insulting *act* itself, make it appear less unjust, while refraining from questioning the competence of the actor. The latter is precisely what we do in the second kind of excuse when we point out that the wrongdoing was the act of a child, a drunk, a madman, etc., that it was committed by someone who was beside himself or incapacitated by stress, as from the effects of a serious illness, and so on. This second type of excuse invites us to view *the actor himself* in a different light, to wit, as someone to whom we cannot unqualifiedly ascribe the qualities that characterize a competent subject. In this case we are supposed to take an objectivating attitude that precludes any moral reproach from the start:

The objective attitude may be emotionally toned in many ways, but not in all ways: It may include repulsion or fear, it may include pity or even love, though not all kinds of love. But it cannot include the range of reactive feelings and attitudes which belong to involvement or participation with others in inter-personal human relationships; it cannot include resentment, gratitude, forgiveness, anger, or the sort of love which two adults can sometimes be said to feel reciprocally for each other. If your attitude towards someone is wholly objective, then though you might fight him, you cannot quarrel with him, and though you may talk to him, even negotiate with him, you cannot reason with him. You can at most *pretend* to quarrel, or to reason, with him.[7]

Strawson concludes that such personal responses on the part of the offended party as resentment are possible only in the performative attitude of a person taking part in interaction. The objectivating attitude of the nonparticipant observer annuls the communicative roles of I and thou, the first and second persons, and neutralizes the realm of moral phenomena as such. The third-person attitude causes this realm of phenomena to vanish.

2

Strawson's remarks are important for methodological reasons as well. The moral philosopher must take up a vantage point from which he can perceive moral phenomena *as* moral phenomena. Strawson shows how different moral feelings are linked to each other internally. The personal responses of the injured party can be compensated for by excuses, as we saw. The aggrieved party, for his part, can forgive an injustice he has suffered. To the feelings of the insulted person corresponds the gratitude felt by someone who is the recipient of a good deed. To the condemnation of a wrong corresponds the admiration we feel for a good act. Our feelings of indifference, contempt, malevolence, satisfaction, recognition, encouragement, consolation, etc., have innumerable nuances. Among them the feelings of guilt and obligation are of course crucial. In trying to explain this web of emotional attitudes and feelings with the tools of linguistic analysis, Strawson is interested primarily in the fact that all these emotions are embedded in a practice of everyday life that is accessible to us only in a performative attitude. This gives the web of moral feelings a certain *ineluctability*: we cannot retract at will our commitment to a lifeworld whose members we are. In comparison, the objectivating attitude toward moral phenomena, which we must first have perceived from a participant's perspective, is secondary: "We look with an objective eye on the compulsive behavior of the neurotic or the tiresome behaviour of a very young child, thinking in terms of treatment or training. But we can sometimes look with something like the same eye on the behaviour of the normal and the mature. We have this resource and can sometimes use it: as a refuge, say, from the strains of involvement; or as an aid to policy; or simply out of intellectual curiosity. Being human, we cannot, in the normal case, do this for long, or altogether."[8]

Strawson's point sheds some light on the position of ethical theories that seek to *reinterpret the moral intuitions of everyday life*

from an observer's perspective. Even if they were true, empiricist ethical theories could have no enlightening impact because they remain fundamentally cut off from the intuitions
of everyday life: "The human commitment to participation in
ordinary inter-personal relationships is, I think, too thorough-
going and deeply rooted for us to take seriously the thought
that a general theoretical conviction might so change our world
that, in it, there were no longer any such things as interpersonal relationships as we normally understand them. . . . A
sustained objectivity of inter-personal attitude, and the human
isolation that would entail, does not seem to be something of
which human beings would be capable, even if some general
truth were a theoretical ground for it."[9] As long as moral
philosophy concerns itself with clarifying the everyday intuitions into which we are socialized, it must be able to adopt, at
least virtually, the attitude of someone who participates in the
communicative practice of everyday life.

3

Strawson's third point leads to the moral core of the emotional
responses discussed above. Indignation and resentment are
directed at a *specific* other person who has violated our integrity.
Yet what makes this indignation moral is not the fact that the
interaction between two concrete individuals has been disturbed but rather the violation of an underlying *normative expectation* that is valid not only for ego and alter but also for all
members of a social group or even, in the case of moral norms
in the strict sense, for all competent actors. This alone explains
the guilt feeling that accompanies the wrongdoer's self-accu-
sation. To the reproaches of the offended party correspond
the scruples of the perpetrator once he realizes that in offending the particular person, he has also violated something impersonal or at least suprapersonal, namely a generalized
expectation that both parties hold. Feelings of guilt and obligation point beyond the particular sphere of what concerns
individual persons in specific situations. Emotional responses
directed against individual persons in specific situations would
be devoid of moral character were they not connected with an
impersonal kind of indignation over some breach of a general-

ized norm or behavioral expectation. It is only their claim to *general* validity that gives an interest, a volition, or a norm the dignity of moral authority.[10]

4

This characteristic of moral validity is related to another observation. There is apparently an inner connection between, on the one hand, the authority of generally accepted norms or commands, i.e., the obligation on the part of those to whom the norm is addressed to do what is enjoined and refrain from doing what is forbidden, and, on the other hand, the impersonality of their claim. Such norms claim that they exist by right and that if necessary, they can be *shown* to exist by right. This means that indignation and reproaches directed against the violation of a norm must in the last analysis be based on a cognitive foundation. The person who makes such a reproach believes that the perpetrator may be able to justify himself by, for example, rejecting as unjustified the normative expectations to which the indignant party is appealing. To say that *I ought* to do something means that I *have good reason*s for doing it.

One would misconceive the nature of these reasons, however, were one to reduce the question What ought I to do? to a question of mere prudence or expediency. The empiricist does precisely that. He reduces the practical question "What ought I to do? to two other questions: What do I want to do? and How can I do it?[11] Nor is anything gained by adopting a position of social utility if the utilitarian reduces the question What ought we to do? to the technical question of the instrumental creation of socially desirable outcomes. In essence, the utilitarian views norms from the outset as instruments that can be justified as more or less appropriate in terms of their social utility:

But the social utility of these practices . . . is not what is now in question. What is in question is the justified sense that to speak in terms of social utility alone is to leave out something vital in our conception of these practices. The vital thing can be restored by attending to that complicated web of attitudes and feelings which form an essential part of the moral life as we know it, and which are quite opposed to objectivity of attitude. Only by attending to this range of attitudes can we recover from the facts as we know them a sense of what we mean, i.e. of *all* we mean when, speaking the language of morals, we speak of desert, responsibility, guilt, condemnation and justice.[12]

At this point Strawson draws together the diverse strands of his argument. The only way to avoid misconstruing what it means to justify a mode of action in moral-practical terms, he insists, is to maintain our focus on the web of moral feelings that is embedded in the communicative practice of everyday life and to situate properly the question What ought I to do? "Inside the general structure or web of human attitudes and feelings of which I have been speaking, there is endless room for modification, redirection, criticism, and justification. But questions of justification are internal to the structure or relate to modifications internal to it. The existence of the general framework of attitudes itself is something we are given with the fact of human society. As a whole, it neither calls for, nor permits, an *external* 'rational' justification."[13]

Strawson's phenomenology of the moral is relevant because it shows that the world of moral phenomena can be grasped only in the performative attitude of participants in interaction, that resentment and personal emotional responses in general point to suprapersonal standards for judging norms and commands, and that the moral-practical justification of a mode of action aims at an aspect *different* from the feeling-neutral assessment of means-ends relations, even when such assessment is made from the point of view of the general welfare. It is no coincidence that Strawson analyzes feelings. Feelings seem to have a similar function for the moral justification of action as sense perceptions have for the theoretical justification of facts.

2 Objectivist and subjectivist approaches to ethics

In his *Examination of the Place of Reason in Ethics* (1950) (which, incidentally, is a telling example of how one can ask the right questions in philosophy without finding the right answers), Stephen Toulmin draws a parallel between feelings and perceptions.[14] In everyday life, expressions of belief like "This is a crooked stick" ordinarily serve as unproblematic mediators in interaction. The same holds for emotive utterances like "How could I do that!" "You ought to help him," "He gave me a rough time," "She behaved splendidly," etc. What happens when utterances like these run into objections is that the claim to validity they raise is challenged. The hearer asks whether the assertion about the stick is true, whether the reproach (or self-reproach), the admonition, or the praise is *right*. The speaker may then tone down her claim and maintain only that the stick *appeared* crooked to her, that she had the definite *sense* that she shouldn't have done that, or that she really did behave splendidly, and so on. She may end up adopting a *physical explanation*, namely that the crookedness she was just talking about is actually an optical illusion that occurs when a straight object is partly submerged in water. This explanation will clear up the problematic state of affairs in which a stick perceived as crooked is in fact straight. In a similar manner, *moral justification* will tend to illuminate a problematic action by excusing, criticizing, or justifying it. An elaborate moral argument is related to the web of moral feelings and attitudes as a theoretical argument is to the stream of perceptions: "In ethics, as in science, incorrigible but conflicting reports of personal experience (sensible or emotional) are replaced by judgments aiming at universality and impartiality—about the 'real value,' the 'real colour,' the 'real shape' of an object, rather than the shape, colour or value one would ascribe to it on the basis of immediate experience alone."[15] Just as theoretical criticism of misleading everyday experiences serves to correct beliefs and expectations, so moral criticism serves to alter modes of action or to correct the judgments we make about them.

The parallel Toulmin draws between the theoretical explanation of facts and the moral justification of modes of action, in other words between the experiential bases of perceptions and feelings respectively, is not all that odd. If "x ought to do y" implies "x has good reasons to do y," questions concerning the decision between alternative norm-guided acts, or the choice between different norms themselves, must admit of truth and falsity. "To believe in the objectivity of morals is to believe that some moral statements are true."[16]

What it means to speak of "moral truth" requires clarification. Alan R. White enumerates ten different reasons that speak to the possibility of normative statements being true or false. As a rule, we utter normative statements in the indicative mood, indicating thereby that normative statements, like descriptive ones, are open to criticism, that is, to refutation and justification. The obvious objection that moral reasoning concerns something that ought to be done rather than the way things stand is met by White in the following way: "In moral discussion about what to do, what we agree on or argue about, assume, discover or prove, doubt or know is not whether *to do* so and so but *that* so-and-so *is* the right, better, or only thing to do. And this is something that can be true or false. I can believe that X ought to be done or is the best thing to do, but I cannot believe a decision any more than I can believe a command or a question. Coming to the decision *to do* so-and-so *is* the best or the right thing to do. Moral pronouncements may entail answers to the question 'What shall I do?' They do not *give* such answers."[17]

Arguments like White's point in the direction of a cognitivist ethics. However, the notion that practical issues admit of truth implies an assimilation of normative to descriptive propositions. If we assume—correctly, I believe—that normative statements can be valid or invalid, and if we interpret the validity claims that are contested in moral arguments in terms of the readily available model of propositional truth, as the expression "moral truth" suggests, then we are led—falsely, I believe—to interpret the possible truth of practical questions as meaning that normative statements can be true or false in the same way that descriptive statements can be true or false. Intuitionism is an example of a theory that assimilates normative statements to such predicative statements as "This table is yellow," "All swans are white," etc. G. E. Moore undertook a detailed investigation of the way the predicates "good" and "yellow" are related.[18] For evaluative predicates he constructs a theory of nonnatural properties that can be grasped in ideal intuitions or read from ideal objects analogously to the way perception grasps the properties of things.[19] In this way Moore wants to show that the truth of substantive normative statements that make intuitive sense can be at least indirectly proved. Reformulating typical normative sentences as predicative sentences, however, puts this kind of analysis on the wrong track.

Expressions such as "good" or "right" should be compared not with predicates of properties like "yellow" or "white" but with higher-level predicates like "true." The statement

(a)   Under given conditions one ought to lie

can be correctly reformulated as

(a')   Under given conditions, it is right (or good in the moral sense) to lie.

It is plain to see that the predicative expression "is right" or "is good" in sentence (a') plays an entirely different logical role than "is yellow" in the sentence

(b)   This table is yellow.

As soon as the value predicate "good" takes on the meaning of "morally good," we can see the asymmetry. The only statements that are comparable are the following reformulations (c) and (d).

(c)   It is right (or commanded) that h.

(d)   It is true (it is the case) that p.

Here h stands for (a) and p stands for (b). The metalinguistic reformulations (c) and (d) make explicit the claims to validity that sentences (a) and (b) implicitly contain. We can see by the form of sentences (c) and (d) that analysis of the attribution of predicates is not the right way to explain the claims to validity embodied in statements (c) and (d). If we want to compare claims to rightness with claims to truth without assimilating the one to the other, we have to clarify how p and h can be *grounded*, how *good* reasons can be adduced for considering (a) and (b) valid or invalid.

In sum, we need to show what is specific to the justification of moral commands. Toulmin saw this need clearly. He writes, "'Rightness' is not a property; and when I asked two people which course of action was the right one I was not asking them about a property—what I wanted to know was whether there was any reason for choosing one course of action rather than another. . . . All that two people need (and all that they have) to contradict one another about in the case of ethical predicates are the *reasons* for doing this rather than that or the other."[20] Toulmin also saw clearly that the subjectivist answer to the weaknesses of the ethical objectivism of Moore and others is only the reverse side of the same coin. Both camps start from the false premise that truth, or the validity of descriptive propositions, and it alone, defines the sense in which a statement, any statement, is accepted as valid.

The intuitionist attempt to grasp moral truths was doomed to failure because normative statements cannot be verified or falsified; that is, they cannot be tested in the same way as descriptive statements. In view of this, the alternative is a wholesale rejection of the idea that practical questions admit of truth. The *subjectivists* do not, of course, deny the grammatical facts, which suggest that people quarrel over moral issues all the time in everyday life as if such quarrels could be decided on the basis of good reasons.[21] But they explain this naive trust in the justifiability of norms and commands as an illusion arising from everyday moral intuitions. In comparison with cognitivists like Strawson, who merely want to make explicit the intuitive knowledge already possessed by competent participants in interaction, ethical skeptics must take on a far more demanding task: they must explain counterintuitively what our moral judgments, contrary to their manifest claim to validity, *really* mean and what functions moral feelings *actually* perform.

The linguistic model for this kind of analysis are sentences with which no discursively redeemable claims to validity are connected. I am thinking of first-person sentences expressing subjective preferences, desires, and aversions, or imperatives with which a speaker tries to get another person to behave in a certain way. The *emotivist* and the *imperativist* approaches try to show that the unclear meaning of normative statements is ultimately derived from the meaning of experiential or imperative statements, or some combination of the two. In this view, the normative semantic components of normative statements express in coded form either subjective attitudes or attempts at persuasion, or both: "'This is good' means roughly the same as 'I approve of this; do as well,' trying to capture by this equivalence both the function of the moral judgment as expressive of the speaker's attitude and the function of the moral judgment as designed to influence the hearer's attitudes."[22]

In his *Language of Morals*, R. M. Hare develops a *prescriptivist model*.[23] Hare broadens the imperativist approach by analyzing normative ("good" and "ought") sentences in terms of a combination of imperatives and evaluations.[24] Here, then, the central semantic component in a normative sentence is the fact that the speaker recommends or prescribes to the hearer a certain option from among alternative courses of action. Since such recommendations and prescriptions are ultimately based on principles arbitrarily adopted by the speaker, however, evaluative sentences of this type are not really suitable as a model for the analysis of normative sentences. Hare's prescriptivism amounts to a form of ethical decisionism. In his theory, the basis for justifying substantive normative sentences is sentences of intention, i.e., sentences by which the speaker expresses his choice of principles, ultimately his choice of a form of life. This choice, on the other hand, is not susceptible of justification.[25]

Compared with emotivist and imperativist versions of ethics in the narrower sense, Hare's version has the advantage of taking into account the fact that we do debate moral issues with reasons. All three metaethical approaches, however, come down to the same skeptical point. The meaning of our moral vocabulary, they declare, consists in reality in saying something which could be said better with experiential sentences, imperatives, or intentional sentences. None of these types of sentences can serve as a vehicle for making a truth claim or for making any claim to validity that requires argumentation. That is why, on this view, the belief in the existence of moral truth is construed as an illusion stemming from the intuitive understanding of everyday life. In short, with a single blow noncognitivist approaches deprive the sphere of everyday moral intuitions of its significance. From a scientific perspective, according to these theories, one can talk about morality only in empirical terms. In so doing, we take an objectivating attitude. We confine ourselves to describing the functions of feelings and sentences that actors view subjectively as moral. Theories such as these have no desire to compete with philosophical ethics. Nor can they. All they do is to pave the way for empirical studies once there is agreement on the premise that moral issues do not admit of truth and that ethical inquiry in the sense of normative theory is meaningless.

This metaethical assertion is by no means as unassailable as the skeptics presume. The noncognitivist position relies primarily on two arguments: first, the fact that disputes about basic moral principles ordinarily do not issue in agreement, and second, the failure, discussed above, of all attempts to explain what it might mean for normative propositions to be true, whether such attempts be along intuitionist lines or in terms of either the classical idea of natural law (which I will not go into here) or an ethics of material value à la Scheler and Hartmann.[26] The first argument loses its force if we can name a principle that makes agreement in moral argumentation possible in principle. The second argument fails if we give up the premise that normative sentences, to the extent to which they are connected with validity claims at all, can be valid or invalid only in the sense of propositional truth.

When employing normative utterances in everyday life, we raise claims to validity that we are prepared to defend against criticism. When we discuss moral-practical questions of the form "What ought I to do?" we presuppose that the answers need not be arbitrary; we trust our ability to distinguish in principle between right norms or commands and wrong ones. But if normative sentences do not admit of truth in the narrow sense of the word "true," that is, *in the same sense* in which descriptive statements can be true or false, we will have to formulate the task of explaining the meaning of "moral truth" or, if that expression is already misleading, the meaning of "normative rightness" in such a way that we are not tempted to assimilate the one type of sentence to the other. We will have to proceed on a weaker assumption, namely that normative claims to validity are *analogous to truth claims*. We will have to return to Toulmin's formulation of the basic question of ethics: "What kind of argument, of reasoning is it proper for us to accept in support of moral decisions?"[27] Toulmin abandons the semantic analysis of expressions and sentences, focusing instead on the issue of the mode in which normative propositions are justified, the *form of the arguments* adduced in defending or rejecting norms and commands, and the criteria for good reasons that motivate us, by dint of insight, to recognize demands as moral obligations. "What kinds of things make a conclusion worthy of belief?"[28] With this query Toulmin makes the transition to the level of a theory of argumentation.

II   The Principle of Universalization as a Rule of Argumentation

The propadeutic comments I have just made were meant to defend the cognitivist approach in ethics against the metaethical diversionary tactics of value skepticism and to lay the groundwork for answering the question of in what sense and in what way moral commands and norms can be justified. In the substantive portion of my reflections (section 3) I will begin by reviewing the role played by normative validity claims in the practice of daily life in order to explain how the deontological claim connected with commands and norms is distinguished from the assertoric claim. I will argue that there are compelling reasons for recasting moral theory in the form of an analysis of moral argumentation. In section 4 I will introduce the principle of universalization (U) as a bridging principle that makes agreement in moral argumentation possible. The version of the principle that I will give excludes any monological application of this rule for argumentation. Finally, in section 5 I will take up certain ideas of Ernst Tugendhat and show that moral justifications are dependent on argumentation actually being carried out, not for pragmatic reasons of an equalization of power, but for internal reasons, namely that real argument makes moral insight possible.

3 Assertoric and normative claims to validity in communicative action

The attempt to ground ethics in the form of a logic of moral argumentation has no chance of success unless we can identify a special type of validity claim connected with commands and norms and can identify it on the level on which moral dilemmas initially emerge: within the horizon of the lifeworld, where Strawson had to look for moral phenomena when he marshalled the evidence of ordinary language against the skeptic. If claims to validity do not appear in the plural there in contexts of communicative action and thus prior to any reflection, we cannot expect a differentiation between truth and normative rightness to occur on the level of argumentation either.

I will not repeat the analysis of action oriented to reaching understanding that I have presented elsewhere,[29] but I would like to review one fundamental idea. I call interactions *communicative* when the participants coordinate their plans of action consensually, with the agreement reached at any point being evaluated in terms of the intersubjective recognition of validity claims. In cases where agreement is reached through explicit linguistic processes, the actors make three different claims to validity in their speech acts as they come to an agreement with one another about something. Those claims are claims to truth, claims to rightness, and claims to truthfulness, according to whether the speaker refers to something in the objective world (as the totality of existing states of affairs), to something in the shared social world (as the totality of the legitimately regulated interpersonal relationships of a social group), or to something in his own subjective world (as the totality of experiences to which one has privileged access). Further, I distinguish between communicative and strategic action. Whereas in strategic action one actor seeks to *influence* the behavior of another by means of the threat of sanctions or the prospect of gratification in order to *cause* the interaction to continue as the first actor desires, in communicative action one actor seeks *rationally* to *motivate* another by relying on the illocutionary binding/bonding effect (*Bindungseffekt*) of the offer contained in his speech act.

The fact that a speaker can rationally motivate a hearer to accept such an offer is due not to the validity of what he says but to the speaker's guarantee that he will, if necessary, make efforts to redeem the claim that the hearer has accepted. It is this guarantee that effects the coordination between speaker and hearer. In the case of claims to truth or rightness, the speaker can redeem his guarantee discursively, that is, by adducing reasons; in the case of claims to truthfulness he does so through consistent behavior. (A person can convince someone that he means what he says only through his actions, not by giving reasons.) As soon as the hearer accepts the guarantee offered by the speaker, obligations are assumed that have consequences for the interaction, obligations that are contained in the meaning of what was said. In the case of orders and directives, for instance, the obligations to act hold primarily for the hearer, in the case of promises and announcements, they hold for the speaker, in the case of agreements and contracts, they are symmetrical, holding for both parties, and in the case of substantive normative recommendations and warnings, they hold asymmetrically for both parties.

Unlike these regulative speech acts, the meaning of a constative speech act gives rise to obligations only insofar as the speaker and the hearer agree to base their actions on situational definitions that do not contradict the propositions they accept as true at any given point. Obligations to act flow directly from the meaning of an expressive speech act in that the speaker specifies what it is that his behavior does not contradict and will not contradict in the future. Owing to the fact that communication oriented to reaching understanding has a validity basis, a speaker can persuade a hearer to accept a speech-act offer by guaranteeing that he will redeem a criticizable validity claim. In so doing, he creates a binding/bonding effect between speaker and hearer that makes the continuation of their interaction possible.

The two *discursively redeemable* claims to validity that are of particular interest to us, claims to propositional truth and claims to normative rightness, play their roles as coordinators of action in different ways. A number of asymmetries beween them suggest that they occupy different "positions" in the communicative practice of everyday life.

On the face of it, *assertoric statements* used in *constative speech acts* appear to be related to *facts* as *normative statements* used in *regulative speech acts* are related to *legitimately ordered interpersonal relations*. The *truth* of propositions seems to signify the *existence* of states of affairs in much the same way as the *rightness* of actions signifies the *observance* of norms. If we look at the matter more closely, however, we notice some interesting differences. The relation of speech acts to norms is not the same as the relation of speech acts to facts. Let us look at the case of moral norms that can be formulated in terms of universal "ought" sentences or commandments:

(a)   One ought not to kill anybody.

(a′)   It is commanded not to kill anybody.

We make reference to norms of action of the above kind in regulative speech acts, and we do so in a variety of ways: by giving orders, making contracts, opening meetings, issuing warnings, granting exceptions, giving advice, etc. A moral norm, however, lays claim to meaning and validity regardless of whether it is promulgated or made use of in a specific way. A norm may be formulated in a statement like (a), but this act of formulating it, i.e., of writing a sentence, *need not* itself by conceived of as a speech act, that is, as something other than the impersonal expression of the norm. Statements such as (a) are commands that we can address *secondarily* in one way or another through speech acts. This has no equivalent in the domain of facts. There are no assertoric propositions that have an existence independent of speech acts, as norms do. If such assertoric statements are to have pragmatic meaning at all, they *must* be used in a speech act. Unlike sentences (a) and (a′), descriptive statements such as "Iron is magnetic" or "It is the case that iron is magnetic" cannot be expressed or used independently of the illocutionary role of a certain type of speech act if they are to retain their assertoric power.

We can account for this asymmetry by saying that claims to truth reside *only* in speech acts, whereas the locus of normative claims to validity is primarily in norms and only derivatively in speech acts.[30] To use an ontological mode of expression, we might say that this asymmetry is due to the fact that the orders of society, which we either conform to or deviate from, are not constituted *independently of validity*, as are the orders of nature, toward which we can assume an objectivating attitude. The social reality that we address in our regulative speech acts has by its very nature an *intrinsic* link to normative validity claims. Claims to truth, on the other hand, have no such intrinsic link to entities; they are inherently related only to the constative speech acts by which we refer to entities when we use fact-stating locutions to represent states of affairs.

Owing to the fact that normative validity claims are built into the universe of norms, the latter reveals a peculiar kind of objectivity vis-à-vis regulative speech acts, an objectivity that the universe of facts does not possess vis-à-vis constative speech acts. To be sure, "objectivity" in this connection refers only to the independence of "objective spirit," for entities and facts are, of course, independent in a completely different sense than is everything we consider part of the social world when we take a norm-conformative attitude. For example, norms are dependent upon the continual reestablishment of legitimately ordered interpersonal relationships. They would assume a utopian character in the negative sense and lose their very meaning if we did not *complement* them, at least in our minds, with actors who might follow them and actions that might fulfill them. States of affairs, for their part, must be assumed to exist independently of whether we formulate them by means of true propositions or not.

Normative claims to validity, then, *mediate a mutual dependence* of language and the social world that does not exist for the relation of language to the objective world. This interlocking of claims to validity that reside in norms and claims to validity raised in regulative speech acts is also connected with the *ambiguous nature* of *normative validity*. While there is an unequivocal relation between existing states of affairs and true propositions about them, the "existence" or social currency of norms says nothing about whether the norms are valid. We must distinguish between the social fact that a norm is intersubjectively recognized and its worthiness to be recognized. There may be good reasons to consider the validity claim raised in a socially accepted norm to be unjustified. Conversely, a norm whose claim to validity is in fact redeemable does not necessarily meet with actual recognition or approval. Gaining acceptance on the part of a norm is encoded in a twofold fashion because our motives for recognizing normative claims to validity are rooted both in convictions and in sanctions, that is, they derive from a complex mixture of rational insight and force. Typically, rationally motivated assent will be combined with empirical *acquiescence*, effected by weapons or goods, to form a belief in legitimacy whose component parts are difficult to isolate. Such alloys are interesting in that they indicate that a positivistic enactment of norms is not sufficient to secure their *lasting* social acceptance. Enduring acceptance of a norm *also* depends on whether, in a given context of tradition, reasons for obedience can be mobilized, reasons that suffice to make the corresponding validity claim at least appear justified in the eyes of those concerned. Applied to modern societies, this means that there is no mass loyalty without legitimacy.[31]

But if in the long run the social currency of a norm depends on its being accepted as valid in the group to which it is addressed and if this recognition is based in turn on the expectation that the corresponding claim to validity can be redeemed with reasons, it follows that there is a connection between the "existence" of norms and the anticipated justifiability of the corresponding "ought" statements, a connection for which there is no parallel in the ontic sphere. While there is an internal connection between the existence of states of affairs and the truth of assertoric statements, there is no inner connection between the existence of states of affairs and the *expectation*, held by a certain group of people, that such statements can be justified. This difference may also explain why, when we ask what makes valid moral judgments possible, we are compelled to proceed *directly* to a logic of practical discourse, whereas determining the conditions for the validity of empirical judgments requires analysis in terms of epistemology and the philosophy of science, an analysis that is, at least initially, independent of a logic of theoretical discourse.

4 The moral principle, or the criterion for generalizing maxims of action

Following Toulmin,[32] I have recently set forth the outlines of a theory of argumentation.[33] I will not discuss that here. In what follows, I presuppose that a theory of argumentation must take the form of an "informal logic," because it is impossible to *force* agreement on theoretical and moral-practical issues either by means of deduction or on the basis of empirical evidence. To the degree to which arguments are deductively valid, i.e., compelling in terms of logical inference, they reveal nothing substantively new. To the degree to which arguments do have substantive content, they are based on experiences and needs/wants that are open to various intepretations in the light of changing theories using changing systems of description. Such experiences and needs/wants thus fail to offer an *ultimate* basis for argumentation.

In theoretical discourse the gap between particular observations and general hypotheses is bridged by some canon or other of induction. An analogous bridging principle is needed for practical discourse.[34] Accordingly, all studies of the logic of moral argumentation end up having to introduce a moral principle as a rule of argumentation that has a function equivalent to the principle of induction in the discourse of the empirical sciences.

Interestingly enough, in trying to identify such a moral principle, philosophers of diverse backgrounds always come up with principles whose basic idea is the same. *All* variants of cognitivist ethics take their bearings from the basic intuition contained in Kant's categorical imperative. What I am concerned with here is not the diversity of Kantian formulations but their underlying idea, which is designed to take into account the impersonal or general character of valid universal commands.[35] The moral principle is so conceived as to exclude as invalid any norm that could not meet with the qualified assent of all who are or might be affected by it. This bridging principle, which makes consensus possible, ensures that only those norms are accepted as valid that express a *general will*. As Kant noted time and again, moral norms must be suitable for expression as "universal laws." The categorical imperative can be understood as a principle that requires the universalizability of *modes of action* and *maxims*, or of the *interests* furthered by them (that is, those embodied in the norms of action). Kant wants to eliminate as invalid all those norms that "contradict" this requirement. He focuses on "that inner contradiction which promptly arises for an agent's maxim when his behavior can lead to its desired goal only upon the condition that it is not universally followed."[36] Admittedly, this and similar versions of the bridging principle imply a requirement of consistency which has led to *formalistic misunderstandings* and *selective interpretations*.

The principle of universalization is by no means exhausted by the requirement that moral norms must take the *form* of unconditionally universal "ought" statements. The *grammatical form* of normative statements alone, which does not permit such sentences to refer to or be addressed to particular groups or individuals, is not a sufficient condition for valid moral commands, for we could give such universal form to commands that are plainly immoral. What is more, in some respects the requirement of formal universality may well be too restrictive; it may make sense to submit nonmoral norms of action (whose range of jurisdiction is socially and spatiotemporally limited) to a practical discourse (restricted in this case to those affected and hence relative), and to test them for generalizability.

Other philosophers subscribe to a less formalistic view of the consistency required by the principle of universality. Their aim is to avoid the contradictions that occur when equal cases are treated unequally and unequal ones equally. R. M. Hare has given this requirement the form of a semantic postulate. As we do when we attribute descriptive predicates ("is red"), so we should attribute normative predicates ("is of value," "is good," "is right") in *conformity with a rule*, using the same linguistic expression in all cases that are the same in the respects relevant to the particular case. Applied to moral norms, Hare's consistency postulate comes to this: every individual, before making a particular norm the basis for his moral judgment, should test whether he can advocate or "will" the adoption of this norm by every other individual in a comparable situation. This or another similar postulate is suitable to serve as a moral principle only if it is conceived as a warrant of impartiality in the process of judging. But one can hardly derive the meaning of impartiality from the notion of consistent language use.

Kurt Baier[37] and Bernard Gert[38] come closer to this meaning of the principle of universalization when they argue that valid moral norms must be generally teachable and publicly defendable. The same is true of Marcus Singer when he proposes the requirement that norms are valid only if they ensure equality of treatment.[39] Yet just as an impartial process of judging is not guaranteed by an empirical check to see that allowance for disagreement has been made, so a norm cannot be considered the expression of the common interest of all who might be affected simply because it seems acceptable to some of them under the condition that it be applied in a nondiscriminatory fashion. The intuition expressed in the idea of the generalizability of maxims intends something more than this, namely, that valid norms must *deserve* recognition by *all* concerned. It is not sufficient, therefore, for *one person* to test whether he can will the adoption of a contested norm after considering the consequences and the side effects that would occur if all persons followed that norm or whether every other person in an identical position could will the adoption of such a norm. In both cases the process of judging is relative to the vantage point and perspective of *some* and not *all* concerned. True impartiality pertains only to that standpoint from which one can generalize precisely those norms that can count on universal assent because they perceptibly embody an interest common to all affected. It is these norms that deserve intersubjective recognition. Thus the impartiality of judgment is expressed in a principle that constrains *all* affected to adopt the perspectives of *all others* in the balancing of interests. The principle of universalization is intended to compel the *universal exchange of roles* that G. H. Mead called "ideal role taking" or "universal discourse."[40] Thus every valid norm has to fulfill the following condition:

(U) *All* affected can accept the consequences and the side effects its *general* observance can be anticipated to have for the satisfaction of *everyone's* interests (and these consequences are preferred to those of known alternative possibilities for regulation).[41]

We should not mistake this principle of universalization (U) for the following principle, which already contains the distinctive idea of an ethics of discourse.

(D) Only those norms can claim to be valid that meet (or could meet) with the approval of all affected in their capacity *as participants in a practical discourse.*

This principle of discourse ethics (D), to which I will return after offering my justification for (U), already *presupposes* that we *can* justify our choice of a norm. At this point in my argument, that presupposition is what is at issue. I have introduced (U) as a rule of argumentation that makes agreement in practical discourses possible whenever matters of concern to all are open to regulation in the equal interest of everyone. Once this bridging principle has been justified, we will be able to make the transition to discourse ethics. I have formulated (U) in a way that precludes a monological application of the principle. First, (U) regulates only argumentation among a plurality of participants; second, it suggests the perspective of real-life argumentation, in which all affected are admitted as participants. In this respect my universalization principle differs from the one John Rawls proposes.

Rawls wants to ensure impartial consideration of all affected interests by putting the moral judge into a fictitious "original position," where differences of power are eliminated, equal freedoms for all are guaranteed, and the individual is left in a condition of ignorance with regard to the position he might occupy in a future social order. Like Kant, Rawls operationalizes the standpoint of impartiality in such a way that every individual can undertake to justify basic norms on his own. The same holds for the moral philosopher himself. It is only logical, therefore, that Rawls views the substantive parts of his study (e.g., the principle of average utility), not as the *contribution* of a participant in argumentation to a process of discursive will formation regarding the basic institutions of late capitalist society, but as the outcome of a "theory of justice," which he as an expert is qualified to construct.

If we keep in mind the action-coordinating function that normative validity claims play in the communicative practice of everyday life, we see why the problems to be resolved in moral argumentation cannot be handled monologically but require a cooperative effort. By entering into a process of moral argumentation, the participants continue their communicative action in a reflexive attitude with the aim of restoring a consensus that has been disrupted. Moral argumentation thus serves to settle conflicts of action by consensual means. Conflicts in the domain of norm-guided interactions can be traced directly to some disruption of a normative consensus. Repairing a disrupted consensus can mean one of two things: restoring intersubjective recognition of a validity claim after it has become controversial or assuring intersubjective recognition for a new validity claim that is a substitute for the old one. Agreement of this kind expresses a *common will*. If moral argumentation is to produce this kind of agreement, however, it is not enough for the individual to reflect on whether he can assent to a norm. It is not even enough for each individual to reflect in this way and then to register his vote. What is needed is a "real" process of argumentation in which the individuals concerned cooperate. Only an intersubjective process of reaching understanding can produce an agreement that is reflexive in nature; only it can give the participants the knowledge that they have collectively become convinced of something.

From this viewpoint, the categorical imperative needs to be reformulated as follows: "Rather than ascribing as valid to all others any maxim that I can will to be a universal law, I must submit my maxim to all others for purposes of discursively testing its claim to universality. The emphasis shifts from what each can will without contradiction to be a general law, to what all can will in agreement to be a universal norm."[42] This version of the universality principle does in fact entail the idea of a cooperative process of argumentation. For one thing, nothing better prevents others from perspectively distorting one's own interests than actual participation. It is in this pragmatic sense that the individual is the last court of appeal for judging what is in his best interest. On the other hand, the descriptive terms in which each individual perceives his interests must be open to criticism by others. Needs and wants are interpreted in the light of cultural values. Since cultural values are always components of intersubjectively shared traditions, the revision of the values used to interpret needs and wants cannot be a matter for individuals to handle monologically.[43]

5 Argumentation versus participation

Discourse ethics, then, stands or falls with two assumptions: (a) that normative claims to validity have cognitive meaning and can be treated *like* claims to truth and (b) that the justification of norms and commands requires that a real discourse be carried out and thus cannot occur in a strictly monological form, i.e., in the form of a hypothetical process of argumentation occurring in the individual mind. Before returning to the debate in ethics between cognitivists and skeptics, I want to discuss a conception developed recently by Ernst Tugendhat, a conception that stands in an oblique relationship to the opposition between those two positions. On the one hand, Tugendhat holds to the intuition that I expressed in the form of a principle of universalization (U), arguing that a norm is justified only if it is "equally good" for each of the persons concerned. According to Tugendhat, the participants themselves must determine whether this is the case in an actual discourse. On the other hand, Tugendhat rejects assumption (a) and opposes interpreting assumption (b) in terms of discourse ethics. Although he wants to avoid skeptical conclusions, he nonetheless shares the skeptical presupposition that the prescriptive validity of norms cannot be conceived as analogous to the propositional validity of truths. But if the prescriptive validity of norms has a volitional rather than a cognitive significance, practical discourse must serve something other than the argumentative clarification of controversial claims to validity. For Tugendhat, discourse is a precautionary measure that, by means of rules of communication, ensures that all concerned have an equal chance to take part in a fair process of compromise formation. The need for argumentation arises from the need to make participation, not cognition, possible. I will begin by sketching the problematic within which Tugendhat develops this thesis.[44]

Statement of the problem

Tugendhat distinguishes semantic rules fixing the meaning of a linguistic expression from pragmatic rules determining how speakers and hearers make communicative use of such expressions. Like the illocutionary components of language, sentences that can be used only communicatively call for a pragmatic analysis, regardless of whether they occur in situations of real speech or only in our minds. Other sentences can, it seems, be stripped of their pragmatic presuppositions and used monologically without detriment to their meaning. They primarily serve thinking and not communication. To this category belong assertoric and intentional sentences, whose full meaning can be explicated in terms of semantic analysis alone. In line with the tradition that goes back to Frege, Tugendhat assumes that the truth of sentences is a semantic matter. According to this view, the justification of sentences is a monological matter. Whether or not one can attribute a predicate to an object, for instance, is a question that any competent subject can decide for himself on the basis of semantic rules. The same is true of intentional sentences. Once again, no intersubjective argumentation is required, even though we might in fact undertake such cooperative argumentation, i.e., several participants might exchange arguments. In contrast to the justification of propositions, the justification of norms is considered by Tugendhat to be not accidentally but *essentially* a communicative endeavor. Whether a controversial norm is equally good for everyone concerned is a question that has to be decided in accordance with pragmatic rules in the context of real discourses. Thus a genuinely pragmatic concept enters the picture when Tugendhat talks about the justification of norms.

The assumption that questions of validity are *nothing but* questions of semantics is crucial to the rest of Tugendhat's analysis. On this presupposition, the pragmatic meaning of justifying a norm cannot pertain to the validity of a norm, at least not when the latter expression is understood as analogous to propositional truth. Instead, there is *something else* hidden behind it, namely a notion of impartiality tied up with a volitional process rather than a judgmental process.

This approach is problematic because of its semanticist assumptions, which I cannot discuss fully here. The semantic concept of truth—or more generally the thesis that the dispute about whether statements are valid or not can be resolved *in foro interno*, in accordance with semantic rules alone—flows directly from an analysis oriented toward predicative statements in a thing-event language.[45] This model is inappropriate because elementary statements like "This ball is red" are component parts of everyday communication; their truth is hardly ever disputed. We have to look for analytically fruitful examples in places where substantive controversies erupt and where claims to truth are systematically questioned. Conceptions of verification derived from a semantic concept of truth lose their plausibility if one looks at the dynamics of the growth of knowledge, especially theoretical knowledge, and the way the scientific community grounds universal existential statements, counterfactual statements, statements with a temporal index, and so on.[46] It is precisely the substantive disagreements that cannot be convincingly resolved on the basis of a monological application of semantic rules. This is the reason why Toulmin found it necessary to develop his pragmatic approach, a theory of informal argumentation.

The argument

If one accepts the above semanticist presuppositions, the question arises why real norm-justifying discourses are necessary at all. What can we mean by justifying norms once the analogy to the justification of propositions has been proscribed? The reasons that appear in practical discourses, Tugendhat answers, are reasons for or against an intention or a decision to accept a particular course of action. The model for this is the justification intrinsic to first-person intentional sentences. I have good reasons for acting in a certain way if it is in my interest to do so, or if it is good for me to realize the corresponding ends. Initially, then, the problem turns on questions of teleological action ("What do I want to do?" and "What can I do?") rather than on the moral question ("What ought I to do?"). Tugendhat introduces the deontological perspective by going from the justification of individual intentions to the justification of the common intentions of a group: "What common course of action do we want to establish for ourselves?" or "To what course of action do we want to commit ourselves?" This brings in a pragmatic element. For if the course of action which needs justification is collective in nature, the members of the collectivity must reach a *common* decision. They have to try to persuade one another that it is in the interest of each that all act as they intend. In the process, one will cite to another the *reasons* he has for willing that an action be declared socially binding. Each member must be convinced that the proposed norm is equally good for all. And this process is what we call practical discourse. Any norm that is put into effect via this route can be called justified because the fact that the decision is reached through a process of argumentation indicates that the norm deserves to be called equally good for all concerned. *this doesn't follow*

If the justification of norms is conceived in this way, according to Tugendhat, the import of practical discourses will also become clear. Their significance cannot be primarily cognitive. For the question to be decided rationally, the question whether a course of action is in a person's interest ultimately has to be answered by that person alone, for intentional sentences are *no* monologically justifiable in accordance with semantic rules. Argumentation as an intersubjective procedure is necessary only because in establishing a collective mode of action, we have to coordinate our individual intentions and come to a joint decision. Only when this decision emerges from argumentation, only when it comes about in accordance with pragmatic rules of discourse, do we consider the resulting norm justified. One has to make sure everyone concerned has had a chance to freely give his consent. Argumentation is designed to prevent some from simply suggesting or prescribing to others what is good for them. On this view, then, argumentation is designed to make possible not *impartiality of judgment* but *freedom from influence* or *autonomy in will formation*. To that extent the rules of discourse themselves have a normative quality, for they neutralize imbalances of power and provide for equal opportunities to realize one's interests.

The form of argumentation thus arises out of the need for participation and the need for an *equalization of power*:

This then seems to me to be the reason why moral questions, and in particular questions of political morality, must be justified in a discourse among those concerned. The reason is not, as Habermas thinks, that the process of moral reasoning is itself essentially communicative, but it is the other way around: one of the rules which result from moral reasoning, which as such may be carried through in solitary thinking, prescribes that only such legal norms are morally justified that are arrived at in an agreement by all concerned. And we can now see that the irreducibly communicative aspect is not a cognitive but a volitional factor. It is the morally obligatory respect for the autonomy of the will of everybody concerned that makes it necessary to require an agreement. (1981, p. 10ff)

This conception of morality would be unsatisfactory even if one accepted the semanticist presupposition on which it rests. It cannot account for an intuition that is very difficult to deny: the idea of impartiality, which cognitivist moral philosophers develop in the form of universality principles, cannot be reduced to the idea of a *balance of power*. Testing a norm to determine whether one can ascribe to it Tugendhat's predicate "equally good for everyone" demands an impartial *judgment* about the interests of all concerned. This requirement is not met by equality of opportunity to make one's own interests prevail. Impartiality in judging cannot be *replaced* by autonomy in will formation. Tugendhat confounds the conditions necessary for the discursive generation of a rationally motivated consensus with the conditions necessary for negotiating a fair compromise. In the first case it is assumed that the parties concerned perceive what is in the common interest of all. In the second case it is assumed that generalizable interests are not at issue. Participants in a practical discourse strive to clarify a common interest, whereas in negotiating a compromise they try to strike a balance between conflicting particular interests. Compromise too has its restrictive conditions. We must assume that a fair balance of interests can come about only when all concerned have equal rights to participation. But these principles of compromise formation in turn require actual practical discourses for justification, and thus they are not subject to the demand for compromise between competing interests.

Tugendhat has to pay a price for equating argumentation with will formation: he gives up the distinction between the validity of norms and their de facto acceptance in society:

To be sure we want the agreement to be a *rational agreement*, an agreement based on arguments, and if possible on moral arguments, and yet what is finally decisive is the *factual agreement*, and we have no right to disregard it by arguing that it was not rational. . . . Here we do have an act which is irreducibly pragmatic, and this precisely because it is not an act of *reason*, but an act of the *will*, an act of collective *choice*. The problem we are confronted with is not a problem of *justification* but of the *participation* in power, of who is to make the decisions about what is permitted and what not. (1981, p. 11)

The conclusions Tugendhat reaches are not in accord with his intention of defending the rational core of moral agreements produced through argumentation against the objectives of ethical skepticism. They are incompatible with an attempt to account for the fundamental intuition that when we say yes or no to norms and commands, we are expressing something more than the arbitrary will of a person who submits to or opposes an imperative claim to power. By conflating validity claims and power claims, Tugendhat cuts the ground out from under his own attempt to differentiate between justified and unjustified norms. He wants to subject the conditions of validity to semantic analysis, separating them from rules of discourse, which are to be analyzed pragmatically. In so doing, he reduces the intersubjective process of justification to a contingent communication event unrelated to validity.

Lumping together the dimension of the validity of norms, which proponents and opponents can argue about with reasons, and the dimension of the social currency of norms that are actually in effect robs normative validity of its autonomous significance. In his impressive analyses, Durkheim warned against the genetic fallacy of reducing the obligatory character of norms to the obedience shown by followers confronted with the power to command and the power to threaten sanctions. This is why Durkheim was interested in the primordial wrong-doing called sacrilege and in norms that predated the advent of the state. The infringement of a norm is punished because the norm claims to be valid by virtue of its moral authority; a norm does not enjoy validity simply because it is linked to sanctions that enforce compliance.[47]

The empiricist reinterpretation of moral phenomena is rooted precisely in the fact that normative validity is erroneously assimilated to the imperatives of power. Tugendhat is following this conceptual strategy when he derives the authority of justified norms from the generalization of imperatives that those concerned address to themselves in the form of intentional statements. But in fact what is expressed in normative validity is the authority of a *general will* shared by all concerned, a will that has been divested of its imperative quality and has taken on a moral quality. This will invokes a universal interest, which we can ascertain through *discourse*, that is, grasp *cognitively* from our perspective as participants.[48]

Tugendhat robs normative validity of its cognitive significance but retains the idea that norms need to be justified. These contradictory intentions combine to produce an intriguing *deficiency of justification* in his theory. Tugendhat starts from the semantic problem of how "equally good for everyone" is to be understood. He must therefore give reasons why norms that deserve this predicate can be considered justified. Justice initially means no more than that the persons concerned have good reasons for deciding on a common course of action, and all religious and metaphysical worldviews are good sources of good reasons. Why should only those reasons be called good that can be subsumed under the predicate "equally good for everyone"? In terms of argumentative strategy, this question has a similar status to the problem (discussed later) of why we should accept the principle of universalization as a rule of argumentation.

Tugendhat refers to the familiar situation in which religious and metaphysical worldviews have lost their credibility and find themselves competing against one another as subjective "gods and demons" unable to underwrite *collectively binding* articles of faith (*Glaubenssätze*). In a situation like this a point of view that is neutral with respect to content—such as that all those concerned should have good reasons for adopting a common course of action—is certainly superior to specific substantive viewpoints dependent on tradition:

Where the moral conceptions relied on higher beliefs, these beliefs also consisted in the belief that something being the case is a reason for wanting to submit to the norm. What is different now is that we have two levels of such beliefs. There is a lower level of *premoral beliefs* which concern the question whether the endorsement of a norm is in the interest of the individual *A* and whether it is in the interest of an individual *B*, etc. It is now only these premoral empirical beliefs that are being presupposed, and the moral belief that the norm is justified if everybody can agree to it is not presupposed but is the result of the communicative process of justifying to each other a common course of action on the basis of those premoral beliefs. (1981, p. 17)

It stands to reason that people with competing value orientations who take part in a process of argumentation will more easily reach agreement on a common course of action if they can have recourse to more abstract points of view that are neutral with respect to the content at issue. But the gains of such an argument are small. First, there could be *other* formal points of view at the *same* level of abstraction that would have an *equivalent* potential for producing agreement. Tugendhat would need to explain why we should prefer the predicate he proposes to another one. Second, the preference for higher-level, more formal considerations becomes plausible only in reference to a contingent situation in which, not by accident, we recognize our contemporary situation. If we put ourselves in a different situation, for instance, one where a single religion has been generally and authentically disseminated, we immediately see that a *different kind of argument* is required to explain why moral norms should be justified through recourse to general principles and procedures and not through an appeal to propositions certified by dogma. To justify the *superiority* of the *reflective mode of justification* and the posttraditional legal and moral ideas developed at that level, a normative theory is required. It is precisely at this point that Tugendhat breaks off his analysis.

This deficiency in justification can be made good only by expressing the meaning of the predicate "equally good for everyone" in a rule of argumentation for practical discourses and not by starting with a semantic explication of it. One can then try to justify this rule of argumentation with an analysis of the pragmatic presuppositions of argumentation as such. In doing so, it will become clear that the idea of impartiality is rooted *in* the structures of argumentation *themselves* and does not need to be *brought in* from the outside as a supplementary normative content.

III Discourse Ethics and Its Bases in Action Theory

With the introduction of the principle of universalization, the first step in the justification of a discourse ethics has been accomplished. We can review the systematic content of the argument in the form of an imaginary debate between an advocate of ethical cognitivism and an advocate of moral skepticism.

The opening round was a matter of opening the die-hard skeptic's eyes to the domain of *moral phenomena*. In the second round the issue was whether practical questions *admit of truth*. We saw that as an ethical subjectivist the skeptic could score some points against the ethical objectivist. The cognitivist could salvage his position by asserting that for normative statements a claim to validity is only *analogous to a truth claim*. The third round opened with the skeptic's realistic observation that it is often impossible to reach a consensus on questions of moral principle, despite the best intentions of all concerned. Faced with a *pluralism of ultimate value orientations*, which seems to support the skeptic's position, the cognitivist has to try to demonstrate the existence of a bridging principle that makes consensus possible. A moral principle having been proposed, the question of cultural relativism occupies the next round of the argumentation. The skeptic voices the objection that (U) represents a hasty generalization of moral intuitions peculiar to our own Western culture, a challenge to which the cognitivist will respond with a *transcendental justification* of his moral principle. In round 5 the skeptic brings in further objections to the strategy of transcendental justification, and the cognitivist meets them with a more cautious version of Apel's argument. In the sixth round, in the face of this promising justification of a discourse ethics, the skeptic can take refuge in a *refusal to enter into discourse*. But as we will see, by doing so he has maneuvered himself into a hopeless position. The theme of the seventh and last round of the debate is the skeptic's revival of the objections to ethical formalism that Hegel brought up in his criticism of Kant. On this issue the astute cognitivist will not hesitate to meet the well-considered reservations of his opponent halfway.

The external form of my presentation does not coincide precisely with the ideal course of the seven-round debate I have just sketched. To counter the deeply ingrained reductionist concept of rationality characteristic of empiricism and the reinterpretation of basic moral experiences that corresponds to it, I stressed (in section 1) the web of moral feelings and attitudes that is interwoven with the practice of everyday life. I turned next (in section 2) to metaethical arguments denying that practical questions admit of truth. These proved to be irrelevant because we abandoned the false identification of normative and assertoric claims to validity and showed (in section 3) that propositional truth and normative rightness play different pragmatic roles in everyday communication. The skeptic was not impressed by this argument and restated his doubts that even the specific claims to validity associated with commands and norms could be justified. This objection fails if one adopts the principle of universalization (introduced in section 4) and can demonstrate (as in section 5) that this moral principle is a rule of argumentation comparable to the principle of induction and is not a principle of participation in disguise.

This is where the debate stands now. Next the skeptic will demand a justification for this bridging principle. In section 6 I will meet the charge of having committed the ethnocentric fallacy with Apel's proposal for a transcendental-pragmatic justification of ethics. I will modify Apel's argument (in section 7) so as to give up any claim to "ultimate justification," without damage to the argument. In section 8 I will defend the principle of discourse ethics against the skeptic's renewed objections by showing that moral arguments are embedded in contexts of communicative action. This internal connection between morality and ethical life does not impose limits on the universality of moral claims of validity, but it does subject practical discourses to constraints to which theoretical discourses are not subject in the same way.

6 Is a justification of the moral principle necessary and possible?

The demand for a justification of the moral principle is hardly unreasonable when one recalls that Kant's categorical imperative, as well as the many variations of the universalization principle put forward by ethical cognitivists following in his footsteps, expresses a moral intuition whose scope is questionable. Certainly only such norms of action as embody generalizable interests correspond to *our* conceptions of justice. But this "moral point of view" might be only the expression of the particular moral ideas of our Western culture. Paul Taylor's objection to Kurt Baier's proposal can be extended to all versions of the universalization principle. In view of the anthropological data available we cannot but concede that the moral code expounded by Kantian moral theories is indeed only one among many:

However deeply our own conscience and moral outlook may have been shaped by it, we must recognize that other societies in the history of the world have been able to function on the basis of other codes. . . . To claim that a person who is a member of those societies and who knows its moral code nevertheless does not have true moral convictions is, it seems to me, fundamentally correct. But such a claim cannot be justified on the ground of our concept of the moral point of view, for that is to assume that the moral code of liberal western society is the only genuine morality.[49]

There are, then, grounds for suspecting that the claim to universality raised by ethical cognitivists on behalf of the moral principle they happen to favor is based on an ethnocentric fallacy. Cognitivists cannot evade the skeptic's demand that it be justified.

Where he does not simply appeal to a "fact of reason," Kant bases his justification of the categorical imperative on the substantive normative concepts of autonomy and free will; by doing so he makes himself vulnerable to the objection that he has committed a *petitio principii*. In any case, the justification of the categorical imperative is so closely intertwined with the overall design of Kant's system that it would not be easy to defend it if the premises were changed. Contemporary moral theorists do not even offer a justification of the moral principle but content themselves with reconstructing pretheoretical knowledge. A case in point is John Rawls's concept of reflective equilibrium.[50] Another example is the constructivist proposal to erect a language of moral argumentation on a systematic basis; the introduction of a moral principle that regulates language is convincing only because it conceptually explicates *extant* intuitions.[51]

I am not dramatizing the situation when I say that faced with the demand for a justification of the universal validity of the principle of universalization, cognitivists are in trouble.[52] The skeptic feels emboldened to recast his *doubts* about the possibility of justifying a universalist morality as an *assertion* that it is impossible to justify such a morality. Hans Albert took this tack with his *Treatise on Critical Reason*[53] by applying to practical philosophy Popper's model of critical testing, which was developed for the philosophy of science and intended to take the place of traditional foundationalist and justificationist models. The attempt to justify moral principles with universal validity, according to Albert, ensnares the cognitivist in a "Münchhausen trilemma" in which he must choose between three equally unacceptable alernatives: putting up with an infinite regress, arbitrarily breaking off the chain of deduction, and making a circular argument. The status of this trilemma, however, is problematic. It arises only if one presupposes a *semantic concept of justification* that is oriented to a deductive relationship between statements and based solely on the concept of logical inference. This deductive concept of justification is obviously too narrow for the exposition of the pragmatic relations between argumentative speech acts. Principles of induction and universalization are introduced as rules of argumentation for the sole purpose of bridging the logical gap in *nondeductive* relations. Accordingly, these bridging principles are not susceptible to deductive justification, which is the only form of justification allowed by the Münchhausen trilemma.

Carrying on this line of argument, Karl-Otto Apel has subjected fallibilism to an illuminating metacritique and refuted the objection to the Münchhausen trilemma.[54] There is no need to go into the details of his argument. More important in the context of our problematic is that Apel has succeeded in revealing the buried dimension of the nondeductive justification of basic ethical norms. He revives the transcendental mode of justification using the tools of a pragmatics of language. One of the key elements of Apel's transcendental-pragmatic line of argumentation is the notion of a *performative contradiction*. A performative contradiction occurs when a constative speech act $k(p)$ rests on noncontingent presuppositions whose propositional content contradicts the asserted proposition p. Following a suggestion by Jaakko Hintikka, Apel illustrates the significance of performative contradictions for understanding the classical arguments of the philosophy of consciousness. The example he chooses is Descartes's "Cogito ergo sum." Descartes's argument can be reconstructed in terms of a performative contradiction by giving the judgment of an imaginary opponent the form of the speech act "I hereby doubt that I exist." The speaker raises a truth claim for the following proposition:

(a)   I do not exist (here and now).

At the same time, by uttering statement (a), he ineluctably makes an existential assumption, the propositional content of which may be expressed,

(b)   I exist (here and now),

where the personal pronoun in both statements refers to one and the same person.[55]

Similarly, Apel uncovers a performative contradiction in the objection raised by the "consistent fallibilist," who in his role as ethical skeptic denies the possibility of grounding moral principles and presents the above-mentioned trilemma. Apel characterizes the argument as follows: The proponent asserts the universal validity of the principle of universalization. He is contradicted by an opponent relying on the Münchhausen trilemma. On the basis of this trilemma the opponent concludes that attempts to ground the universal validity of principles are meaningless. This the opponent calls the principle of fallibilism. But the opponent will have involved himself in a performative contradiction if the proponent can show that in making his argument, he has to make assumptions that are inevitable in *any* argumentation game aiming at critical examination and that the propositional content of those assumptions contradicts the principle of fallibilism. This is in fact the case, since in putting forward his objection, the opponent necessarily assumes the validity of at least those logical rules that are irreplaceable if we are to understand his argument as a refutation. In taking part in the process of reasoning, even the consistent fallibilist has already accepted as valid a minimum number of unavoidable rules of criticism. Yet this state of affairs is incompatible with the principle of fallibilism.

This debate about a "minimal logic," which is currently being carried out among critical rationalists,[56] is of interest to Apel insofar as it refutes the skeptic's claim that it is impossible to ground moral principles. But it does not thereby relieve the ethical cognitivist of the burden of proof. This controversy has also drawn attention to the fact that the injunction to avoid performative contradictions applies not only to individual speech acts and arguments but to argumentative speech in general. In "argumentation as such" Apel has gained a reference point that is as fundamental for the analysis of unavoidable rules as the "I think" or "consciousness as such" is for the philosophy of reflection. Just as someone interested in a theory of knowledge cannot adopt a standpoint outside his own cognitive acts (and thus remains caught in the self-referentiality of the subject of cognition), so too a person engaged in developing a theory of moral argumentation cannot adopt a standpoint outside the situation defined by the fact that he is taking part in a process of argumentation (e.g., with a skeptic who is following his every move like a shadow). For him, the situation of argumentation is just as inescapable as the process of cognition is for the transcendental philosopher. The theorist of argumentation becomes aware of the self-referentiality of his arguments as the epistemologist becomes aware of the self-referentiality of his knowledge. Such awareness means giving up futile attempts at a deductive grounding of "ultimate" principles and returning to the explication of "unavoidable," (i.e., universal and necessary) presuppositions. At this point the moral theorist will experimentally assume the role of the skeptic to determine whether the skeptic's rejection of a specific moral principle involves him in a performative contradiction with the inescapable presuppositions of moral argumentation as such. In this indirect way the cognitivist can demonstrate to the skeptic that in involving himself in a specific argument with the goal of refuting ethical cognitivism, the skeptic must inevitably subscribe to certain tacit presuppositions of argumentation that are incompatible with the propositional content of his objection. Apel turns this form of performative refutation of the skeptic into a mode of justification, which he describes as follows: "If, on the one hand, a presupposition cannot be challenged in argumentation without actual performative self-contradiction, and if, on the other hand, it cannot be deductively grounded without formal-logical petitio principii, then it belongs to those transcendental-pragmatic presuppositions of argumentation that one must always (already) have accepted, if the language game of argumentation is to be meaningful."[57]

Thus the necessary justification of the proposed moral principle could take the following form: every argumentation, regardless of the context in which it occurs, rests on pragmatic presuppositions from whose propositional content the principle of universalism (U) can be derived.

7 The structure and status of the transcendental-pragmatic argument

Having established that a transcendental-pragmatic justification of the moral principle is in fact possible, I will now present the argument itself. I will begin in section 1 by enumerating certain conditions that all transcendental-pragmatic arguments must satisfy. I will then use these criteria to assess two of the best known proposals of this kind, namely those of R. S. Peters and K. O. Apel. In section 2 I will present a version of the transcendental-pragmatic argument that can stand up to the familiar objections against it. Finally, in section 3 I will show that this justification of discourse ethics cannot have the status of an ultimate justification and why there is no need to claim this status for it.

1

Following Collingwood, a type of philosophical analysis has gained credence in England that corresponds quite closely to the procedure Apel terms "transcendental pragmatics." A. J. Watt calls it "analysis of the presuppositions of a mode of discourse." Watt characterizes the structure of this approach as follows:

The strategy of this form of argument is to accept the skeptical conclusion that these principles are not open to any proof, being presuppositions of reasoning rather than conclusions from it, but to go on to argue that commitment to them is rationally inescapable because they must, logically, be assumed if one is to engage in a mode of thought essential to any rational human life. The claim is not exactly that the principles are *true*, but that their adoption is not a result of mere social convention or free personal decision: that a mistake is involved in repudiating them while continuing to use the form of thought and discourse in question.[58]

Collingwood's influence shows up in the application of presuppositional analysis to the way specific *questions* are posed and dealt with: "A presuppositional justification would show that one was committed to certain principles by raising and considering a certain range of *questions*."[59] The purpose of such arguments is to prove that certain discourses entail inescapable presuppositions; moral principles have to be derivable from the propositional content of such presuppositions. The significance of these arguments is proportional to the degree of generality of the discourses that entail substantive normative presuppositions. Strictly speaking, arguments cannot be called transcendental unless they deal with discourses, or the corresponding competences, so general that it is impossible to replace them by functional equivalents; they must be constituted in such a way that they can be replaced only with discourses or competences of the same kind. Accordingly, it is of the utmost importance to specify the precise object domain to which presuppositional analysis is to be applied.

Yet the delineation of an object domain must not already prejudge the normative content of its presuppositions, or one will be guilty of a *petitio principii* that could have been avoided. R. S. Peters tries to avoid both pitfalls. He limits himself to practical discourses, i.e., to processes of reaching understanding designed to answer practical questions of the form What ought I to do? In restricting himself to these issues, Peters hopes to single out an order of discourses for which there are no substitutes and at the same time to avoid normative prejudgments in the demarcation of practical discourses:

It is always possible to produce *ad hominem* arguments pointing out what any individual must actually presuppose in saying what he actually says. But these are bound to be very contingent, depending upon private idiosyncrasies, and would obviously be of little use in developing a general ethical theory. Of far more importance are arguments pointing to what any individual *must* presuppose in so far as he uses a public form of discourse in seriously discussing with others or with himself what he ought to do. In a similar way one might inquire into the presuppositions of using scientific discourse. These arguments would be concerned not with prying into individual idiosyncrasies but with probing public presuppositions.[60]

Only these *public* presuppositions are comparable to the transcendental preconditions on which the Kantian analysis was focused. Only of them can one say that they are inescapable presuppositions of irreplaceable discourses and in that sense universal.[61]

Peters proceeds to derive certain basic norms from the presuppositions of practical discourses: first a fairness principle ("All people's claims should be equally considered") and then more concrete principles like freedom of thought and expression. Yet instead of identifying the relevant presuppositions of practical discourses one by one and subjecting their content to systematic analysis, Peters offers some merely *ad hoc* reflections. In my view, Peters's analyses are by no means without merit, but in the form he gives them they are open to two objections.

The first objection is a variant of the charge of a *petitio principii* to the effect that in the presuppositions of discourse Peters finds only the normative substance that he had previously put into his implicit definition of practical discourse. This objection could be raised against Peters's semantic deduction of the principle of equal treatment, for example.[62]

Apel tries to meet this objection by extending presuppositional analysis to the preconditions of argumentative speech *as such*, as opposed to restricting it to *moral* argumentation. He wants to show that any subject capable of speech and action necessarily makes substantive normative presuppositions as soon as the subject engages in any discourse with the intention of critically examining a hypothetical claim to validity. With this argumentative strategy Apel reaches even the skeptic who insists on a metaethical treatment of questions of moral theory and consequently refuses to be drawn into *moral* argumentation. Apel wants to make this kind of skeptic aware that no sooner does he object (and defend his objection) than he commits himself to an "argumentation game" and thus to presuppositions that entangle him in a performative contradiction. Peters too makes occasional use of this more radical version of presuppositional analysis as, for example, when grounding the principle of freedom of opinion:

The argument need not be based simply on the manifest interest of anyone who seriously asks the question "what ought I to do?" For the principle of liberty, at least in the sphere of opinion, is also surely a (general presupposition of this form of) discourse into which any rational being is initiated when he laboriously learns to reason. In matters where reason is paramount it is argument rather than force of inner illumination that is decisive. The conditions of argument include letting any rational being contribute to a public discussion. . . .[63]

Admittedly, a second objection can be raised against such arguments, one that is not so easily refuted. True as it may be that freedom of opinion, in the sense of freedom from external interference in the process of opinion formation, is one of the inescapable pragmatic presuppositions of every argumentation, the fact remains that what the skeptic is now forced to accept is no more than the notion that as a *participant* in a process of *argumentation* he has implicitly recognized a principle of freedom of opinion. This argument does not go far enough to convince him in his capacity as an *actor* as well. The validity of a norm of action, as for example a publicly guaranteed constitutional right to freedom of expression, cannot be justified in this fashion. It is by no means self-evident that rules that are unavoidable *within* discourses can also claim to be valid for regulating action *outside* of discourses. Even if participants in an argumentation are forced to make substantive normative presuppositions (e.g., to respect one another as competent subjects, to treat one another as equal partners, to assume one another's truthfulness, and to cooperate with one another),[64] they can still shake off this transcendental-pragmatic compulsion when they leave the field of argumentation. The necessity of making such presuppositions is not transferred directly from discourse to action. In any case, a separate justification is required to explain why the normative content discovered in the pragmatic presuppositions of *argumentation* should have the power to *regulate action*.[65]

One cannot demonstrate a transfer of this kind as Apel and Peters try to do, namely by deriving basic ethical norms *directly* from the presuppositions of argumentation. Basic norms of law and morality fall outside the jurisdiction of moral theory; they must be viewed as substantive principles to be justified in practical discourses. Since historical circumstances change, every epoch sheds its own light upon fundamental moral-practical ideas. Nevertheless, in such practical discourses we always already make use of substantive normative rules of argumentation. It is *these rules* alone that transcendental pragmatics is in a position to derive.

2

We must return to the justification of the principle of universalization. We are now in a position to specify the role that the transcendental-pragmatic argument can play in this process. Its function is to help to show that the principle of universalization, which acts as a rule of argumentation, is implied by the presuppositions of argumentation in general. This requirement is met if the following can be shown:

Every person who accepts the universal and necessary communicative presuppositions of argumentative speech and who knows what it means to justify a norm of action implicitly presupposes as valid the principle of universalization, whether in the form I gave it above or in an equivalent form.

It makes sense to distinguish three levels of presuppositions of argumentation along the lines suggested by Aristotle: those at the logical level of products, those at the dialectical level of procedures, and those at the rhetorical level of processes.[66] First, reasoning or argumentation is designed to *produce* intrinsically cogent arguments with which we can redeem or repudiate claims to validity. This is the level at which I would situate the rules of a minimal logic currently being discussed by Popperians, for example, and the consistency requirements proposed by Hare and others. For simplicity I will follow the catalog of presuppositions of argumentation drawn up by R. Alexy.[67] For the logical-semantic level, the following rules[68] can serve as *examples*:

(1.1)   No speaker may contradict himself.

(1.2)   Every speaker who applies predicate F to object A must be prepared to apply F to all other objects resembling A in all relevant aspects.

(1.3)   Different speakers may not use the same expression with different meanings.

The presuppositions of argumentation at this level are logical and semantic rules that have no ethical content. They are not a suitable point of departure for a transcendental-pragmatic argument.

In *procedural* terms, arguments are processes of reaching understanding that are ordered in such a way that proponents and opponents, having assumed a hypothetical attitude and being relieved of the pressures of action and experience, can test validity claims that have become problematic. At this level are located the pragmatic presuppositions of a special form of interaction, namely everything necessary for a search for truth organized in the form of a competition. Examples include recognition of the accountability and truthfulness of all participants in the search. At this level I also situate general rules of jurisdiction and relevance that regulate themes for discussion, contributions to the argument, etc.[69] Again I cite a few examples from Alexy's catalog of rules:

(2.1)   Every speaker may assert only what he really believes.

(2.2)   A person who disputes a proposition or norm not under discussion must provide a reason for wanting to do so.

Some of these rules obviously have an ethical import. At this level what comes to the fore are presuppositions common both to discourses and to action oriented to reaching understanding as such, e.g., presuppositions about relations of mutual recognition.

But to fall back here directly on the basis of argumentation in action theory would be to put the cart before the horse. Yet the presuppositions of an unrestrained competition for better arguments are relevant to our purpose in that they are irreconcilable with traditional ethical philosophies that have to protect a dogmatic core of fundamental convictions from all criticism.

Finally, in *process* terms, argumentative speech is a process of communication that, in light of its goal of reaching a rationally motivated agreement, must satisfy improbable conditions. In argumentative speech we see the structures of a speech situation immune to repression and inequality in a particular way: it presents itself as a form of communication that adequately approximates ideal conditions. This is why I tried at one time to describe the presuppositions of argumentation as the defining characteristics of an ideal speech situation.[70] I cannot here undertake the elaboration, revision, and clarification that my earlier analysis requires, and accordingly, the present essay is rightly characterized as a sketch or a proposal. The intention of my earlier analysis still seems correct to me, namely the reconstruction of the general symmetry conditions that every competent speaker who believes he is engaging in an argumentation must presuppose as adequately fulfilled. The presupposition of something like an "unrestricted communication community," an idea that Apel developed following Peirce and Mead, can be demonstrated through systematic analysis of performative contradictions. Participants in argumentation cannot avoid the presupposition that, owing to certain characteristics that require formal description, the structure of their communication rules out all external or internal coercion other than the force of the better argument and thereby also neutralizes all motives other than that of the cooperative search for truth.

Following my analysis, R. Alexy has suggested the following rules of discourse for this level:[71]

(3.1)   Every subject with the competence to speak and act is allowed to take part in a discourse.

(3.2)   a. Everyone is allowed to question any assertion whatever.

　　　　 b.　Everyone is allowed to introduce any assertion whatever into the discourse.

　　　　 c.　Everyone is allowed to express his attitudes, desires, and needs.[72]

(3.3)   No speaker may be prevented, by internal or external coercion, from exercising his rights as laid down in (3.1) and (3.2).

A few explanations are in order here. Rule (3.1) defines the set of potential participants. It includes all subjects without exception who have the capacity to take part in argumentation. Rule (3.2) guarantees all participants equal opportunity to contribute to the argumentation and to put forth their own arguments. Rule (3.3) sets down conditions under which the rights to universal access and to equal participation can be enjoyed equally by all, that is, without the possibility of repression, be it ever so subtle or covert.

If these considerations are to amount to more than a definition favoring an ideal form of communication and thus prejudging everything else, we must show that these rules of discourse are not mere *conventions*; rather, they are inescapable presuppositions.

The presuppositions themselves are identified by convincing a person who contests the hypothetical reconstructions offered that he is caught up in performative contradictions.[73] In this process I must appeal to the intuitive preunderstanding that every subject competent in speech and action brings to a process of argumentation. Here I will content myself with discussing a few examples, indicating what such an analysis might actually look like.

The statement

(1)   Using good reasons, I finally convinced H that p

can be read as someone's report on the outcome of a discourse. In this discourse the speaker, by using reasons, motivated the hearer to accept the truth claim connected with the assertion that p, that is, to consider p true. Central to the meaning of the word "convince" is the idea that a subject other than the speaker adopts a view on the basis of good reasons. This is why the statement

(2)   *Using lies, I finally convinced H that p

is nonsensical. It can be revised to

(3)   Using lies, I finally talked H into believing that p.

I can refer someone to a dictionary to look up the meaning of the verb "to convince." But that will not explain *why* statement (2) is a semantic paradox that can be resolved by statement (3). To explain that, I can start with the internal connection between the expressions "to convince someone of something" and "to come to a reasoned agreement about something." In the *final* analysis, convictions rest on a consensus that has been attained discursively. Now statement (2) implies that H has formed his conviction under conditions that simply do not permit the formation of convictions. Such conditions contradict the pragmatic presuppositions of argumentation as such (in this case rule (2.1)). This presupposition holds not only for particular instances but inevitably for every process of argumentation. I can prove this by making a proponent who defends the truth of statement (2) aware that he thereby gets himself into a performative contradiction. For as soon as he cites a reason for the truth of (2), he enters a process of argumentation and has thereby accepted the presupposition, among others, that he can never *convince* an opponent of something by resorting to lies; at most, he can talk him into believing something to be true. But then the content of the assertion to be justified contradicts one of the presuppositions the proponent must operate with if his statement is to be regarded as a justification.

Similarly, performative contradictions can be demonstrated in the statements of a proponent who tries to justify the following sentence:

(4) *Having excluded persons $A, B, C, \ldots$ from the discussion by silencing them or by foisting our interpretation on them, we were able to convince ourselves that N is justified.

Here $A, B, C, \ldots$ are assumed to be among the persons who would be affected by putting norm N into effect and to be indistinguishable in their capacity as *participants in argumentation* in all relevant respects from the other participants. In any attempt to justify statement (4), a proponent necessarily contradicts the presuppositions set out in rules (3.1) to (3.3).

In giving these presuppositions the form of rules, Alexy may well be promoting the misconception that all actual discourses must conform to these rules. In many cases this is clearly not so, and in all cases we have to be content with approximations. This misconception may have something to do with the ambiguity of the world "rule." Rules of discourse in Alexy's sense are not *constitutive* of discourses in the sense in which chess rules are constitutive of real chess games. Whereas chess rules *determine* the playing of actual chess games, discourse rules are merely the *form* in which we present the implicity adopted and intuitively known pragmatic presuppositions of a special type of speech, presuppositions that are adopted implicitly and known intuitively. If one wanted to make a serious comparison between argumentation and chess playing, one would find that the closest equivalents to the rules of chess are the rules for the construction and exchange of arguments. These rules must be followed in *actual fact* if error-free argumentation is to take place in real life. By contrast, discourse rules (3.1) to (3.3) state only that participants in argumentation must assume these conditions to be approximately realized, or realized in an approximation adequate enough for the purpose of argumentation, regardless of whether and to what extent these assumptions are counterfactual in a given case or not.

Discourses take place in particular social contexts and are subject to the limitations of time and space. Their participants are not Kant's intelligible characters but real human beings driven by other motives in addition to the one permitted motive of the search for truth. Topics and contributions have to be organized. The opening, adjournment, and resumption of discussions must be arranged. Because of all these factors, institutional measures are needed to sufficiently neutralize empirical limitations and avoidable internal and external interference so that the idealized conditions always already presupposed by participants in argumentation can at least be adequately approximated. The need to institutionalize discourses, trivial though it may be, does not contradict the partly counterfactual content of the presuppositions of discourse. On the contrary, attempts at institutionalization are subject in turn to normative conceptions and their goal, which spring *spontaneously* from our intuitive grasp of what argumentation is. This assertion can be verified empirically by studying the authorizations, exemptions, and procedural rules that have been used to institutionalize theoretical discourse in science or practical discourse in parliamentary activity.[74] To avoid the fallacy of misplaced concreteness, one must carefully differentiate between rules of discourse and conventions serving the institutionalization of discourses, conventions that help to actualize the ideal content of the presuppositions of argumentation under empirical conditions.

If after these cursory remarks we accept the rules tentatively set down by Alexy (pending a more detailed analysis), we have at our disposal, in conjunction with a weak idea of normative justification (i.e., one that does not prejudge the matter), premises that are strong enough for the derivation of the universalization principle (U).

If every person entering a process of argumentation must, among other things, make presuppositions whose content can be expressed in rules (3.1) to (3.3) and if we understand what it means to discuss hypothetically whether norms of action ought to be adopted, then everyone who seriously tries to

discursively redeem normative claims to validity intuitively accepts procedural conditions that amount to implicitly acknowl-
edging (U). It follows from the aforementioned rules of
discourse that a contested norm cannot meet with the consent
of the participants in a practical discourse unless (U) holds,
that is,

Unless all affected can *freely* accept the consequences and the
side effects that the *general* observance of a controversial norm
can be expected to have for the satisfaction of the interests of
each individual.

But once it has been shown that (U) can be grounded upon
the presuppositions of argumentation through a transcendental-pragmatic derivation, discourse ethics itself can be formulated in terms of the principle of discourse ethics (D), which
stipulates,

Only those norms can claim to be valid that meet (or could
meet) with the approval of all affected in their capacity as
participants in a practical discourse.[75]

The justification of discourse ethics outlined here avoids confusions in the use of the term "moral principle." The only
moral principle here is the universalization principle (U), which
is conceived as a rule of argumentation and is part of the logic
of practical discourses. (U) must be carefully distinguished
from the following:

• Substantive principles or basic norms, which can only be the
subject matter of moral argumentation

• The normative content of the presuppositions of argumentation, which can be expressed in terms of rules, as in (3.1) to
(3.3)

• The principle of discourse ethics (D), which stipulates the
basic idea of a moral theory but does not form part of a logic
of argumentation

Previous attempts to ground discourse ethics were flawed
because they tended to collapse *rules, contents, presuppositions* of
argumentation and in addition confused all of these with moral

principles in the sense of principles of philosophical ethics. (D) is the assertion that the philosopher as moral theorist ultimately seeks to justify. The program of justification I have outlined in this essay describes what I regard as the most promising *road* to that goal. This road is the transcendental-pragmatic justification of a rule of argumentation with normative content. This rule is selective, to be sure, but it is also formal. It is not compatible with all substantive legal and moral principles, but it does not prejudge substantive regulations, as it is a rule of argumentation only. All contents, no matter how fundamental the action norm involved may be, must be made to depend on real discourses (or advocatory discourses conducted as substitutes for them). The moral theorist may take part in them as one of those concerned, perhaps even as an expert, but he cannot conduct such discourses by *himself alone*. To the extent to which a moral theory touches on substantive areas—as Rawls's theory of justice does, for example—it must be understood as a contribution to a discourse among citizens.

3

F. Kambartel has characterized the transcendental-pragmatic justification of discourse ethics as a procedure whereby a proponent tries to convince an opponent "who asks for justification of a rational principle put forth by someone else that his intention in asking the question, rightly understood, already involves an acceptance of that same principle."[76] The question arises what status this kind of justification may claim for itself. There are two schools of thought on the subject. The first refuses to speak of justification at all, since, as G. F. Gethmann points out, the recognition of something that is presupposed, in contrast to the recognition of something that is justified, is always hypothetical in the sense of being dependent on the prior acceptance of some end. The transcendental pragmatist counters this by pointing out that the necessity of accepting as valid the propositional content of inescapable presuppositions is all the less hypothetical the more general the discourses and competences are to which the presuppositional analysis of transcendental pragmatics is applied. The end of argumentation, the argument continues, is not something we can treat quite so arbitrarily as the contingent ends of action. The former is so intimately interwoven with the intersubjective form of life to which subjects competent in speech and action belong that there is no way we can either posit or bypass it.

The second school of thought saddles transcendental pragmatics with the far-reaching claim to "ultimate justification." Ultimate justification, as W. Kuhlmann emphasizes, is supposed to create an absolutely secure basis of unerring knowledge, a basis that is immune to the fallibilism of all experiential knowledge:

What I cannot meaningfully dispute (i.e. without contradicting myself) because it is necessarily presupposed in a process of meaningful argumentation, and what for the same reason I cannot meaningfully justify by deriving it deductively (except at the price of a *petitio principii*), is therefore a secure, *unshakable basis*. As participants in a process of argumentation, we have necessarily always already accepted the propositions and rules that belong to these presuppositions. We are unable to question them skeptically, either to dispute their validity or to adduce reasons for their validity.[77]

In other words, the type of argument that H. Lenk calls *petitio tollendi* serves only to demonstrate the inevitability of certain conditions and rules. It can be used only to show an opponent that he makes performative use of a *tollendum*, that is, of the very thing he wants to negate.

Demonstrating the existence of performative contradictions helps to identify the rules necessary for any argumentation game to work; if one is to argue at all, there are no substitutes. The fact that there are *no alternatives* to these rules of argumentation is what is being proved; the rules themselves are not being *justified*. True, the participants must have accepted them as a "fact of reason" in setting out to argue. But this kind of argument cannot accomplish a transcendental deduction in the Kantian sense. The same thing holds for Apel's transcendental-pragmatic analysis of the presuppositions of argumentation as for Strawson's transcendental-semantic analysis of the presuppositions of judgments of experience. As G. Schönrich puts it,

The conceptual system underlying our experience owes its necessity to its being without alternatives. It is proved by showing that any attempt to develop an alternative system of concepts fails because it makes use of structural elements of the system it seeks to replace. . . . As long as Strawson's method remains confined to immanent conceptual relationships of implication, it is impossible for him to justify a conceptual system a priori, since it is in principle an open question whether the subjects of cognition will change their way of thinking about the world at some point or not.[78]

Schönrich warns provocatively against overburdening this *weak form of transcendental analysis*: "The acceptance of certain conceptual relationships of implication wrung from the skeptic through cunning can have no more than quasi-empirical validity."[79]

The explanation for Apel's stubborn retention of the claim of transcendental pragmatics to ultimate justification lies, I believe, in his inconsistent recourse to motifs of thought that he himself discredited in the paradigm shift from the philosophy of consciousness to the philosophy of language, a shift which he promoted vigorously. In his interesting essay "The A Priori of the Communication Community and the Foundations of Ethics," Apel refers, not coincidentally, to Fichte, who sought to "dissolve the fact of reason in its mere facticity" through "co-enactment and re-enactment informed by insight" (*einsichtigen Mit- und Nachvollzug*).[80] Although Apel speaks of Fichte's "residual metaphysical dogmatism," he bases the transcendental-pragmatic claim to ultimate justification, if I understand him correctly, on the equation of propositional truth with the experience of certitude—an equation which can be made only in the reflective reenactment of something previously done intuitively, that is, only under the conditions of a philosophy of consciousness. Once we are on the analytic level of the pragmatics of language, it becomes impossible to make the above equation. This becomes clear when we isolate the steps in the justification as outlined above and present them one by one. My programmatic justification of discourse ethics requires all of the following:

1. A definition of a universalization principle that functions as a rule of argumentation

2. The identification of pragmatic presuppositions of argumentation that are inescapable and have a normative content

3. The explicit statement of that normative content (e.g., in the form of discourse rules)

4. Proof that a relation of material implication holds between steps (3) and (1) in connection with the idea of the justification of norms

Step (2) in the analysis, for which the search for performative contradictions provides a guide, relies upon a maieutic method that serves

2a. to make the skeptic who presents an objection aware of presuppositions he knows intuitively,

2b. to cast this pretheoretical knowledge in an explicit form that will enable the skeptic to recognize his intuitions in this description,

2c. to corroborate, through counterexamples, the proponent's assertion that there are no alternatives to the presuppositions he has made explicit.

Substeps (2b) and (2c) contain unmistakable hypothetical elements. The description we employ to pass from knowing how to knowing that is a hypothetical reconstruction that can provide only a more or less correct rendering of intuitions. It needs maieutic confirmation. Similarly, the assertion that there is no alternative to a given presupposition, that it is one of the inescapable (i.e., necessary and general) presuppositions, has the status of an assumption. Like a lawlike hypothesis (*Gesetzeshypothese*), it must be checked against individual cases. To be sure, the intuitive knowledge of rules that subjects capable of speech and action must use if they are to be able to participate in argumentation is in a certain sense not fallible. But this is not true of *our reconstruction* of this pretheoretical knowledge and the claim to universality that we connect with it. The *certainty* with which we put our knowledge of rules into practice does not extend to the *truth* of proposed reconstructions of presuppositions hypothesized to be general, for we have to put our reconstructions up for discussion in the same way in which the logician or the linguist, for example, presents his theoretical descriptions.

No harm is done, however, if we deny that the transcendental-pragmatic justification constitutes an ultimate justification. Rather, discourse ethics then takes its place among the reconstructive sciences concerned with the rational bases of knowing, speaking, and acting. If we cease striving for the foundationalism of traditional transcendental philosophy, we acquire new corroborative possibilities for discourse ethics. In competition with other ethical approaches, it can be used to describe empirically existing moral and legal ideas. It can be built into theories of the development of moral and legal consciousness at both the sociocultural and the ontogenetic levels and in this way can be made susceptible to indirect corroboration.

Nor need moral philosophy maintain the claim to ultimate justification because of its presumed relevance for the lifeworld. The *moral* intuitions of everyday life are not in need of clarification by the philosopher. In this case the therapeutic self-understanding of philosophy initiated by Wittgenstein is for once, I think, appropriate. Moral philosophy does have an enlightening or clarificatory role to play vis-à-vis the confusions that it has created in the minds of the educated, that is, to the extent to which value skepticism and legal positivism have established themselves as professional ideologies and have infiltrated everyday consciousness by way of the educational system. Together skepticism and positivism have misinterpreted and thus neutralized the intuitions people acquire in a quasi-natural manner through socialization. Under extreme conditions they can contribute to the moral disarmament of academics already in the grip of a cultivated skepticism.[81]

8 Morality and ethical life (*Sittlichkeit*)

The dispute between the cognitivist and the skeptic has not yet been definitively settled. The skeptic is not satisfied with the surrender of the claim to ultimate justification and the prospect of indirect confirmation of the theory of discourse. (1) He can question the soundness of the transcendental-pragmatic derivation of the moral principle. And even if he has to grant that discourse ethics can be justified in this way, he still has enough ammunition for one parting shot: (2) he can join the ranks (revived for political reasons) of the neo-Aristotelians and neo-Hegelians, who point out that discourse ethics does not represent much of a gain for the real concern of philosophical ethics, since discourse ethics offers at best an empty formalism whose practical consequences would even be disastrous. I will respond to these last two skeptical objections only to the extent necessary to clarify the action-theoretical bases of discourse ethics. Because morality is always embedded in what Hegel called ethical life (*Sittlichkeit*), discourse ethics is always subject to limitations, though not limitations that can devalue its critical function or strengthen the skeptic in his role as an advocate of a counterenlightenment.

1

The fact that the transcendental-pragmatic strategy of justification depends on the objections of a skeptic is not wholly to its advantage. Such arguments are telling only with an opponent who does his proponent the favor of entering into an argumentation. A skeptic who sees in advance that he will be caught in performative contradictions will reject the game of wits from the outset. The *consistent skeptic* will deprive the transcendental pragmatist of a basis for his argument. He may, for example, take the attitude of an ethnologist vis-à-vis his own culture, shaking his head over philosophical argumentation as though he were witnessing the unintelligible rites of a strange tribe. Nietzsche perfected this way of looking at philosophical matters, and Foucault has now rehabilitated it. When this happens, the debate suddenly changes. If the cognitivist persists in his analysis, he will now be talking only *about* the skeptic, not *with* him. At this point the cognitivist usually throws up his hands, confessing he has no further remedy for this dropout posture of the skeptic. He will say that a willingness to argue and to think about one's actions must really be presupposed if the whole concern of moral theory is not to become pointless. There may be, he will continue, a residue of decisionism that cannot be disproved by argumentation. This, he will grant, is where the volitional moment comes into its own.

It seems to me that the moral theorist ought not to leave it at that. A skeptic who could wrest the topic from the cognitivist's grip merely with his behavior might not have the last word, but he would be performatively right, so to speak—he would assert his position mutely and impressively.

At this juncture in the discussion, if we can still call it that, it helps to keep in mind that through his behavior the skeptic voluntarily terminates his membership in the community of beings who argue—no less and no more. By refusing to argue, for instance, he cannot, even indirectly, deny that he moves in a shared sociocultural form of life, that he grew up in a web of communicative action, and that he reproduces his life in that web. In a word, the skeptic may reject morality, but he cannot reject the ethical substance (*Sittlichkeit*) of the life circumstances in which he spends his waking hours, not unless he is willing to take refuge in suicide or serious mental illness. In other words, he cannot extricate himself from the communicative practice of everyday life in which he is continually forced to take a position by responding yes or no. As long as he is still alive *at all*, a Robinson Crusoe existence through which the skeptic demonstrates mutely and impressively that he has dropped out of communicative action is inconceivable, even as a thought experiment.

As we have seen, in reaching an understanding about something in the world, subjects engaged in communicative action orient themselves to validity claims, including assertoric and normative validity claims. This is why there is no form of sociocultural life that is not at least implicitly geared to maintaining communicative action by means of argument, be the actual form of argumentation ever so rudimentary and the institutionalization of discursive consensus building ever so inchoate. Once argumentation is conceived as a special form of rule-governed interaction, it reveals itself to be a reflective form of action oriented toward reaching an understanding. Argumentation derives the pragmatic presuppositions we found at the procedural level from the presuppositions of communicative action. The reciprocities undergirding the mutual recognition of competent subjects are already built into action oriented toward reaching an understanding, the action in which argumentation is *rooted*. That is why the radical skeptic's refusal to argue is an empty gesture. No matter how consistent a dropout he may be, he cannot drop out of the communicative practice of everyday life, to the presuppositions of which he remains bound. And these in turn are at least partly identical with the presuppositions of argumentation as such.

Of course, one would need to see in detail what normative content a presuppositional analysis of action oriented toward reaching an understanding can uncover. Alan Gewirth, for example, tries to derive basic ethical norms from the structures and general pragmatic presuppositions of goal-directed action.[82] He applies presuppositional analysis to the concept of the capacity to act spontaneously and teleologically, in order to show that every rational actor is forced to view as goods the latitude he has to act, or more generally, all resources for the realization of his ends. Interestingly, however, the teleological concept of action is inadequate to provide a transcendental-pragmatic justification of the notion of a *right* to such "necessary goods," as opposed to the idea of the goods themselves.[83] If instead the concept of communicative action is chosen as a basis, one gets, via the same methodological route, a concept of rationality strong enough to *extend* the transcendental-pragmatic derivation of the moral principle to the basis of validity of action oriented toward reaching an understanding.[84] I cannot develop this idea farther here.[85]

If the concept of teleological action is replaced by the more comprehensive concept of action oriented toward reaching an understanding and the latter is made the basis of a transcendental-pragmatic analysis, the skeptic will return to the scene with the argument that a concept of social action that has a built-in normative content necessarily prejudges the moral theory to be developed.[86] On the assumption that action oriented toward success and action oriented toward reaching an understanding are mutually exclusive types of action, opting for a move from communicative to strategic action seems to give the skeptic a new opportunity. He might insist not only on not arguing but also on not acting communicatively, thereby for the *second time* knocking the ground out from under a presuppositional analysis that traces discourse back to action.

To meet this new objection, the cognitivist has to be able to show that contexts of communicative action represent an order for which there is no substitute. I will dispense with conceptual arguments here and content myself with a factual observation intended to make the centrality of communicative action clear. The possibility of *choosing* between communicative and strategic action exists only abstractly; it exists only for someone who takes the contingent perspective of an individual actor. From the perspective of the lifeworld to which the actor belongs, these modes of action are not matters of free choice. The symbolic structures of every lifeworld are reproduced through three processes: cultural tradition, social integration, and socialization. As I have shown elsewhere,[87] these processes operate only in the medium of action oriented toward reaching an understanding. There is no other, equivalent medium in which these functions can be fulfilled. Individuals acquire and sustain their identity by appropriating traditions, belonging to social groups, and taking part in socializing interactions. That is why they, as individuals, have a choice between communicative and strategic action only in an abstract sense, i.e., in individual cases. They do not have the option of a long-term absence from contexts of action oriented toward reaching an understanding. That would mean regressing to the monadic isolation of strategic action, or schizophrenia and suicide. In the long run such absence if self-destructive.

2

If the skeptic has followed the argumentation that has gone on in his presence and has seen that his demonstrative exit from argumentation and action oriented toward reaching an understanding leads to an existential dead end, he may finally be ready to accept the justification of the moral principle that I have proposed and the principle of discourse ethics that I have introduced. He does so, however, only to draw upon the remaining possibilities for argumentation; he calls into question the meaning of a formalistic ethics of this kind. Rooting the practice of argumentation in the lifeworld contexts of communicative action calls to mind Hegel's critique of Kant, which the skeptic will now bring to bear against the cognitivist.

Albrecht Wellmer has formulated this objection as follows:

In the idea of a "discourse free from domination" we only seem to have gained an objective criterion for "assessing" the practical rationality of individuals or societies. In reality it would be an illusion to believe that we could emancipate ourselves from the normatively charged facticity of our historical situation with its traditional values and criteria of rationality and see history as a whole, and our position in it, "from the sidelines," so to speak. An attempt in this direction could end only in theroetical arbitrariness and practical terror.[88]

There is no need for me to reiterate the counterarguments Wellmer develops in his brilliant study. What I will do instead is to briefly review those aspects of the critique of formalism that deserve consideration.

1 The principle of discourse ethics (D) makes reference to a *procedure*, namely the discursive redemption of normative claims to validity. To that extent discourse ethics can properly be characterized as *formal*, for it provides no substantive guidelines but only a procedure: practical discourse. Practical discourse is not a procedure for generating justified norms but a procedure for testing the validity of norms that are being proposed and hypothetically considered for adoption. That means that practical discourses depend on content brought to them from outside. It would be utterly pointless to engage in a practical discourse without a horizon provided by the lifeworld of a specific social group and without real conflicts in a concrete situation in which the actors consider it incumbent upon them to reach a consensual means of regulating some controversial social matter. Practical discourses are always related to the concrete point of departure of a disturbed normative agreement. These antecedent disruptions determine the topics that are up for discussion. This procedure, then, is not formal in the sense that it abstracts from content. Quite the contrary, in its openness, practical discourse is dependent upon contingent content being fed into it from outside. In discourse this content is subjected to a process in which particular values are ultimately discarded as being not susceptible to consensus. The question now arises as to whether this very selectivity might not make the procedure unsuitable for resolving practical questions.

2 If we define practical issues as issues of the good life, which invariably deal with the totality of a particular form of life or the totality of an individual life history, then ethical formalism is incisive in the literal sense: the universalization principle acts like a knife that makes razor-sharp cuts between evaluative statements and strictly normative ones, between the good and the just. While cultural values may imply a claim to intersubjective acceptance, they are so inextricably intertwined with the totality of a particular form of life that they cannot be said to claim normative validity in the strict sense. By their very nature, cultural values are at best *candidates* for embodiment in norms that are designed to express a general interest.

Participants can distance themselves from norms and normative systems that have been set off from the totality of social life only to the extent necessary to assume a hypothetical attitude toward them. Individuals who have been socialized cannot take a hypothetical attitude toward the form of life and the personal life history that have shaped their own identity. We are now in a position to define the scope of application of a deontological ethics: it covers only practical questions that can be debated rationally, i.e., those that hold out the prospect of consensus. It deals not with value preferences but with the normative validity of norms of action.

3 It remains for us to deal with the hermeneutic objection that the discourse-ethical procedure for justifying norms is based on an extravagant idea whose practical consequences may even be dangerous. The principle of discourse ethics, like other principles, cannot regulate problems concerning its own application. The application of rules requires a practical prudence that is *prior to* the practical reason that discourse ethics explicates. Prudence itself is not subject to rules of discourse. If that is so, the principle of discourse ethics can be effective only if it makes use of a faculty that links it with the local conventions of a hermeneutic point of departure and draws it back within the provincialism of a particular historical horizon.

This objection cannot be disputed as long as problems of application are viewed from a *third-person perspective*. The hermeneuticist's reflective insight, however, does not undercut the claim of the principle of discourse ethics to transcend all local conventions. No participant in argumentation can escape this claim as long as he takes a *performative attitude*, confronts normative claims to validity seriously, and does not objectify norms as social facts, i.e., avoids reducing them to something that is simply found in the world. The transcending force of validity claims that are dealt with in a straightforward manner has an empirical impact as well, and the hermeneuticist's reflective insight cannot catch up with it. The history of human rights in modern constitutional states offers a wealth of examples showing that once principles have been recognized, their application does not fluctuate wildly from one situation to another but tends to have a *stable direction*. Through the reflecting mirror of different interest positions, the universal content of these norms itself makes those concerned aware of the partiality and selectivity of applications. Applications can distort the meaning of the norm itself; we can operate in a more or less biased way in the dimension of prudent application. *Learning processes* are possible in this dimension too.[89]

4 In the face of foundationalist programs one must stress the fact that practical discourses are in fact subject to limitations. What these are has been shown with consummate clarity by Albrecht Wellmer in his unpublished manuscript "Reason and the Limits of Rational Discourse":

• Practical discourses—which must address, among other things, the question of how adequately needs are interpreted—are intimately linked with two other forms of argumentation: aesthetic and therapeutic criticism. These two forms of argumentation are not subject to the premise we posit for strict discourses, namely that *in principle* a rationally motivated agreement must always be reachable, where the phrase "in principle" signifies the counterfactual reservation "if argumentation were conducted openly and continued long enough." But if in the last analysis forms of argumentation make up a system and cannot be isolated from one another, the fact that practical discourse, with its stricter claim, is related (along with theoretical and explicative discourse) to forms of argumentation with more lenient criteria represents a liability for the former, a liability that originates in the sociohistorical situatedness of reason.

• Practical discourses cannot be relieved of the burden of social conflicts to the degree that theoretical and explicative discourses can. They are less free of the burdens of action because contested norms tend to upset the balance of relations of intersubjective recognition. Even if it is conducted with discursive means, a dispute about norms is still rooted in the struggle for recognition.

• Like all argumentation, practical discourses resemble islands threatened with inundation in a sea of practice where the pattern of consensual conflict resolution is by no means the dominant one. The means of reaching agreement are repeatedly thrust aside by the instruments of force. Hence, action that is oriented toward ethical principles has to accommodate itself to imperatives that flow not from principles but from strategic necessities. On the one hand, the problem posed by an ethics of responsibility that is mindful of the temporal dimension is in essence trivial, since the perspective that an ethics of responsibility would use for a future-oriented assessment of the indirect effects of collective action can be derived from discourse ethics itself. On the other hand, these problems do give rise to questions of a political ethics that deals with the aporias of a political practice whose goal is radical emancipation and that must take up those themes that were once part of Marxian revolutionary theory.

These limitations of practical discourses testify to the power history has over the transcending claims and interests of reason. The skeptic for his part tends to give an overdrawn account of these limits. The key to understanding the problem is that moral judgments, which provide demotivated answers to decontextualized questions, require an offsetting *compensation*. If we are clear about the feats of abstraction to which universalist moralities owe their superiority to conventional ones, the old problem of the relationship between morality and ethical life appears in a different, rather trivial light.

For the hypothesis-testing participant in a discourse, the relevance of the experiential context of his lifeworld tends to

pale. To him, the normativity of existing institutions seems just
as open to question as the objectivity of things and events. In
a discursive framework we perceive the lived world of the
communicative practice of everyday life from an artificial, retrospective point of view: as we hypothetically consider claims
to validity, the world of institutionally ordered relations becomes *moralized*, just as the world of existing states of affairs
becomes *theoretized*. Facts and norms that had previously gone
unquestioned can now be true or false, valid or invalid. Moreover, in the realm of subjectivity, modern art inaugurated a
comparable thrust toward problematization. The world of lived
experiences is aestheticized, that is, freed of the routines of
everyday perception and the conventions of everyday action. For
this reason we do well to look at the relationship of morality
and ethical life as part of a more complex whole.

According to Max Weber, one of the features of Western
rationalism is the creation in Europe of expert cultures that
deal with cultural traditions reflectively and in so doing isolate
the cognitive, aesthetic-expressive, and moral-practical components from one another. These cultures specialize in questions of truth, questions of taste, or questions of justice. With
the internal differentiation into what Weber calls "spheres of
value" (i.e., scientific production, art and art criticism, and law
and morality), the elements that make up an almost indisso-
luble syndrome in the lifeworld are dissociated at the cultural
level. It is only with these value spheres that reflective perspectives emerge, perspectives from which the lifeworld appears as practice with which theory is to be mediated, as life
with which art is to be reconciled (in line with the surrealist
credo), or ethical life to which morality must be related.

From the viewpoint of a participant in moral argumentation,
the lifeworld that he has put at a distance, a world in which
unproblematic cultural givens of cognitive, expressive, or
moral origin are interwoven with one another, appears as the
sphere of ethical life. In this sphere, duties are so inextricably
tied to concrete habitual behavior that they derive their self-
evident quality from background convictions. In the sphere of
ethical life, questions of justice are posed only within the horizon of questions concerning the good life, questions which

have *always already been answered*. Under the unrelenting moralizing gaze of the participant in discourse this totality has lost its quality of naive acceptance, and the normative power of the factual has weakened. Familiar institutions can be transformed into so many instances of problematic justice. Under this gaze the store of traditional norms has disintegrated into those norms that can be justified in terms of principles and those that operate only de facto. The fusion of validity and social acceptance that characterizes the lifeworld has disintegrated. With this, the practice of everyday life separates into the component of the practical (into norms and values that can be subjected to the demands of strict moral justification) and into another component that cannot be moralized (a component that comprises the particular value orientations integrated to form individual and collective modes of life).

To be sure, cultural values too transcend de facto behavior. They congeal into historical and biographical syndromes of value orientations through which subjects can distinguish the good life from the reproduction of mere life. But ideas of the good life are not something we hold before us as an abstract "ought." Rather, they shape the identities of groups and individuals in such a way that they form an intrinsic part of culture or personality. Thus the development of the moral point of view goes hand in hand with a differentiation within the practical into *moral questions* and *evaluative questions*. Moral questions can in principle be decided rationally, i.e., in terms of *justice* or the generalizability of interests. Evaluative questions present themselves at the most general level as issues of the *good life* (or of self-realization); they are accessible to rational discussion only *within* the unproblematic horizon of a concrete historical form of life or the conduct of an individual life.

If we consider the abstraction achieved by morality, two things become clear: (1) the increase in rationality achieved when we isolate issues of justice and (2) the problems of mediating morality and ethical life that arise therefrom. Within the horizon of the lifeworld, practical judgments derive both their concreteness and their power to motivate action from their inner connection to unquestioningly accepted ideas of the good life, in short, from their connection to ethical life and its institutions. Under these conditions, problematization can never be so profound as to risk all the assets of the existing ethical substance. But the abstractive achievements required by the moral point of view do precisely that. This is why Kohlberg speaks of a transition to the *postconventional* stage of moral consciousness. At this stage, moral judgment becomes dissociated from the local conventions and historical coloration of a particular form of life. It can no longer appeal to the naive validity of the context of the lifeworld. Moral answers retain only the rationally motivating force of insights. Along with the naive self-certainty of their lifeworld background they lose the thrust and efficacy of empirical motives for action. To become effective in practice, every universalist morality has to make up for this loss of concrete ethical substance, which is initially accepted because of the cognitive advantages attending it. Universalist moralities are dependent on forms of life that are rationalized in that they make possible the prudent application of universal moral insights and support motivations for translating insights into moral action. Only those forms of life that meet universalist moralities halfway in this sense fulfill the conditions necessary to reverse the abstractive achievements of decontextualization and demotivation.

Notes

1. A MacIntyre, *After Virtue* (London, 1981), p. 52. M. Horkheimer, *Eclipse of Reason* (New York, 1974), chapter 1, pp. 3–57.

2. R. Wimmer, *Universalisierung in der Ethik* (Frankfurt, 1980).

3. W. K. Frankena, *Ethics* (Englewood Cliffs, N.J., 1973), chapter 6.

4. See chapters 1 and 8 of my *Theory of Communicative Action*, 2 vols. (Boston, 1984, 1987).

5. P. F. Strawson, *Freedom and Resentment* (London, 1974). It should be noted that Strawson is concerned with a different theme.

6. Nietzsche too saw a genetic link between the *ressentiment* of those who have been injured or insulted and a universalistic morality of sympathy. On this point, see J. Habermas, "The Entwinement of Myth and Enlightenment," in *The Philosophical Discourse of Modernity* (Cambridge, Mass., 1987), pp. 106–130.

7. Strawson (1974), p. 9.

8. Strawson (1974), p. 9.

9. Strawson (1974), p. 11ff. Strawson here refers to a determinism that exposes the competence actors impute to each other as deceptive.

10. Strawson (1974), p. 15.

11. On the differentiation of possible answers to these three classes of questions, see L. Krüger, "Über das Verhältnis von Wissenschaftlichkeit und Rationalität," in H. P. Duerr, ed., *Der Wissenschaftler und das Irrationale* (Frankfurt, 1981), vol. 2., pp. 91ff.

12. Strawson (1974), p. 22.

13. Strawson (1974), p. 23.

14. S. Toulmin, *An Examination of the Place of Reason in Ethics* (Cambridge, 1970), pp. 121ff.

15. Toulmin (1970), p. 125.

16. K. Nielsen, "On Moral Truth," in N. Rescher, ed., *Studies in Moral Philosophy* (Oxford, 1968), pp. 9ff.

17. A. R. White, *Truth* (New York, 1971), p. 61.

18. G. E. Moore, *Principia Ethica* (Cambridge, 1903), especially chapter 1.

19. G. E. Moore, "A Reply to My Critics," in P. A. Schilpp, ed., *The Philosophy of G. E. Moore* (Evanston, 1942).

20. Toulmin (1970), p. 28.

21. A. J. Ayer, "On the Analysis of Moral Judgments," in M. Munitz, ed., *A Modern Introduction to Ethics* (New York, 1958), p. 537.

22. MacIntyre (1981), p. 12. See also C. L. Stevenson, *Ethics and Language* (London, 1945), chapter 2.

23. R. M. Hare, *The Language of Morals* (Oxford, 1952).

24. Hare (1952), p. 3.

25. Compare the interesting remarks on "complete justification" by Hare: "The truth is that, if asked to justify as completely as possible any decision, we have to bring in both effects—to give content to the decision—and principles, and the effects in general of observing those principles, and so on, until we have satisfied our inquirer. Thus a complete justification of a decision would consist of a complete account of its effects, together with a complete account of the principles which it observed, and the effects of observing those principles, for of course it is the effects (what obeying them in fact consists in) which give content to the principles too. Thus, if pressed to justify a decision completely, we have to give a complete specification of the *way of life* of which it is a part." Hare (1952), pp. 68ff. Following Max Weber, Hans Albert has developed a different version of decisionism on the basis of Popper's critical rationalism, most recently in his *Fehlbare Vernunft* (Tübingen, 1980).

26. On the historical background of the philosophy of value, of which Moore and Scheler are merely two variants, see the excellent chapter entitled "Values," in H. Schnädelbach, *Philosophy in Germany 1831–1933* (Cambridge, 1984).

27. Toulmin (1970), p. 64.

28. Toulmin (1970), p. 74.

29. Habermas (1984), chapter 3, "Social Action, Purposive Activity, and Communication," p. 273ff.

30. At most we can compare theories, as higher-level systems of propositions, with norms. But it is debatable whether theories can be said to be true or false in the same sense as the descriptions, predictions, and explanations that we derive from them, whereas norms for their part are right or wrong in the same sense as the actions that satisfy or violate them.

31. J. Habermas, "Legitimation Problems in the Modern State," in Habermas, *Communication and the Evolution of Society* (Boston, 1979), pp. 178ff. On the relation between the justification of norms, their being put into effect, and their being accepted, see also W. Kuhlmann, "Ist eine philosophische Letztbegründung von Normen möglich?" in *Funkkolleg Ethik*, Studienbegleitbrief 8 (Weinheim, 1981), p. 32.

32. S. Toulmin, *The Uses of Argument* (Cambridge, 1958).

33. J. Habermas, "Wahrheitstheorien," in H. Fahrenbach, ed., *Festschrift für W. Schulz* (Pfullingen, 1973), pp. 211ff. J. Habermas, *The Theory of Communicative Action*, vol. 1. (Boston, 1984), pp. 22ff.

34. On the logic of practical discourse, see T. McCarthy, *The Critical Theory of Jürgen Habermas* (Cambridge, Mass., 1978), pp. 310ff.

35. Wimmer (1980), pp. 174ff.

36. G. Patzig, *Tatsachen, Normen, Sätze* (Stuttgart, 1980), p. 162.

37. Kurt Baier, *The Moral Point of View* (London, 1958).

38. Bernard Gert, *Moral Rules* (New York, 1976).

39. Marcus Singer, *Generalization in Ethics* (New York, 1961).

40. G. H. Mead, "Fragments on Ethics," in *Mind, Self, and Society* (Chicago, 1934), pp. 379ff. See also H. Joas, *G. H. Mead: A Contemporary Reexamination of His Thought* (Cambridge, Mass., 1985), and J. Habermas, *The Theory of Communicative Action*, vol. 2 (Boston, 1987), pp. 92ff.

41. With reference to B. Gert's *Moral Rules*, p. 72, G. Nunner-Winkler has raised the objection that (U) is unable to single out from among the norms that fulfill the stated conditions those that are moral in the narrow sense and to exclude others (e.g., "You ought to smile when you say hello to people"). This objection is met when one proposes to call moral only those norms that are strictly universalizable, i.e., those that are invariable over historical time and across social groups. This usage of the moral theorist does not, of course, coincide with that of the sociologist and the historian, who tend to describe epoch-specific and culture-specific rules as moral rules if they are accepted as such by the members of the group under study.

42. T. McCarthy (1978), p. 326.

43. S. Benhabib, "The Methodological Illusions of Modern Political Theory: The Case of Rawls and Habermas," in *Neue Hefte für Philosophie* 21 (1982) 47ff.

44. In what follows I am referring to the third of Tugendhat's Christian Gauss lectures at Princeton University, entitled "Morality and Communication" (ms., 1981). Subsequently published in German in E. Tugendhat, *Probleme der Ethik* (Stuttgart, 1984), pp. 108ff.

45. E. Tugendhat, *Traditional and Analytical Philosophy* (Cambridge, 1982).

46. M. Dummett, "What Is a Theory of Meaning?" in G. Evans and J. McDowell, eds., *Truth and Meaning* (Oxford, 1976), pp. 67ff.

47. Habermas (1987), vol. 2, pp 47ff.

48. This aspect was captured by G. H. Mead's concept of the "generalized other." See Habermas (1987), vol. 2, pp. 37ff and pp. 92ff.

49. P. Taylor, "The Ethnocentric Fallacy," *Monist* 47 (1963): 570.

50. J. Rawls, *A Theory of Justice* (Cambridge, Mass., 1971), pp. 20ff and 48ff.

51. P. Lorenzen and O. Schwemmer, *Konstruktive Logik, Ethik und Wissenschaftstheorie* (Mannheim, 1973), pp. 107ff.

52. Wimmer (1980), pp. 358f.

53. H. Albert, *Treatise on Critical Reason* (New York, 1985).

54. K. O. Apel, "The A Priori of the Communication Community and the Foundations of Ethics," in Apel, *Towards a Transformation of Philosophy* (London, 1980), pp. 225ff.

55. K. O. Apel, "The Problem of Philosophical Foundations Grounding in Light of a Transcendental Pragmatics of Language," in K. Baynes, J. Bohman, and T. McCarthy, eds., *After Philosophy* (Cambridge, Mass., 1987), pp. 250–290.

56. H. Lenk, "Philosophische Logikbegründung und rationaler Kritizismus," in *Zeitschrift für Philosophische Forschung* 24 (1970): 183ff.

57. Apel (1987), p. 277.

58. A. J. Watt, "Transcendental Arguments and Moral Principles," *Philosophical Quarterly* 25 (1975): 40.

59. Watt (1975), p. 41.

60. R. S. Peters, *Ethics and Education* (London, 1974), pp. 114f.

61. Peters himself makes this point: "If it could be shown that certain principles are necessary for a form of discourse to have meaning, to be applied or to have point, then this would be a very strong argument for the justification of the principles in question. They would show what anyone must be committed to who uses it seriously. Of course, it would be open for anyone to say that he is not so committed because he does not use this form of discourse or because he will give it up now that he realizes

its presuppositions. This would be quite a feasible position to adopt in relation, for instance, to the discourse of witchcraft or astrology; for individuals are not necessarily initiated into it in our society, and they can exercise their discretion about whether they think and talk in this way or not. Many have, perhaps mistakenly, given up using religious language, for instance, because they have been brought to see that its use commits them to, e.g., saying things which purport to be true for which the truth conditions can never be produced. But it would be a very difficult position to adopt in relation to moral discourse. For it would entail a resolute refusal to talk or think about what ought to be done." Peters (1974), pp. 115f.

62. Peters (1974), p. 121.

63. Peters (1974), p. 181.

64. Kuhlmann (1981), 64ff.

65. This constitutes a revision of assertions I made earlier. See J. Habermas and N. Luhmann, *Theorie der Gesellschaft oder Sozialtechnologie* (Frankfurt, 1971), pp. 136ff. Compare Apel (1980), pp. 276ff.

66. B. R. Burleson, "On the Foundation of Rationality," *Journal of the American Forensic Association* 1979: 112ff.

67. R. Alexy, "Eine Theorie des praktischen Diskurses," in W. Oelmüller, ed., *Normenbegründung, Normendurchsetzung* (Paderborn, 1978).

68. Alexy (1978), p. 37. The numbering has been changed.

69. To the degree to which these are of a special kind and cannot be distilled from the general meaning of a competition for better arguments, they are *institutional* mechanisms that belong to a *different* level of analysis (see below).

70. Habermas, "Wahrheitstheorien" (1973), pp. 211ff.

71. Alexy (1978), p. 40.

72. This presupposition is obviously irrelevant for theoretical discourses, since they only test assertoric validity claims. All the same, it is one of the pragmatic presuppositions of argumentation as such.

73. In what follows, Habermas contrasts *überzeugen* and *überreden*, here translated as "convince" and "talk into." The contrast is more emphatic in German than in English; *überzeugen* implies the use of argument, while "to cause to believe by argument" is one but not the only meaning of "convince." (Translator's note)

74. See J. Habermas, "Die Utopie des guten Herrschers," in Habermas, *Kleine Politische Schriften*, vols. 1–4 (Frankfurt, 1981), pp. 318ff.

75. A somewhat different formulation of the same principle can be found in F. Kambartel, "Moralisches Argumentieren," in Kambartel, ed., *Praktische Philosophie und konstruktive Wissenschaftstheorie*, (Frankfurt, 1974), pp. 54ff. According to Kambartel, those norms for which the consent of all concerned can be obtained through "rational dialogue" are justified. Justification is based on "a rational dialogue (or the outline of such a dialogue) leading to an agreement by all participants that the orientation which is being questioned can be agreed to by all concerned in an imaginary situation of undistorted communication" (p. 68).

76. F. Kambartel, "Wie ist praktische Philosophie konstruktiv möglich?" in Kambartel (1974), p. 11.

77. Kuhlmann (1981), p. 57.

78. G. Schönrich, *Kategorien und transzendentale Argumentation* (Frankfurt, 1981), pp. 196f.

79. Schönrich (1981), p. 200.

80. Apel (1980), p. 273 (translation altered). The quote by Fichte goes as follows: "Our method almost always is (a) to do something, whereby we are doubtless guided by a law of reason working in us. In this case, what we are . . . is still a facticity. Then we set about (b) to study and discover the law that guided our mechanically determined doing. What we at first apprehended immediately we now apprehend mediately through the principle and ground of its thusness, that is, we grasp the genesis of its determinacy. We thus progress from the factual analysis of parts to their genetic analysis. The genetic can also be factual but in a different way. This is why we are forced to go beyond it to examine its genesis, and so on, until we reach absolute genesis, the genesis of the science of knowledge." J. G. Fichte, *Werke*, ed. F. Medicus (Leipzig, 1910), vol. 4, p. 206.

81. When we talk about the political relevance of an ethics of discourse, things are different to the degree to which the ethics of discourse affects the moral-practical basis of the legal system or any political aspect transcending the private sphere of morality. In this regard, that is, in regard to providing guidance for an emancipatory practice, discourse ethics can acquire a significance for orienting action. It does so, however, not as an ethics, that is, not prescriptively in the direct sense, but indirectly, by becoming part of a critical social theory that can be used to interpret situations, as for example when it is used to differentiate between particular and universalizable interests.

82. A. Gewirth, *Reason and Morality* (Chicago, 1978).

83. A. MacIntyre has shown this to be the case: "Gewirth argues that anyone who holds that the prerequisites for his exercise of rational agency are necessary goods is logically committed to holding also that he has a right to these goods. But quite clearly the introduction of the concept of a right needs justification both because it is at this point a concept quite new to Gewirth's argument *and* because of the special character of the concept of right. It is first of all clear that the claim that I have a right to do or to have something is a quite different type of claim from the claim that I need or want or will be benefited by something. From the first—if it is the only relevant considera-tion—it follows that others ought not to interfere with my attempts to do or have whatever it is, whether it is for my own good or not. From the second it does not. And it makes no difference what kind of good or benefit is at issue." MacIntyre (1981), pp. 64f.

84. Habermas (1984), vol. 1, chapters 1 and 3. See also Stephen K. White, "On the Normative Structure of Action," *Review of Politics* 44 (1982): 282ff.

85. R. S. Peters has propagated this sort of analytical strategy in another context: "To say . . . that men ought to rely more on their reason, that they ought to be more concerned with first-hand justification, is to claim that they are systematically falling down on a job on which they are already engaged. It is not to commit some version of the naturalistic fallacy by basing a demand for a type of life on features of human life which make it distinctively human. For this would be to repeat the errors of the

old Greek doctrines of function. Rather it is to say that human life already bears witness to the demands of reason. Without some acceptance by men of such demands their life would be unintelligible. But given the acceptance of such demands they are proceeding in a way which is inappropriate to satisfying them. Concern for truth is written into human life." R. S. Peters, *Education and the Education of Teachers* (London, 1977), pp. 104f.

86. This question is sharply posed by T. McCarthy in W. Oelmüller, ed., *Transzendentalphilosophische Normenbegründungen* (Paderborn, 1979), p. 134ff.

87. Habermas (1987), vol. 2, pp. 140ff.

88. A. Wellmer, *Praktische Philosophie und Theorie der Gesellschaft* (Konstanz, 1979), pp. 40f.

89. I am referring to Tugendhat's concept of "normative learning" as presented in G. Frankenberg and U. Rödel, *Von der Volkssouveränität zum Minderheitenschutz* (Frankfurt, 1981).

Moral Consciousness and Communicative Action

The discourse theory of ethics, for which I have proposed a program of philosophical justification,[1] is not a self-contained endeavor. Discourse ethics advances universalistic and thus very strong theses, but the status it claims for those theses is relatively weak. Essentially, the justification involves two steps. First, a principle of universalization (U) is introduced. It serves as a rule of argumentation in practical discourses. Second, this rule is justified in terms of the substance of the pragmatic presuppositions of argumentation as such in connection with an explication of the meaning of normative claims to validity. The universalization principle can be understood on the model of Rawls's "reflective equilibrium" as a reconstruction of the everyday intuitions underlying the impartial judgment of moral conflicts of action. The second step, which is designed to set forth the universal validity of (U), a validity that extends beyond the perspective of a particular culture, is based on a transcendental-pragmatic demonstration of universal and necessary presuppositions of argumentation. We may no longer burden these arguments with the status of an a priori transcendental deduction along the lines of Kant's critique of reason. They ground only the fact that there is no identifiable alternative to our kind of argumentation. In this respect, discourse ethics, like other reconstructive sciences, relies solely on hypothetical reconstruction for which plausible confirmation

I would like to thank Max Miller and Gertrud Nunner-Winkler for their critical comments on a draft of this essay.

must be sought.[2] Initially, of course, the place to look for such confirmation is at the level on which discourse ethics competes with other moral theories. But a theory of this kind is also open to, indeed dependent upon, *indirect* validation by *other* theories that are consonant with it. I view the theory of the development of moral consciousness advanced by Lawrence Kohlberg and his coworkers as an example of the latter kind of validation.[3]

Kohlberg holds that the development of the capacity for moral judgment from childhood to adolescence and adult life follows an invariant pattern. The normative reference point of the developmental path that Kohlberg empirically analyzes is a principled morality in which we can recognize the main features of discourse ethics. From the standpont of ethics, the consonance between psychological theory and normative theory consists in this case in the following: Opponents of universalistic ethics generally bring up the fact that different cultures have *different* conceptions of morality. To oppose relativistic objections of this kind, Kohlberg's theory of moral development offers the possibility of (a) reducing the empirical diversity of existing moral views to variation in the *contents*, in contrast to the universal *forms*, of moral judgment and (b) explaining the remaining structural differences between moralities as differences in the stage of development of the capacity for moral judgment.

Yet the consonance in the results of these two theories would seem to be deprived of its significance by the internal links between them. Kohlberg's theory of moral development makes use of the insights of philosophical ethics in the description of the cognitive structures underlying principle moral judgment. In making a normative theory like that of Rawls an integral part of an empirical theory, the psychologist at the same time subjects it to indirect testing. Empirical corroboration of the assumptions derived from developmental psychology extends, then, to *all* components of the theory from which the confirmed hypotheses were derived. This means we must give precedence to the moral theory that survives such a test better than others. I consider reservations about the circular character of this verification process to be unfounded.

The empirical corroboration of an emperical theory that *presupposes* as valid the fundamental assumptions of a norma- tive theory cannot, I admit, pass for an *independent* corrobora- tion of the normative theory. But independence postulates have been shown to be too strong in several respects. For example, the data used to test an empirical theory cannot be described independently of the language of the same theory. Similarly, two competing emperical theories cannot be evalu- ated independently of the paradigms furnishing their basic concepts. On the meta- or intertheoretical level, the only gov- erning principle is that of coherence. We want to find out what elements fit together, which is a bit like doing a jigsaw puzzle. The reconstructive sciences designed to grasp universal com- petences break through the hermeneutic circle in which the *Geisteswissenschaften*, as well as the interpretive social sciences, are trapped. But the hermeneutic circle closes on the meta- theoretical level even for a genetic structuralism, that, like the theories of moral development derived from Piaget, attempts to deal with problems posed in an ambitious universalist form.[4] In such a case, looking for independent proof is a waste of time. It is only a question of seeing whether the descriptions produced with the aid of *several* theoretical spotlights can be integrated into a relatively reliable map.

If one adopts criteria of coherence to govern the *division of labor* between *philosophical ethics* and a *developmental psychology* designed to rationally reconstruct the pretheoretical knowledge of competently judging subjects, philosophy and science must change their self-perceptions.[5] This division of labor is no more compatible with the claim to exclusivity previously raised by the program of unified science on behalf of the standard form of the nomological empirical sciences than it is with transcen- dental philosophy and its foundationalist aim of ultimate justification. Once transcendental arguments have been dis- engaged from the language game of the philosophy of reflec- tion and reformulated along Strawsonian lines, recourse to the synthetic functions of self-consciousness loses its plausibility. The objective of transcendental deduction loses its meaning, and the hierarchical relation claimed to exist between the a priori knowledge of foundations and the a posteriori knowledge of phenomena loses its basis. A reflective grasp of what Kant had captured with the image of the subject's constitutive achievements, or as we would say today, the reconstruction of the general and necessary presuppositions under which subjects capable of speech and action reach understanding about something in the world—such striving for knowledge on the part of the philosopher is no less fallible than anything else that has ever been exposed to the grueling and cleansing process of scientific discussion and has stood up, at least for the time being.[6]

A nonfoundationalist self-understanding of this kind does more, however, than simply relieve philosophy of tasks that have overburdened it. It not only takes something away from philosophy; it also provides it with the opportunity for a certain naïveté and a new self-confidence in its cooperative relationship with the reconstructive sciences. A relationship of mutual dependence becomes established.[7] Thus, to return to the matter at hand, not only does moral philosophy depend on indirect confirmation from a developmental psychology of moral consciousness; the latter in turn is built on philosophical assumptions.[8] I will investigate this interdependence by using Kohlberg as an example.

I The Fundamental Philosophical Assumptions of Kohlberg's Theory

Coming from the tradition of American pragmatism, Lawrence Kohlberg has a clear conception of the philosophical bases of his theory.[9] His philosophical views on the "nature of moral judgment" were originally inspired by G. H. Mead. But since the publication of A Theory of Justice (1971), he has used John Rawls's ethics, which takes its bearings from Kant and modern natural-law theory, to sharpen them: "These analyses point to the features of a 'moral point of view,' suggesting truly moral reasoning involves features such as impartiality, universalizability, reversibility and prescriptivity."[10] The premises Kohlberg borrows from philosophy can be grouped under three headings: cognitivism, universalism, and formalism.

In section 1 below I will elaborate on why I think discourse ethics is better suited than any other ethical theory to explain the moral point of view in terms of premises of cognitivism, universalism, and formalism. In section 2 I want to show that the concept of constructive learning used by Piaget and Kohlberg is necessary to discourse ethics as well. Discourse ethics is thus well suited to the description of cognitive structures that emerge from learning processes. Section 3 shows how discourse ethics can complement Kohlberg's theory by virtue of its connection with a theory of communicative action. In the sections that follow I will use this internal relation to establish a plausible basis for a vertical reconstruction of the developmental stages of moral judgment.

1

All cognitivist moral theories in the tradition of Kant take into account the three aspects Kohlberg focuses on to explain the idea of the moral. The advantage of the position Apel and I defend is that the basic cognitivist, universalist, and formalist assumptions can be derived from the moral principle grounded in discourse ethics. I have previously proposed the following formulation of this principle:

(U)   For a norm to be valid, the consequences and side effects that its *general* observance can be expected to have for the satisfaction of the particular interests of *each* person affected must be such that *all* affected can accept them freely.

Cognitivism   Since the universalization principle is a rule of argumentation enabling us to reach consensus on generalizable maxims, the justification of (U) demonstrates at the same time that moral-practical issues can be decided on the basis of reasons. Moral judgments have cognitive content. They represent more than expressions of the contingent emotions, preferences, and decisions of a speaker or actor.[11] Discourse ethics refutes *ethical skepticism* by explaining how moral judgments can be justified. Any developmental theory of the capacity for moral judgment must presuppose this possibility of distinguishing between right and wrong moral judgments.

Universalism It follows directly from (U) that anyone who takes part in argumentation of any sort is in principle able to reach the same judgments on the acceptability of norms of action. By justifying (U), discourse ethics rejects the basic assumptions of *ethical relativism*, which holds that the validity of moral judgments is measured solely by the standards of rationality or value proper to a specific culture or form of life. A theory of moral development that attempts to outline a general path of development would be doomed to failure from the start if moral judgments could not claim universal validity.

Formalism   (U) works like a rule that eliminates as nongeneralizable content all those concrete value orientations with which particular biographies or forms of life are permeated. Of the evaluative issues of the good life it thus retains only issues of justice, which are normative in the strict sense. They alone can be settled by rational argument. With its justification of (U), discourse ethics sets itself in opposition to the fundamental assumptions of *material ethics*. The latter is oriented to issues of happiness and tends to ontologically favor some particular type of ethical life or other. By defining the sphere of the normative validity of action norms, discourse ethics sets the domain of moral validity off from the domain of cultural value *contents*. Unless one operates with a strictly deontological notion of normative rightness or justice such as this, one cannot isolate those questions accessible to rational decision from the mass of practical issues. Kohlberg's moral dilemmas are designed around the latter.

Yet this does not exhaust the contents of discourse ethics. While its *universalization principle* furnishes a rule of argumentation, the *principle of discourse ethics* (D) expresses the fundamental idea of moral theory that Kohlberg borrowed from G. H. Mead's communication theory as the notion of "ideal role taking."[12] This principle postulates the following:

(D) Every valid norm would meet with the approval of all concerned if they could take part in a practical discourse.

Discourse ethics does not set up substantive orientations. Instead, it establishes a *procedure* based on presuppositions and designed to guarantee the impartiality of the process of judging. Practical discourse is a procedure for testing the validity of hypothetical norms, not for producing justified norms. It is this proceduralism that sets discourse ethics apart from *other* cognitivist, universalist, and formalist ethical theories, and thus from Rawls's theory of justice as well. (D) makes us aware that (U) merely expresses the normative content of a procedure of discursive will formation and must thus be strictly distinguished from the substantive content of argumentation. *Any* content, no matter how fundamental the action norms in question may be, must be made subject to real discourse (or advocatory discourses undertaken in their place). The principle of discourse ethics prohibits singling out with philosophical authority any specific normative contents (as, for example, certain principles of distributive justice) as the definitive content of moral theory. Once a normative theory like Rawls's theory of justice strays into substantive issues, it becomes just one contribution to practical discourse among many, even though it may be an especially competent one. It no longer helps to ground the moral point of view that characterizes practical discourses *as such*.

The fundamental assumptions of cognitivism, universalism, and formalism discussed above are already contained within a procedural definition of the moral. Such a definition also allows for a sufficiently sharp demarcation within moral judgment between cognitive structures and contents. The discursive procedure, in fact, reflects the very operations Kohlberg postulates for moral judgments at the postconventional level: complete *reversibility* of the perspectives from which participants produce their arguments; *universality*, understood as the inclusion of all concerned; and the *reciprocity* of equal recognition of the claims of each participant by all others.

2

Discourse ethics singles out (U) and (D) as characteristics of moral judgment that can serve as normative points of reference in describing the development of the capacity for moral judgment. Kohlberg distinguishes *six stages of moral judgment*. They can be regarded as *gradual approximations* in the dimensions of reversibility, universality, and reciprocity to structures of impartial or just judgments about morally relevant conflicts of action. Below I quote Kohlberg's summary of his moral stages.

Level A, preconventional level

Stage 1, the stage of punishment and obedience
Content: Right is literal obedience to rules and authority, avoiding punishment, and not doing physical harm.

1. What is right is to avoid breaking rules, to obey for obedience' sake, and to avoid doing physical damage to people and property.

2. The reasons for doing right are avoidance of punishment and the superior power of authorities.

Stage 2, the stage of individual instrumental purpose and exchange

1. What is right is following rules when it is to someone's immediate interest. Right is acting to meet one's own interests and needs and letting others do the same. Right is also what is fair; that is, what is an equal exchange, a deal, an agreement.

2. The reason for doing right is to serve one's own needs or interests in a world where one must recognize that other people have their interests, too.

Level B, conventional level

Stage 3, the stage of mutual interpersonal expectations, relationships, and conformity
Content: The right is playing a good (nice) role, being concerned about the other people and their feelings, keeping loyalty and trust with partners, and being motivated to follow rules and expectations.

1. What is right is living up to what is expected by people close to one or what people generally expect of people in one's role as son, sister, friends, and so on. "Being good" is important and means having good motives, showing concern about others. It also means keeping mutual relationships, maintaining trust, loyalty, respect, and gratitude.

2. Reasons for doing right are needing to be good in one's own eyes and those of others, caring for others, and because if one puts oneself in the other person's place one would want good behavior from the self (Golden Rule).

Stage 4, the stage of social system and conscience maintenance
Content: The right is doing one's duty in society, upholding the social
order, and maintaining the welfare of society or the group.

1. What is right is fulfilling the actual duties to which one has agreed.
Laws are to be upheld except in extreme cases where they conflict
with other fixed social duties and rights. Right is also contributing to
society, the group, or institution.

2. The reasons for doing right are to keep the institution going as a
whole, self-respect or conscience as meeting one's defined obligations,
or the consequences: "What if everyone did it?"

Level C, postconventional and principled level

Moral decisions are generated from rights, values or principles that
are (or could be) agreeable to all individuals composing or creating
a society designed to have fair and beneficial practices.

Stage 5, the stage of prior rights and social contract or utility
Content: The right is upholding the basic rights, values, and legal
contracts of a society, even when they conflict with the concrete rules
and laws of the group.

1. What is right is being aware of the fact that people hold a variety
of values and opinions, that most values and rules are relative to
one's group. These "relative" rules should usually be upheld, however, in the interest of the impartiality and because they are the social
contract. Some nonrelative values and rights such as life, and liberty,
however, must be upheld in any society and regardless of majority
opinion.

2. Reasons for doing right are, in general, feeling obligated to obey
the law because one has made a social contract to make and abide by
laws, for the good of all and to protect their own rights and the rights
of others. Family, friendship, trust, and work obligations are also
commitments or contracts freely entered into and entail respect for
the rights of others. One is concerned that laws and duties be based
on rational calculation of overall utility: "the greatest good for the
greatest number."

Stage 6, the stage of universal ethical principles
Content: This stage assumes guidance by universal ethical principles
that all humanity should follow.

1. Regarding what is right, Stage 6 is guided by universal ethical
principles. Particular laws or social agreements are usually valid because they rest on such principles. When laws violate these principles,
one acts in accordance with the principle. Principles are universal
principles of justice: the equality of human rights and respect for the

dignity of human beings as individuals. These are not merely values that are recognized, but are also principles used to generate particular decisions.

2. The reason for doing right is that, as a rational person, one has seen the validity of principles and has become committed to them.[13]

Kohlberg conceives the transition from one stage to the next as *learning*. Moral development means that a child or adolescent rebuilds and differentiates the cognitive structures he already has so as to be better able to solve the same sort of problems he faced before, namely, how to solve relevant moral dilemmas in a consensual manner. The young person himself sees this moral development as a learning process in that at the higher stage he must be able to explain whether and in what way the moral judgments he had considered right at the previous stage were wrong. Kohlberg interprets this learning process as a constructive achievement on the part of the learner, as would Piaget. The cognitive structures underlying the capacity of moral judgment are to be explained neither primarily in terms of environmental influences nor in terms of inborn programs and maturational processes. They are viewed instead as outcomes of a creative reorganization of an existing cognitive inventory that is inadequate to the task of handling certain persistent problems.

Discourse ethics is compatible with this constructivist notion of learning in that it conceives discursive will formation (and argumentation in general) as a reflective form of communicative action and also in that it postulates a *change of attitude* for the transition from action to discourse. A child growing up, and caught up, in the communicative practice of everyday life is not able at the start to effect this attitude change.

In argumentation, claims to validity that heretofore served actors as unquestioned points of orientation in their everyday communication are thematized and made problematic. When this happens, the participants in argumentation adopt a hypothetical attitude to controversial validity claims. The validity of a contested norm is put in abeyance when practical discourse begins. The issue is then whether or not the norm *deserves* to be recognized, and that issue will be decided by a contest between proponents and opponents of the norm. The attitude change accompanying the passage from communicative action to discourse is no different for issues of justice than for issues of truth. In the latter case, what had previously been considered facts in naive dealings with things and events must now be regarded as something that may or may not be the case. Just as "facts" are thus transformed into "states of affairs," so social norms to which one is accustomed are transformed into possibilities for regulation that can be accepted as valid or rejected as invalid.

If by way of a thought experiment we compress the adolescent phase of growth into a single critical instant in which the individual for the first time—yet pervasively and intransigently—assumes a hypothetical attitude toward the normative context of his lifeworld, we can see the nature of the problem that every person must deal with in passing from the conventional to the postconventional level of moral judgment. The social world of legitimately regulated interpersonal relations, a world to which one was naively habituated and which was unproblematically accepted, is abruptly deprived of its quasi-natural validity.

If the adolescent cannot and does not want to go back to the traditionalism and unquestioned identity of his past world, he must, on penalty of utter disorientation, reconstruct, at the level of basic concepts, the normative orders that his hypothetical gaze has destroyed by removing the veil of illusions from them. Using the rubble of devalued traditions, traditions that have been recognized to be merely conventional and in need of justification, he erects a new normative structure that must be solid enough to withstand critical inspection by someone who will henceforth distinguish soberly between socially accepted norms and valid norms, between de facto recognition of norms and norms that are *worthy* of recognition. At first principles inform his plan for reconstruction; these principles govern the generation of valid norms. Ultimately all that remains is a procedure for a rationally motivated choice among principles that have been recognized in turn as in need of justification. In contrast to moral action in everyday life, the shift in attitude that discourse ethics requires for the procedure it singles out as crucial, the transition to argumentation, has something unnatural about it: it marks a break with the ingenuous straightforwardness with which people have raised the claims to validity on whose intersubjective recognition the communicative practice of everyday life depends. This unnaturalness is like an echo of the developmental catastrophe that historically once devalued the world of traditions and thereby provoked efforts to rebuild it at a higher level. In this sense, what Kohlberg conceives as a constructive learning process operating at *all* levels is built into the transition (which has become routine for the adult) from norm-guided action to norm-testing discourse.

3

Having dealt with the *normative reference point* of moral development in Kohlberg's theory in section 1 and with his concept of *learning* in section 2, I will now turn to an analysis of his *stage model*. Here too Kohlberg follows Piaget by setting up a model of the developmental stages of a specific competence, in this case the capacity for moral judgment. Kohlberg describes this model in terms of three strong hypotheses:

• The stages of moral judgment form an invariant, irreversible, and consecutive sequence of discrete structures. This assumption precludes the possibility that different experimental subjects will reach the same goal by different developmental paths, that the same subject will regress from a higher to a lower stage, and that stages will be skipped in the course of a subject's development.

• The stages of moral judgment form a hierarchy in that the cognitive structures of a higher stage dialectically sublate those of the lower one, that is, the lower stage is replaced and at the same time preserved in a reorganized, more differentiated form.

• Every stage of moral judgment can be characterized as a structured whole. This assumption precludes the possibility that at a given point in time an experimental subject will have to judge different moral content at different levels. Not precluded are so-called *décalage* (realignment) phenomena, which indicate a step by step anchoring of newly acquired structures.

The key component of this model is obviously the second hypothesis. The other two hypotheses can be toned down or modified, but the notion of a path of development which can be described in terms of a *hierarchically ordered sequence of structures* is absolutely crucial to Kohlberg's model of developmental stages. For Kohlberg as for Piaget, synonymous with this concept of a hierarchical order is the concept of a logic of development. This expression reflects the awkward situation they found themselves in: In the sequences of stages, the cognitive structures that they assumed were *internally* related in intuitively evident ways eluded analysis in terms of exclusively logicosemantic concepts. Kohlberg justifies the developmental logic of his six stages of moral judgment by correlating them with corresponding sociomoral perspectives. I quote his summary of these perspectives below:

1. This stage takes an egocentric point of view. A person at this stage doesn't consider the interests of others or recognize they differ from actor's, and doesn't relate two points of view. Actions are judged in terms of physical consequences rather than in terms of psychological interests of others. Authority's perspective is confused with one's own.

2. This stage takes a concrete individualistic perspective. A person at this stage separates own interests and points of view from those of authorities and others. He or she is aware everybody has individual interests to pursue and these conflict, so that right is relative (in the concrete individualistic sense). The person integrates or relates conflicting individual interests to one another through instrumental exchange of services, through instrumental need for the other and the other's goodwill, or through fairness giving each person the same amount.

3. This stage takes the perspective of the individual in relationship to other individuals. A person at this stage is aware of shared feelings, agreements, and expectations, which take primacy over individual interests. The person relates points of view through the "concrete Golden Rule," putting oneself in the other person's shoes. He or she does not consider generalized "system" perspective.

4. This stage differentiates societal point of view from interpersonal agreement or motives. A person at this stage takes the viewpoint of the system, which defines roles and rules. He or she considers individual relations in terms of place in the system.

5. This stage takes a prior-to-society perspective—that of a rational individual aware of values and rights prior to social attachments and contracts. The person integrates perspectives by formal mechanisms of agreement, contract, objective impartiality, and due process. He or she considers the moral point of view and the legal point of view, recognizes they conflict, and finds it difficult to integrate them.

6. This stage takes the perspective of a moral point of view from which social arrangements derive or on which they are grounded. The perspective is that of any rational individual recognizing the nature of morality or the basic moral premise of respect for other persons as ends, not means.[14]

Kohlberg describes these sociomoral perspectives in such a way that their correlations with stages of moral judgment seem intuitively correct. This plausibility is achieved, however, at the cost of a description in which the sociocognitive conditions of moral judgment have already been blended with the structures of those judgments. Moreover, the sociocognitive conditions lack sufficient analytical rigor to make it immediately evident why this sequence represents a hierarchy in the sense of a logic of development. Perhaps these reservations can be cleared up if we replace Kohlberg's sociomoral perspectives with the stages of perspective taking developed by Robert Selman.[15] This is indeed a step in the right direction, but it does not suffice for a justification of moral stages, as I will presently show.

It remains to be demonstrated that Kohlberg's descriptions of moral stages do in fact satisfy the conditions of a stage model conceived in terms of a logic of development. This is a problem of conceptual analysis. It is my impression that empirical research will not advance our understanding here until we have an interesting and sufficiently precise proposal for a solution of the problem in the form of a hypothetical reconstruction. What follows is an attempt to establish whether discourse ethics can contribute to the solution of this problem.

Discourse ethics uses transcendental arguments to demonstrate that certain conditions are unavoidable. Such arguments are geared to convincing an opponent that he makes performative use of something he expressly denies and thus gets caught up in a performative contradiction.[16] In grounding (U) I am specifically concerned to identify the pragmatic presuppositions indispensable to any argumentation. Anyone who participates in argumentation has already accepted these substantive normative conditions—there is no alternative to them. Simply by choosing to engage in argumentation, participants are forced to acknowledge this fact. This transcendental-pragmatic demonstration serves to make us aware of the extent of the conditions under which we always already operate when we argue; no one has the option of *escaping to alternatives*. The absence of alternatives means that those conditions are, in fact, inescapable for us.

This "fact of reason" cannot be deductively *grounded*, but it can be *clarified* if we take the further step of conceiving argumentative speech as a special case—in fact, a privileged derivative—of action oriented toward reaching understanding. Only when we return to the level of action theory and conceive discourse as a continuation of communicative action by other means can we understand the true thrust of discourse ethics. The reason we can locate the content of (U) in the communicative presuppositions of argumentation is that argumentation is a reflective form of communicative action and the structures of action oriented toward reaching understanding always already presuppose those very relationships of reciprocity and mutual recognition around which *all* moral ideas revolve in everyday life no less than in philosophical ethics. Like Kant's appeal to the "fact of reason," this thrust of discourse ethics has a naturalistic ring to it, but it is by no means a naturalistic fallacy. Both Kant and the proponents of discourse ethics rely on a type of argument that draws attention to the inescapability of the general presuppositions that *always already* underlie the communicative practice of everyday life and that cannot be picked or chosen like makes of cars or value postulates. This type of argument is made from the reflective point of view, not from the empiricist attitude of an objectivating observer.

The transcendental mode of justification reflects the fact that practical discourse is embedded in contexts of communicative action. To that extent discourse ethics points to, and itself depends upon, a theory of communicative action. We can expect a contribution to the vertical reconstruction of stages of moral consciousness from the theory of communicative action, for the latter focuses on structures of linguistically mediated, norm-governed interaction, structures that *integrate* what psychology analytically separates, to wit, perspective taking, moral judgment, and action.

Kohlberg saddles sociomoral perspectives with the job of grounding a logic of development. His social perspectives are supposed to express capacities for social cognition. The stages of social perspective do not, however, match Selman's stages of perspective taking. It may be wise to separate two dimensions that are associated in Kohlberg's description: the perspective structures themselves and the justice conceptions derived from the sociocognitive inventory at any particular point. There is no need to bring in these normative aspects on the sly, because a moral dimension is intrinsic to the basic concepts of the "social world" and "norm-governed interaction"

Kohlberg's construction of social perspectives also seems to be based on the concepts of a conventional role structure. At stage 3 the child learns these role structures in their particularity and generalizes them at stage 4. The axis around which the social perspectives turn, as it were, is the social world as the sum total of the interactions a social group considers legitimate because they are institutionally ordered. At the first two stages the child does not yet have these concepts, and at the last two stages he has reached a standpoint at which he leaves concrete society behind and from which he can test the validity of existing norms. With this transition the fundamental concepts in which the social world was constituted for the young person are transformed directly into basic moral concepts. I would like to trace these links between social cognition and morality, using the theory of communicative action. The attempt to clarify Kohlberg's social perspectives in this framework should have a number of advantages.

The idea of action oriented toward reaching understanding implies two notions that require clarification: that of the social world and that of norm-guided interaction. The sociomoral perspective developed at stages 3 and 4 and used reflectively at stages 5 and 6 can be set within a system of *world perspectives* that, in conjunction with a system of *speaker perspectives*, underlies communicative action. Moreover, the nexus between conceptions of the world and claims to validity opens the possibility of linking the reflective attitude toward the social world (Kohlberg's "prior-to-society perspective") with the hypothetical attitude of a participant in argumentation who thematizes corresponding normative validity claims. This enables us to explain why the moral point of view, conceived in terms of discourse ethics, emerges when the conventional role structure is made reflexive.

This action-theoretic approach suggests that we should understand the development of sociomoral perspectives in the context of the *decentering of* the young person's *understanding of the world*. It also draws attention to the structures of interaction themselves, which set the parameters for the constructive learning of basic sociocognitive concepts in children and adolescents. The concept of communicative action is well suited to serve as a point of reference for the reconstruction of stages of interaction. These *stages of interaction* can be described in terms of the perspective structures implemented in different types of action. To the extent to which these perspectives, embodied and integrated in interactions, fit readily into the scheme of a logic of development, it will be possible to ground stages of moral judgment by tracing Kohlberg's moral stages first to social perspectives and ultimately to stages of interaction. This is my objective in what follows.

I propose to begin by reviewing in part II some of the tenets of the theory of communicative action in order to show that the concept of the social world forms an integral part of a decentered understanding of the world, which in turn forms the basis of action oriented toward reaching understanding. In part III, I will focus on two specific stages of interaction. Studies of perspective taking by Flavell and Selman will serve as my point of departure. The bulk of part III will trace the restructuring of preconventional types of action in two directions: strategic action and normatively regulated action. Part IV deals with a conceptual analysis of how the introduction of a hypothetical attitude into communicative action makes the exacting form of communication called discourse possible, how the moral point of view arises when a reflective stance is taken vis-à-vis the social world, and finally, how stages of moral judgment can be traced back to stages of interaction via social perspectives. This justification of moral stages in terms of a logic of development will have to prove its mettle in subsequent empirical research. For now I will use my reflections only to illuminate some of the anomalies and unresolved problems with which Kohlberg's theory is currently faced (part V).

II   The Perspective Structure of Action Oriented toward Reaching Understanding

In section 1 I review some conceptual aspects of action oriented toward reaching understanding. Section 2 provides an outline of how the related concepts of the social world and normatively regulated action emerge from a decentered understanding of the world.

1

Since I have given a detailed account of the concept of communicative action elsewhere,[17] I will confine myself at this point to reviewing the most important aspects of this formal-pragmatic study.

Orientation toward success versus orientation toward reaching understanding   Social interactions vary in terms of how cooperative and stable or, conversely, how conflictual and unstable they are. The question in social theory of what makes social order possible has a counterpart in action theory: How can (at least two) participants in interaction coordinate their plans in such a way that alter is in a position to link his actions to ego's without a conflict arising, or at least without the risk that the interaction will be broken off? If the actors are interested solely in the *success*, i.e., the *consequences* or *outcomes* of their actions, they will try to reach their objectives by influencing their opponent's definition of the situation, and thus his decisions or motives, through external means by using weapons or goods, threats or enticements. Such actors treat each other *strategically*. In such cases, coordination of the subjects' actions depends on the extent to which their egocentric utility calculations mesh. The degree of cooperation and the stability is determined by the interest positions of the participants. By contrast, I speak of *communicative* action when actors are prepared to harmonize their plans of action through internal means, committing themselves to pursuing their goals only on the condition of an agreement—one that already exists or one to be negotiated—about definitions of the situation and prospective outcomes. In both cases the teleological structure of action is presupposed inasmuch as the actors are assumed to have the ability to act purposively and an interest in carrying out their plans. They differ in that for the *model of strategic action*, a structural description of action directly oriented toward success is sufficient, whereas the *model of action oriented toward reaching understanding* must specify the preconditions of an agreement, to be reached communicatively, that allows alter to link his actions to ego's.[18]

Reaching agreement as a mechanism for coordinating actions   The concept of communicative action is set out in such a way that the acts of reaching understanding that coordinate the action plans of several actors, thus forging a complex of interactions out of goal-directed behavior, cannot in turn be reduced to teleological action.[19] The kind of agreement that is the goal of efforts to reach understanding depends on rationally motivated approval of the substance of an utterance. Agreement cannot be imposed or brought about by manipulating one's partner in interaction, for something that *patently* owes its existence to external pressure cannot even be *considered* an agreement. The generation of convictions can be analyzed in terms of the model of taking a position on the offer contained in a speech act. Ego's speech act can be successful only if alter accepts the offer contained in it by taking an affirmative position, however implicitly, on a claim to validity that is in principle criticizable.[20]

Action situation and speech situation   If we define action in general as mastering situations, then the concept of communicative action highlights two aspects of this mastering: the teleological one of implementing an action plan and the communicative one of arriving at a shared interpretation of the situation, or more generally, of reaching consensus. A *situation* denotes a segment of a lifeworld that has been delimited in terms of a specific theme. A *theme* arises in connection with the interests and objectives of actors. It defines the *range* of matters that are *relevant* and can be thematically focused on. Individual *action plans* help put a theme in relief and determine the *current need for consensual understanding* that must be met through the activity of interpretation. In these terms the action situation is at the same time a speech situation in which the actors take turns playing the *communicative roles* of speaker, addressee, and bystander. To these roles correspond first- and second-person *participant perspectives* as well as the third-person *observer perspective* from which the I-thou relation is observed as an intersubjective complex and can thus be objectified. This system of *speaker perspectives* is intertwined with a system of *world perspectives* (see below).

The lifeworld as background . Communicative action can be understood as a circular process in which the actor is two things in one: an *initiator* who masters situations through actions for which he is accountable and a *product* of the traditions surrounding him, of groups whose cohesion is based on solidarity to which he belongs, and of processes of socialization in which he is reared.

The actor stands face to face with that situationally relevant segment of the lifeworld that impinges on him as a problem, a problem he must resolve through his own efforts. But in another sense, the actor is carried or supported from behind, as it were, by a lifeworld that not only forms the *context* for the process of reaching understanding but also furnishes *resources* for it. The shared lifeworld offers a storehouse of unquestioned cultural givens from which those participating in communication draw agreed-upon patterns of interpretation for use in their interpretive efforts.

These ingrained cultural background assumptions are only one component of the lifeworld. The solidarity of groups integrated through values and the competences of socialized individuals also serve as resources for action oriented toward reaching understanding, although in a different way than cultural traditions.[21]

The process of reaching an understanding between world and lifeworld
The lifeworld, then, offers both an intuitively preunderstood *context* for an action situation and *resources* for the interpretive process in which participants in communication engage as they strive to meet the need for agreement in the action situation. Yet these participants in communicative action must reach understanding *about something in the world* if they hope to carry out their action plans on a consensual basis, on the basis of some jointly defined action situation. In so doing, they presuppose a formal concept of the world (as the sum total of existing states of affairs) as the reference system in the context of which they can decide what is and what is not the case. The depiction of facts, however, is only one among several functions of the process of reaching understanding through speech. Speech acts serve not only to represent (or presuppose) states and events—in which case the speaker makes reference to something in the *objective world*. They also serve to produce (or renew) interpersonal relationships—in which case the speaker makes reference to something in the *social world* of legitimately ordered interactions. And they serve to express lived experience, that is, they serve the process of self-representation—in which case the speaker makes reference to something in the *subjective world* to which he has privileged access. It is this reference system of precisely three worlds that communicative actors make the basis of their efforts to reach understanding. Thus, agreement in the communicative practice of everyday life rests simultaneously on intersubjectively shared propositional knowledge, on normative accord, and on mutual trust.

Relations to the world and claims to validity   A measure of whether or not participants in communication reach agreement is the yes or no position taken by the hearer whereby he accepts or rejects the claim to validity that has been raised by the speaker. In the attitude oriented toward reaching understanding, the speaker raises with *every* intelligible utterance the claim that the utterance in question is true (or that the existential presuppositions of the propositional content hold true), that the speech act is right in terms of a given normative context (or that the normative context that it satisfies is itself legitimate), and that the speaker's manifest intentions are meant in the way they are expressed.

When someone rejects what is offered in an intelligible speech act, he denies the validity of an utterance in at least one of three respects: *truth*, *rightness*, or *truthfulness*. His "no" signals that the utterance has failed to fulfill at least one of its three functions (the representation of states of affairs, the maintenance of an interpersonal relationship, or the manifestation of lived experience) because the utterance is not in accordance with either *the* world of existing states of affairs, *our* world of legitimately ordered interpersonal relations, or *each participant's own* world of subjective lived experience. These aspects are not clearly distinguished in normal everyday communication. Yet in cases of disagreement or persistent problematization, competent speakers can differentiate between the aforementioned three *relations to the world*, thematizing individual validity claims and focusing on something that confronts them, whether it be something objective, something normative, or something subjective.

World perspectives Having explicated the above structural properties of action oriented toward reaching understanding, we are in a position to identify the *options* a competent speaker has. If the above analysis is correct, he essentially has the choice between a *cognitive*, an *interactive*, and an *expressive* mode of *language use*. To these modes correspond three different classes of speech acts—the *constative*, the *regulative*, and the *representative*—which permit the speaker to concentrate, in terms of a universal validity claim, on issues of truth, justice, or taste (i.e., personal expression). In short, he has a choice among three basic attitudes, each entailing a different perspective on the world. In addition, the decentered understanding of the world enables him to confront external nature not only in an *objectivating* attitude but also in a *norm-conformative* or an *expressive* one, to confront society not only in a norm-conformative attitude but also in an objectivating or an expressive one, and to confront inner nature not only in an expressive attitude but also in an objectivating or a norm-conformative one.

2

A *decentered understanding of the world* presupposes that relations to the world, claims to validity, and basic attitudes have become differentiated. This process springs from something else in turn, the *differentiation between lifeworld and world*. Every consciously enacted process of communication recapitulates, as it were, this differentiation, which has been laboriously acquired in the ontogenesis of the capacity for speech and action. The spheres of things about which we can reach a fallible agreement at a given point become detached from the diffuse background of the lifeworld with its absolute certainties and intuitive presence. As this differentiation progresses, the demarcation becomes ever sharper. On one side we have the horizon of unquestioned, intersubjectively shared, nonthematized certitudes that participants in communication have "at their backs." On the other side, participants in communication face the communicative contents constituted within a world: objects that they perceive and manipulate, norms that they observe or violate, and lived experiences to which they have privileged access and which they can express. To the extent to which participants in communication can conceive of what they reach agreement on as *something in a world*, something detached from the lifeworld background from which it emerged, what is explicitly *known* comes to be distinguished from what is implicitly *certain*. To that extent the content they communicate takes on the character of knowledge linked with a potential for reasoning, knowledge that claims validity and can be criticized, that is, knowledge that can be argued about on the basis of reasons.[22]

For the matter under discussion it is important to distinguish between world perspectives and speaker perspectives. On the one hand, participants in communication must have the competence to adopt, when necessary, an objectivating attitude to a given state of affairs, a norm-conformative attitude to legitimately ordered interpersonal relations, and an expressive attitude to their own lived experience; they must also be able to vary these attitudes in relation to each of the three worlds. If, on the other hand, they want to reach a *shared* understanding *about something* in the objective, social, or subjective world, they must also be able to take the attitudes connected with the communicative roles of the first, second, or third person.

The decentered understanding of the world is thus characterized by a complex structure of perspectives. It combines two things: first, perspectives that are grounded in the formal three-world reference system and *linked with the different attitudes toward the world*, and second, perspectives that are built into the speech situation itself and *linked to the communicative roles*. The grammatical correlates of these world and speaker perspectives are the three basic modes of language use on the one hand and the system of personal pronouns on the other.

A crucial point in my argument is that the *development* of this complex structure of perspectives also provides us with the key to the desired justification of moral stages in terms of a logic of development. Before discussing the relevant literature in the next two sections, I will explain the basic idea that will govern my analysis.

First, I am convinced that *the ontogenesis of speaker and world perspectives* that leads to a decentered understanding of the world can be explained only in connection with the development of the corresponding structures of interaction. If, like Piaget, we start from action, i.e., from the active confrontation and interaction between an individual who learns constructively and his environment, it makes sense to assume that the complex system of perspectives sketched above develops from two roots: the observer perspective, acquired by the child as a result of his perceptual-manipulative contact with the physical environment, and the reciprocal I-thou perspectives that the child adopts as a result of symbolically mediated contacts with reference persons (in the framework of interactive socialization processes). The observer perspective is later consolidated as the objectivating attitude toward external nature (or the world of existing states of affairs), while the I-thou perspective is perpetuated in the form of first- and second-person attitudes linked to the communicative roles of speaker and hearer. This stabilization occurs by virtue of a reshaping and differentiation of the original perspectives. The observer perspective is integrated with the system of world perspectives, whereas the I-thou perspective is rounded out into a system of speaker perspectives. The development of structures of interaction can serve as a guide in reconstructing these processes.

Second, I will argue that the *completion of a system of speaker perspectives* takes place in two major developmental steps. From a structural point of view, the preconventional stage of interaction can be understood as an implementation, in types of action, of the I-thou perspectives learned through experience in the roles of speaker and hearer. Next, the introduction of an observer perspective into the realm of interaction and its linkage with the I-thou perspective permits a reorganization of action coordination at a higher level. The complete system of speaker perspectives is the result of these two transformations. It is only after the transition to the conventional stage of interaction has been completed that the communicative roles of the first, second, and third persons become fully integrated.

The *completion of the system of world perspectives* takes a different route. In reconstructing this process we can refer back to the observation that the conventional stage of interaction is characterized by the rise of two new contrasting types of action: strategic action and norm-governed interaction. Owing to the integration of the observer perspective into the sphere of interaction, the child learns to perceive interactions, and his own participation in them, as occurrences in an objective world. This makes possible the development of a purely success-oriented type of action as an extrapolation of conflict behavior guided by self-interest. At the same time that strategic action is being acquired through practice, its opposite, nonstrategic action, comes into view. Once the *perception* of social interaction is differentiated in this way, the growing child cannot avoid the necessity of also reorganizing types of nonstrategic action that had been left behind in his development, so to speak, to bring them into line with the conventional level. What this means is that a social world of norm-guided interactions open to thematization comes to be set off against the background of the lifeworld.

Third, I will argue that the introduction of an observer perspective into the domain of interactions also provides the impetus for constituting a social world and for judging actions according to whether or not they conform to or violate socially recognized norms. For its members, a social world consists of norms defining which interactions belong to the totality of justified interpersonal relations and which do not. Actors who accept the validity of such a set of norms are members of the same social world. The concept of a social world is linked with the norm-conformative attitude, that is, the *perspective* from which a speaker relates to accepted norms.[23]

The basic sociocognitive concepts of the social world and of norm-governed interaction thus evolve within the framework of a decentered understanding of the world, which in turn stems from a differentiation of speaker and world perspectives. These very complex presuppositions of Kohlberg's social perspectives should finally provide the key to deriving stages of moral judgment from stages of interaction.

What follows has the limited purpose of making a plausible case for the foregoing hypotheses about the ontogenesis of speaker and world perspectives, on the basis of existing empirical studies. At best, a hypothetical reconstruction of this kind can serve as a guide to further research. Admittedly, my hypotheses do require distinctions not easy to operationalize, distinctions between (a) communicative roles and speaker perspectives, (b) implementations of these speaker perspectives in different types of interactions, and (c) the perspective structure of an understanding of the world that permits a choice between basic attitudes to the objective, social, and subjective worlds. I am aware of the difficulty that results from the fact that I have to bring these distinctions *from the outside* to bear on material derived from previous research.

III   The Integration of Participant and Observer Perspectives and the Restructuring of Preconventional Types of Action

In section 1 below I will interpret R. Selman's stages of perspective taking in terms of the step-by-step construction of a system of speaker perspectives that are fully reversible. Section 2 describes four different types of interaction in which I-thou perspectives are embodied. I then go on to assess the significance of the introduction of an observer perspective into the sphere of interaction, with particular reference to the restructuring of interest-guided conflict behavior as strategic action. Section 3 will reconstruct the transformation of authority-governed action and interest-governed cooperative behavior into normatively regulated action in order to demonstrate that the complex perspective structure of action oriented to reaching understanding cannot develop in any other way.

1

Selman characterizes three stages of perspective taking in terms of conceptions of persons and relationships. He summarizes his stages as follows:[24]

Level 1, differentiated and subjective perspective taking (about ages 5 to 9)

Concepts of persons: differentiated At Level 1, the key conceptual advance is the clear differentiation of physical and psychological characteristics of persons. As a result, intentional and unintentional acts are differentiated and a new awareness is generated that each person has a unique subjective covert psychological life. Thought, opinion, or feeling states within an individual, however, are seen as unitary, not mixed.

Concepts of relations: subjective The subjective perspectives of self and other are clearly differentiated and recognized as potentially different. However, another's subjective state is still thought to be legible by simple physical observation. Relating of perspectives is conceived of in one-way, unilateral terms, in terms of the perspective of and impact on one actor. For example, in this simple one-way conception of relating of perspectives and interpersonal causality, a gift makes someone happy. Where there *is* any understanding of two-way reciprocity, it is limited to the physical—the hit child hits back. Individuals are seen to respond to action with like action.

Level 2, self-reflective/second-person and reciprocal perspective taking (about ages 7 to 12)

Concepts of persons: self-reflective/second-person Key conceptual advances at Level 2 are the growing child's ability to step mentally outside himself or herself and take a self-reflective or second-person

perspective on his or her own thoughts and actions *and* on the realization that others can do so as well. Persons' thought or feeling states
are seen as potentially multiple, for example, curious, frightened,
and happy, but still as groupings of mutually isolated and sequential
or weighted aspects, for example, mostly curious and happy and a
little scared. Both selves and others are thereby understood to be
capable of doing things (overt actions) they may not want (intend) to
do. And persons are understood to have a dual, layered social orientation: visible appearance, possibly put on for show, and the *truer*
hidden reality.

Concepts of relations: reciprocal   Differences among perspectives are
seen relativistically because of the Level 2 child's recognition of the
uniqueness of each person's ordered set of values and purposes. A
new two-way reciprocity is the hallmark of Level 2 concepts of relations. It is a reciprocity of thoughts and feelings, not merely actions.
The child puts himself or herself in another's shoes and realizes the
other will do the same. In strictly mechanical-logical terms, the child
now sees the infinite regress possibility of perspective taking (I know
that she knows that I know that she knows . . . etc.). The child also
recognizes that the outer appearance–inner reality distinction means
selves can deceive others as to their inner states, which places accuracy
limits on taking another's inner perspective. In essence, the two-way
reciprocity of this level has the practical result of detente, wherein
both parties are satisfied, but in relative isolation: two single individuals seeing self and other, but not the relationship system between
them.

**Level 3, third-person and mutual perspective taking (about ages 10
to 15)**

Concepts of persons: third-person   Persons are seen by the young adolescent thinking at Level 3 as systems of attitudes and values fairly
consistent over the long haul, as opposed to randomly changeable
assortments of states as at Level 2. The critical conceptual advance is
toward ability to take a true third-person perspective, to step outside
not only one's own immediate perspective, but outside the self as a
system a totality. There are generated notions of what we might call
an "observing ego," such that adolescents do (and perceive other
persons to) simultaneously see themselves as both actors and objects,
simultaneously acting and reflecting upon the effects of action on
themselves, reflecting upon the self in interaction with the self.

Concepts of relations: mutual   The third-person perspective permits
more than the taking of another's perspective on the self; the truly
third-person perspective on relations which is characteristic of Level
3 *simultaneously* includes and coordinates the perspectives of self and
other(s), and thus the system or situation and all parties are seen
from the third-person or generalized other perspective. Whereas at

Level 2, the logic of infinite regress, chaining back and forth, was indeed apparent, its implications were not. At Level 3, the limitations and ultimate futility of attempts to understand interactions on the basis of the infinite regress model become apparent and the third-person perspective of this level allows the adolescent to abstractly step outside an interpersonal interaction and simultaneously and mutually coordinate and consider the perspectives (and their inter-actions) of self and other(s). Subjects thinking at this level see the need to coordinate reciprocal perspectives, and believe social satis-faction, understanding, or resolution must be mutual and coordi-nated to be genuine and effective. Relations are viewed more as ongoing systems in which thoughts and experiences are mutually shared.[25]

The process of language acquisition comes to an end between the ages of five and nine.[26] The incomplete perspective taking that typifies Selman's level 1 already rests on a firm foundation of linguistically mediated intersubjectivity. If, following G. H. Mead, we start from the assumption that the growing child acquires an understanding of identical meanings, i.e., intersub-jectively valid conventions of meaning as he repeatedly assumes the perspectives and attitudes of a reference person in an interactional context, then the development of *action* perspec-tives studied by Selman continues on from the now completed development of perspective taking in the domain of speech perspectives. Having learned to speak, the child already knows how to address an utterance to a hearer with communicative intent. Conversely, he also knows what it is to understand another person's utterance from the perspective of the person to whom it is addressed. The child has mastered a reciprocal I-thou relation between speaker and hearer when he is able to distinguish saying from doing. At that point the child differ-entiates between acts of seeking understanding with a hearer—that is, speech acts and their equivalents—and acts that have an impact on physical or social objects. Thus our point of departure is a situation where reciprocal speaker-hearer rela-tions have been established at the level of *communication* but not yet at the level of *action*. The child understands what alter *means* when he states, demands, announces, or wants some-thing; ego also knows how alter *comprehends* ego's utterances. This reciprocity between speaker and hearer perspectives, which relates to what is being *said,* is not yet a reciprocity of *action orientations*; in any event, it does not automatically affect the actor's structure of expectations, that is, the perspectives from which actors make and pursue their plans for action. The *coordination of action plans* necessitates a *meshing of action perspectives* beyond the reciprocity of speaker perspectives. In what follows I will interpret Selman's stages in these terms.[27]

At level 1 Selman postulates that the child distinguishes between the interpretive and action perspectives of the various participants in interaction. But in judging the actions of others, he is unable to simultaneously maintain his own point of view and step into the other's shoes, which is why he is also unable to judge his own actions from the standpoint of others.[28] The child is beginning to differentiate between the outer world and the inner worlds of privileged access. However, the sharply delineated basic sociocognitive concepts of the world of normativity that Kohlberg posits for the conventional stage of social perspectives are lacking. At Selman's level 1, the child correctly uses sentences expressing statements, requests, wishes, and intentions. No clear meaning is as yet attached to normative sentences; imperatives are not yet dichotomized into those which represent the speaker's subjective claim to power and those which represent a normative, i.e., nonpersonal claim to validity.[29]

The first step toward bringing about the coordination of the action plans of various interacting participants on the basis of a shared definition of the situation is to *extend the reciprocal relationship between speaker and hearer to the relationship between actors* who interpret a shared *action situation* in terms of their diverse plans and from different perspectives. It is no coincidence that Selman identifies this stage of perspective taking as the second-person perspective. With the passage to level 2, the young person learns to make a reversible connection between the action perspectives of speaker and hearer. He can now assume the action perspective of another, and he knows that the other can also assume his (ego's) action perspective. Ego and alter can take each other's attitudes toward their own action orientations. In this way the first- and second-person *communicative* roles are extended to the coordination of *actions*.

The perspective structure built into the performative attitude of a speaker now determines not only linguistic understanding but also interaction as such. The I-thou perspectives of speaker and hearer thereby take on the function of coordinating action.

With the transition to level 3, this structure of perspectives again changes as the observer perspective is introduced into the field of interaction. Granted, children have long since been able to make correct use of third-person pronouns in reaching understanding *about* other persons, their utterances, their possessions, and so forth. They have also already learned to take an objectivating attitude toward things and events that can be perceived and manipulated. Now, however, the young adolescent learns to turn from the observer perspective back to an interpersonal relationship, in which he engages in a performative attitude along with another participant in interaction. The performative attitude is coupled with the neutral attitude of a person who is present but remains uninvolved, in other words, the attitude of a person who witnesses an interactive event in the role of a listener or viewer. This makes it possible to *objectify the reciprocity of action orientations* attained at earlier levels and to become aware of that reciprocity in its *systemic aspect*.

The system of action perspectives is now complete. This completion signifies the actualization of the system of speaker perspectives that exists *in nuce* in the grammar of personal pronouns. This in turn makes possible a new way to organize conversation.[30] The new structure consists of the ability to view the reciprocal interlocking of action orientations in the first and second persons from the perspective of the third person. Once interaction has been restructured in this way, participants can not only take one another's action perspectives but also exchange the participant perspective for the observer perspective and transform the one into the other. At level 3 of perspective taking, the constitution of the social world, for which level 2 represented a preparation, is brought to completion. To show how this occurs, I will first have to identify the types of interaction that are restructured in the passage from level 2 to level 3 to become strategic and norm-guided action.

2

Selman's theory was initially developed on the basis of material from clinical interviews conducted after the experimenter had shown two filmed stories. One of these short films is about a girl named Holly. The dilemma Holly gets into stems from the conflict between a promise she has made to her father and her relationship with a girlfriend who needs her help.[31] The story is set up so that the two action systems to which children of that age typically belong, family and friends, come into conflict. James Youniss has made a comparative structural analysis of the social relations between children and adults on the one hand and between children in the same age group on the other.[32] He characterizes these relations in terms of different forms of reciprocity. A nonsymmetrical form of reciprocity, *complementarity between behavioral expectations of different kinds*, tends to obtain whenever authority is unequal, as in the family. By contrast, a *symmetry between behavioral expectations of the same kind* obtains in egalitarian friendships. With respect to the co-ordination of actions, a consequence of authority-governed complementarity is that one person controls the other's contribution to the interaction; interest-governed reciprocity, in contrast, means that the participants exercise mutual control over their contributions to the interaction.

It appears that authority-governed complementary and in-terest-governed symmetrical social relations define two *different types of interaction* that can embody the *same perspective structure*, namely the reciprocity of action perspectives typical of Selman's level 2 of perspective taking. In both types of action we find implemented the I-thou perspectives that speaker and hearer assume vis-à-vis one another. According to Selman, children at this level also possess analogously structured concepts of be-havioral expectation, authority, motives for action, and the ability to act. This sociocognitive inventory enables them to differentiate between the outer world and the inner world of a person, to impute intentions and need dispositions, and to distinguish intentional from unintentional acts. Children thereby also acquire the ability to control interactions by de-ception if necessary.

Moral Consciousness and Communicative Action

In cooperative relationships the participants renounce the use of deception. In authority-governed relationships the dependent partner cannot resort to deception, even in cases of conflict. Hence, the option of influencing alter's behavior by means of deception exists only when ego construes the social relationship as symmetrical and interprets the action situation in terms of conflicting needs. For ego's and alter's behavior to be *competitive*, the impact they have on one another must be *reciprocal*. This sort of competition also occurs, it is true, within the institutional framework of the family, where there is an objective differential in authority between the generations. In that case, however, the child behaves toward members of the older generation as though the relationship were symmetrical.

It is therefore advisable to distinguish preconventional types of action not in terms of action systems but in terms of the more abstract criterion of forms of reciprocity (table 1). In cases 2 and 4, conflicts are resolved by means of different strategies. Where the child sees himself as dependent (case 2), he will try to resolve the conflict between his own needs and alter's demands by avoiding threatened sanctions. The considerations that will guide his action resemble in their structures the judgments of Kohlberg's first moral stage. Where the child sees power as distributed equally (case 4), he may try to avail himself of the possibilities for deception that exist in symmetrical relations. J. H. Flavell has simulated this case using a coin experiment.[33]

The psychological study of perspective taking began with this special case, which is one of the four types of interaction. Here is how Flavell set up this famous experiment: two cups are put upside down on a table. They conceal different

Table 1
Preconventional types of action

Forms of reciprocity	Action orientations	
	Cooperation	Conflict
Authority-governed complementarity	1	2
Interest-governed symmetry	3	4

amounts of money, one nickel and two nickels respectively. Each cup bears a label in plain view indicating the number of nickels hidden under the cup. The experimental subjects are shown that the relationship between the inscription and the actual amount hidden can be varied at will. The subject's task is to secretly distribute the coins in such a way that another person who is called into the room will fail to guess where the greater amount is hidden, because he has been deceived, and will end up with nothing. The experiment is defined in such a way that the subjects accept the framework of elementary competitive behavior; they try to *influence* the decisions of the other *indirectly*. The participants proceed on the assumptions that each pursues only his particular interests, monetary or otherwise, that each knows the other's interest, that they are forbidden to reach an understanding directly (which is why they have to infer hypothetically how the other is going to behave), that deception on both sides is necessary or at least permitted, and that the normative claims to validity that might be bound up with the rules of the game may not be questioned within the framework of the game. The point of the game is clear: alter will try to win as much as he can, an ego is to prevent this. If the experimental subjects have the perspective structure of Selman's level 2, they will choose what Flavell calls strategy B: the child assumes that alter is guided by monetary considerations and will therefore think that the two nickels are under the one-nickel cup; his rationale is, Alter thinks I want to fool him by *not* putting the two nickels under the two-nickel label.

This is an experimentally produced example of competitive behavior that entails a reciprocal I-thou perspective (table 1, case 4). It is easy to trace the reorganization of the preconventional stage of interaction in this type of action. Experimental subjects who are able to engage in Selman's level 3 of perspective taking will choose Flavell's strategy C: they will turn the spiral of reflection one more time, taking into account that alter sees through ego's strategy B (and the reciprocity of action perspectives underlying it). An adolescent acquires this insight as soon as he has learned to objectify the reciprocal relations between ego and alter from the observer perspective and view them as a system. In principle, he is now in a position even to

recognize the structure of this two-person game, which is that
if both partners act rationally, the chance of losing is as great
as the chance of winning, no matter what ego decides to do.

Strategy C is characteristic of a type of action that is possible
only at the conventional stage of interaction if, as I have suggested, Selman's more complex level 3 of perspective taking is
required for this stage.[34] In these terms the restructuring of
preconventional competitive behavior into strategic action is
marked by a coordination of observer and participant
perspectives.

The concept of the acting subject is also affected by this shift.
Ego is now in a position to attribute stability over time to alter's
pattern of attitudes and preferences. Alter stops being perceived as someone whose actions are determined by shifting
needs and interests and is now perceived as a subject who
intuitively follows rules of rational choice. Beyond this, however, *no* structural change in the sociocognitive inventory is
required. In all other respects the preconventional inventory
is adequate for the strategic actor. It suffices for him to derive
behavioral expectations from imputed intentions, to understand motives in terms of orientation to rewards and punish-
ments, and to interpret authority as the power to promise or
threaten positive or negative sanctions (table 2).

Unlike elementary competitive behavior (table 1, case 4), the
three *other* types of preconventional action cannot be adapted
quite so economically to the conventional stage of interaction.

3

Up to this point I have been looking at the development of
strategic action as it comes to be differentiated from competitive behavior. The hypothesis I favor explains the transition to
the conventional stage of interaction in terms of an amalgamation of the observer and I-thou perspectives into a system
of action perspectives that can be transformed into one another. This amalgamation is attended by a completion of the
system of speaker perspectives, at which point the organization
of dialogue reaches a new level. This latter development need
not concern us here. Instead, I want to examine at this juncture

Moral Consciousness and Communicative Action

Table 2
The transition to the conventional stage of interaction: From
preconventional competitive behavior to strategic action

| Types of action | Sociocognitive inventory | | | |
	Perspective structures	Structure of behavioral expectations	Concept of authority	Concept of motivation
Preconventional competitive behavior	Reciprocal interconnection of action perspectives (Selman's level 2, Flavell's strategy B)	Particular behavior pattern; ascription of latent intentions	Externally sanctioned arbitrary rule of reference persons	Orientation toward punishment and reward
Strategic action	Coordination of observer and participant perspectives (Selman's level 3, Flavell's strategy C)			

how the other three preconventional action types (table 1, cases 1 to 3) change when the transition to the conventional stage of interaction occurs.

Once again I will restrict myself to the structural features of this change, leaving aside the question of how the restructuring of action perspectives might be explained dynamically. All I want to do is propose an analytical distinction between two paths of development, one for normatively regulated action and the other for strategic action. Let me characterize the problematic situation that forms the point of departure for this transition:

• Neither the action-orienting authority of reference persons nor the immediate orientation to individual needs is sufficient to meet the demand for coordination.

• Competitive behavior already has a new basis in strategic action; it has thus been disengaged from an *immediate* orientation to individual needs.

• A polarization of the attitude oriented toward success and the attitude of action oriented toward reaching understanding has been established, and this forces the child to choose between two types of action: one involving deception and the other being free of it. The choice has become both compulsory and normal.

In this situation, preconventional modes of coordinating action come under pressure in areas of behavior not dominated by competition. The sociocognitive inventory has to be restructured to make room for a mechanism of nonstrategic (or understanding-oriented) coordination of action. This mechanism must be independent both of authority relations to actual reference persons and of direct links to the actor's own interests. This stage of conventional but nonstrategic action requires basic sociocognitive concepts revolving around the notion of a suprapersonal will. The notion of behavioral expectations that are covered by this supra-personal authority (i.e., the notion of a social role) levels the difference between alien imperatives and one's own intentions, transforming both the notion of authority and the notion of interest.

Selman (1980) and Damon have given accounts of the development of the concepts of friendship, person, group, and authority during middle childhood.[35] These accounts agree in their essentials. As observations by human ethologists of early mother-child interaction show, these basic concepts undergo an extremely complex development that extends back to the first months of life.[36] From this store of early social ties and intersubjective relations, discrete sociocognitive capacities emerge through a process of differentiation that extends to middle childhood. It would appear that these capacities are used only selectively in the realm of competitive behavior. For preconventional competitive behavior can be transformed into strategic action without the introduction of an observer perspective into the sphere of interaction affecting the sociocognitive inventory as a whole. The passage to normatively regulated action, on the other hand, does require a global reconstruction, which Selman traces in four different dimensions.[37] One possible explanation why this global reconstruction is required is that reorganization along this line of development involves the three preconventional types of action that preclude deception and rely instead on consensus. Studies of children's cooperative behavior in dealing with problems of distribution and peer group conflicts at various age levels provide empirical access to rudimentary prototypes of normatively regulated action.[38] As the child advances in age and cognitive maturity, his ability to solve interpersonal problems in his peer group grows continually. This ability is a good indicator of the mechanisms for coordinating action that are available to him at different stages of development.

In what follows I will limit myself to two concepts: suprapersonal authority and action norm. These concepts are constitutive for the strict concept of the social world as the sum total of legitimately ordered interpersonal relationships. At the preconventional level the child views authority and friendship relations as relations of exchange (e.g., exchange of obedience for security or guidance, of demand for reward, of one achievement for another or for a show of confidence). At the conventional stage, however, the notion of exchange no longer fits the now reorganized relations.[39] At this point the child's views of social bonds, authority, and loyalty become dissociated from specific reference persons and contexts. They are transformed into the normative concepts of moral obligation, the legitimacy of rules, the normative validity of authoritative commands, and so on.

Preparation for this step takes place at the second stage of interaction, i.e., in a framework of reciprocal action orientations, as the growing child (A) learns particularistic behavior patterns by interacting with a specific reference person (B).[40] I have proposed a reconstruction of this transition elsewhere.[41] My proposal, however, is concerned only with issues of conceptual analysis.

What the child initially sees behind particular behavioral expectations is only the authority of a concrete person, an imposing person who is the object of emotional cathexis. The task of passing to the conventional stage of interaction consists in reworking the imperative arbitrary will of a dominant figure of this kind into the authority of a suprapersonal will detached from this specific person. As we know, Freud and Mead alike assumed that particular behavior patterns become detached from the context-bound intentions and speech acts of specific individuals and take on the external form of social norms to the extent that the sanctions associated with them are *internalized* by taking the attitudes of others, that is, to the extent that they are assimilated into the personality of the growing child and thus made independent of the sanctioning power of concrete reference persons. In the process the imperative significance of expectation changes in such a way that the individual wills of A and B are now subordinated to a *combined* will *delegated* to a *generalized* social-behavioral expectation. In this way there arises for A a *higher-level imperative* that is a generalized pattern applicable to all members of a social group. Both A and B appeal to it when uttering an imperative or wish.

Whereas Freud inquired into the psychodynamic facets of this process, Mead was interested in the *sociocognitive conditions of internalization*. He explained why it is that particular behavior patterns can be generalized only when A has learned to take an objectivating attitude toward his own actions and knows how to divorce the reciprocal system of action perspectives governing A and B from the contingent context of their encounter. Only when A in his interaction with B adopts the attitude of an impartial member of their social group toward them both can he become aware of the *interchangeability* of his and B's positions. A realizes that what he thought was a special behavior pattern applicable only to this particular child and these particular parents has always been for B the result of an intuitive understanding of the norms that govern relations between children and parents in general. As he learns to internalize concrete expectations, A forms the concept of a social behavior pattern that applies to *all* group members, a pattern in which the places are not reserved for alter and ego but can in principle be taken by any member of their social group.

The social generalization of behavior patterns also impinges on the meaning of their imperative aspect. Henceforth A will view interactions in which A, B, C, D, . . . express or obey imperatives and wishes as carrying out the *collective will of a group* to which A and B jointly subordinate their arbitrary wills. Behind the *social role* is the authority of a generalized group-specific imperative representing the united power of a concrete group that demands and receives loyalty. In this process the forms of reciprocity inherent in social relations also change. When the persons concerned play their social roles knowing that as members of a social group they are *entitled* to expect certain actions from others in given situations and at the same time *obliged* to fulfill the justified behavioral expectations of others, they are basing themselves on a symmetrical form of reciprocity even though the *contents* of the roles are still distributed in a complementary fashion among the different group participants.

The group's power to punish and reward, which stands behind social roles, loses the character of a higher-stage imperative only when the growing child once again internalizes the power of institutions (which at first confronts him as a fact of life) and anchors it internally as a system of behavioral controls. Only when *A* has learned to conceive of group sanctions as his own sanctions, which he *himself* has set up against *himself*, does he have to *presuppose* his consent to a norm whose violation he punishes in this way. Unlike socially generalized imperatives, institutions possess a validity that is derived from intersubjective recognition, the approval of all concerned. The affirmative responses underlying this consensus have at first an ambiguous status. To be sure, they *no longer* simply denote the "yes" of the compliant hearer responding to an imperative. A "yes" of this kind is equivalent to an intentional sentence referring to the action required; it is merely an expression of an arbitrary will uninformed by a norm. On the other hand, "yes" responses at this particular stage do *not yet* have the character of affirmative responses to criticizable validity claims. If it were otherwise, one would have to assume that the mere acceptance of norms of action is always and everywhere based on some rationally motivated agreement by all concerned. What speaks against this assumption is the repressiveness indicated by the fact that most norms take effect in the form of social control. Conversely, however, to the extent to which it is exercised through group-specific norms, social control is not based on repression *alone*.

This equivocal traditionalist understanding is already based on a conception of the legitimacy of norms of action. Within the horizon of this conception, social roles can cease to be properties of primary groups and can become generalized components of a system of norms. What emerges is a world of legitimately ordered interpersonal relations. Similarly, the concept of role behavior is transformed into that of norm-guided interaction. Through reference to the legitimate validity of norms, duties become distinct from inclinations, and responsible action from contingent or unintended violations. Table 3 provides an overview of the corresponding changes in the sociocognitive inventory, which I will not dwell on at this point.

IV On Grounding Moral Stages in a Logic of Development

Having proposed a reconstruction of two stages of interaction along the lines suggested by studies of perspective taking, I will now return to my initial query, namely the question whether Kohlberg's social perspectives can be linked with stages of interaction in such a way as to permit a plausible grounding of moral stages in a logic of development. I will begin by looking at the question of how the considerations raised so far bear on the ontogenesis of a decentered understanding of the world that is structurally rooted in action oriented toward reaching understanding (section 1 below). To do this, I will need to introduce discourse as a third stage of interaction. Introducing the hypothetical attitude into the domain of interaction and passing from communicative action to discourse signify, in reference to the social world, a moralization of existing norms. This devaluation of naively accepted institutions makes necessary a transformation of the sociocognitive inventory of the conventional stage into basic concepts that are moral in the immediate sense (section 2). Finally, I will assemble those aspects of a logic of development in terms of which social perspectives can be correlated with specific stages of interaction and the corresponding forms of moral consciousness can be justified *as stages* (section 3).

1

Following Selman, I can characterize the preconventional stage of interaction in terms of reciprocity between the action per-

Table 3
The transition to the conventional stage of interaction: From preconventional cooperative behavior to norm-governed action

Types of action	Basic sociocognitive concepts			
	Perspective structure	Structure of behavioral expectations	Concept of authority	Concept of motivation
Interaction controlled by authority; cooperation based on self-interest	Reciprocal interconnection of action perspectives (Selman's level 2)	Particular behavior pattern	Authority of reference persons; externally imposed sanctions	Loyalty to persons; orientation toward punishment and reward
Role behavior	Coordination of observer and participant perspectives (Selman's level 3)	Social generalization of behavior patterns: roles	Internalized authority of supraindividual will (*Willkür*): loyalty	Duty vs. inclination
Norm-governed interaction		Social generalization of roles: system of norms	Internalized authority of an impersonal collective will (*Wille*): legitimacy	

spectives of participants. These, I argued, represent the implementation of speaker perspectives in action types, more specifically, the implementation of the I-thou perspectives previously acquired by the child along with the communicative roles of speaker and hearer. The conventional stage of interaction is characterized by a system of action perspectives that comes into being when the observer perspective is joined to the participant perspective of the previous stage. This insertion of the observer perspective into the field of interaction makes it possible (a) to link the third-person role to the communicative roles of the first and second persons and thus to complete the system of speaker perspectives (which has an effect on the level of the organization of dialogue). The new perspective structure is a necessary precondition (b) for the transformation of interest-governed conflict behavior into strategic action and (c) for the formation of the basic sociocognitive concepts that structure normatively regulated action. As the social world of legitimately ordered interpersonal relations is taking shape, (d) a norm-conformative attitude and its corresponding perspective are generated. They supplement the basic attitudes and world perspectives linked with the inner and outer worlds. The linguistic correlate of this system of world perspectives is the three basic modes of language use that every competent speaker is able to distinguish and combine when he takes a performative attitude. Processes (a) to (d) satisfy the structural preconditions of a communicative action (e) in which individual plans of action are coordinated by means of a mechanism for reaching understanding through communication. Normatively regulated action represents one among several pure types of action oriented toward reaching understanding.[42]

In connection with the types of action analyzed so far, the differentiated form of communicative action is of interest only in that it has a corresponding form of reflection, ie., discourse, which constitutes a third stage of interaction, albeit one in which the pressure to act is minimized. Argumentation serves to focus on and test validity claims that are initially raised implicitly in communicative action and are naively carried along with it. Argumentation is characterized by the hypothetical attitude of those who take part in it. From this perspective, things and events become states of affairs that may or may not exist. Similarly, this perspective transforms existing norms, norms that are empirically recognized or socially accepted, into norms that may or may not be valid, that is, worthy of recognition. Whether assertoric statements are true and whether norms (or the corresponding normative statements) are right thus become matters for discussion.

This third stage of interaction sees a further growth in the complexity of the perspective structure. At the conventional stage the reciprocal participant perspectives and the observer perspective, two elements that developed at the preconventional stage but were not yet coordinated, are joined. In a similar fashion, the two systems of speaker perspectives and world perspectives, two systems that had been fully developed at the second stage but not yet coordinated, are joined at the third stage. On the one hand, the system of world perspectives, which has been refracted, as it were, by the hypothetical attitude, is constitutive of the claims to validity that are thematized in argumentation. On the other hand, the system of fully reversible speaker perspectives is constitutive of the framework within which participants in argumentation can reach rationally motivated agreement. In discourse, then, the two systems must be put in relationship to one another.

This increasingly complex perspective structure can be intuitively grasped in the following terms. At the conventional stage the characteristic innovation was the actor's ability to view himself in reciprocal relation to others as a participant in a process of action and *at the same time* to step outside and observe himself as a constituent part of interaction. At that stage the perspectives had to interlock in an interpersonal framework of interaction: the observer perspective achieved specificity and was joined with the third-person communicative role of the disinterested observer. Similarly, in agreement attained through discourse, the actors rely, in the act of consenting, on the complete reversibility of their relations with other participants in the argumentation and *at the same time* attribute the position they take to the persuasive force of the better argument, no matter how their consensus was reached in actual fact. Here too the perspectives interlock in an interpersonal

framework of communication whose presuppositions are improbable: world perspectives that have been refracted by reflection are linked up with the roles of opponents and
proponents who criticize and defend validity claims.

What typifies the development of interaction is not only the
growing ability to coordinate *perspectives* that used to exist in
isolation but also the greater degree of integration of previously separate *types of interaction*. As we have seen, the type I
have called role behavior represents successful integration of
two forms of reciprocity that developed in different types of
action at the first stage of interaction. Complementary and
symmetrical relations are synthesized even before a mature
concept of normative validity is available. That synthesis occurs
in the notion of a higher-level suprapersonal imperative in
which the intersubjective authority of a common will is expressed. Yet the price paid for this synthesis is a polarity, with
straegic action on one side and normatively regulated action
on the other. Only at the third stage of interaction is this split
overcome. What happens in argumentation is that the success-
orientation of competitors is assimilated into a form of communication in which action oriented toward reaching understanding is continued by other means. In argumentation,
proponents and opponents engage in a *competition with arguments* in order to convince one another, that is, in order to
reach a consensus. This dialectical role structure makes forms
of disputation available for a cooperative search for truth.
Argumentation can exploit the conflict between success-oriented competitors for the purpose of achieving consensus so
long as the arguments are not reduced to mere means of
influencing one another. In discourse what is called the *force*
of the better argument is wholly unforced. Here convictions
change internally via a process of rationally motivated attitude
change.

2

As he passes into the postconventional stage of interaction, the
adult rises above the naïveté of everyday life practice. Having
entered the quasi-natural social world with the transition to the

conventional stage of interaction, he now leaves it behind. As he becomes a participant in discourse, the relevance of his experiential context pales, as do the normativity of existing orders and the objectivity of things and events. On the plane of metacommunication the only perspectives on the lived world left to him are retrospective ones. In the light of hypothetical claims to validity the world of existing states of affairs is theoretized, that is, becomes a matter of theory, and the world of legitimately ordered relations is moralized, that is, becomes a matter of morality. This moralization of society—that is, of the normatively integrated structure of relationships that the growing child initially had to appropriate through construction—undermines the normative power of the factual: from the isolated viewpoint of deontological validity, institutions that have lost their quasi-natural character can be turned into so many instances of problematic justice. Problematization of this sort, in turn, arrests the process of communicative action before it is completed. It severs the ties between the social world and the surrounding lifeworld, and it jolts the intuitive certainties that flow into the social world from the lifeworld. Interactions now appear in a different light. When they become subject to judgment from a purely moral point of view, interactions emancipate themselves from parochial conventions but also lose the vigorous historical coloration of a particular form of life. Interactions become strangely abstract when they come under the aegis of principled autonomous action.

As the social world is dissociated from the context of a form of life that used to be its ever present background of certitude and habituation and is put at a distance by participants in discourse who take a hypothetical attitude, the uprooted and now free-floating systems of norms require a *different* basis. This new basis has to be achieved through a reorganization of the fundamental sociocognitive concepts available at the preceding stage of interaction. The means to the solution of this problem is the very same perspective structure of a fully decentered understanding of the world that created the problem in the first place. Norms of action are now conceived as subject to other norms in turn. They are subordinated to principles, or higher-level norms. The notion of the legitimacy of norms of action is now divided into the components of mere de facto recognition and worthiness to be recognized. The social currency of existing norms is no longer equivalent to the validity of justified norms. To these differentiations within the concepts of norm and normative validity corresponds a parallel differentiation in the concept of duty. Respect for the law is no longer considered an ethical motive per se. To heteronomy, that is, dependence on existing norms, is opposed the demand that the agent make the validity rather than the social currency of a norm the determining ground of his action.

With this concept of autonomy, the notion of the capacity for responsible action also changes. Responsibility becomes a special case of accountability, the latter here meaning the orientation of action toward an agreement that is rationally motivated and conceived as universal: to act morally is to act on the basis of insight.

The concept of the capacity to act that develops at the postconventional stage of interaction makes it clear that moral action is a case of normatively regulated action in which the actor is oriented toward reflectively tested claims to validity. Intrinsic to moral action is the claim that the settling of action conflicts is based on justified reasoning alone. Moral action is action guided by moral insight.

This strict concept of morality can evolve only at the postconventional stage. To be sure, even at earlier stages there is an intuitive grasp of the moral linked with a conception of consensual resolution of action conflicts. But at these earlier stages actors are relying on ideas of, shall I say, the good and just life, ideas that make possible a transitive ordering of conflicting needs. Only at the postconventional stage is the social world uncoupled from the stream of cultural givens. This shift makes the autonomous justification of morality an unavoidable problem. The very perspectives that make consensus possible are now at issue. Independently of contingent commonalities of social background, political affiliation, cultural heritage, traditional forms of life, and so on, competent actors can now take a moral point of view, *a point of view distanced from the controversy,* only if they cannot avoid accepting that point of view even when their value orientations diverge. Consequently, this moral reference point must be derived from the structure in which all participants in interaction *always already* find themselves insofar as they act communicatively. As discourse ethics shows, a point of reference of this kind is contained in the general pragmatic presuppositions of argumentation as such.

The passage to principled moral judgment is only a first, incomplete step in the adult's dissociation from the traditional world of existing norms. The principles governing our judgments about norms (principles of distributive justice, for instance) are principles in the plural, and they themselves require justification. The moral point of view cannot be found in a first principle, nor can it be located in an ultimate justification that would lie outside the domain of argumentation. Justificatory power resides only in the discursive procedure that redeems normative claims to validity. And this justificatory power stems in the last analysis from the fact that argumentation is rooted in communicative action. The sought-after moral point of view that precedes all controversies originates in a fundamental reciprocity that is built into action oriented toward reaching understanding. This reciprocity first appears in the form of authority-governed complementarity and interest-governed symmetry. Later it manifests itself in the reciprocity of behavioral expectations that are linked together in social roles and in the reciprocity of rights and obligations that are linked together in norms. Finally, it shows up as ideal role taking in discourse and insures that the right to universal access to, and equal opportunity for participation in argumentation is enjoyed freely and equally. At this third stage of interaction, then, an idealized form of reciprocity becomes the defining characteristic of a cooperative search for truth on the part of a potentially unlimited communication community. To that extent morality as grounded by discourse ethics is based on a pattern inherent in mutual understanding in language from the beginning.

3

Having reviewed the sociocognitive inventory and the perspective structure of the three stages of interaction, I would like to return to the sociomoral perspectives from which Kohlberg's stages of moral judgment are directly derived. With the help of these social perspectives Kohlberg defines the points of view in terms of which a transitive order of contested interests can be established and conflicts settled consensually. These points of view owe their existence to the combination of a given perspective structure with the corresponding idea of the good and just life, as I will demonstrate. As the two right-hand columns of table 4 show, the first of these two components requires no explanation. The second, however, does.

On the face of it, it is difficult to understand how the normative component of the social perspectives, namely the conception of justice, emerges from the sociocognitive inventory of the corresponding stages of interaction.

In trying to explain this process, one has to take into account the fact that the normatively integrated fabric of social relations is moral *in and of itself*, as Durkheim has shown. The basic moral phenomenon is the binding force of norms, which can be violated by acting subjects. All basic concepts that are constitutive of normatively regulated action, then, already have a moral dimension, which is merely being actualized and fully employed when people judge conflicts and violations of norms. With the formation of the social world and the transition to norm-guided interaction, all social relations take on an *implicitly* ethical character. Golden rules and obedience to the law are ethical imperatives that merely sue, as it were, for what is already implicit in social roles and norms prior to any actual moral conflict: the complementarity of behavioral expectations and the symmetry of rights and duties.

The conformity to role expectations and norms, which assures consensus, flows naturally from the sociocognitive inventory only because at the conventional stage the social world is still embedded in the lifeworld and reinforced by its certainties. At this point, morality (*Moralität*) and the ethics (*Sittlichkeit*) of an unquestioned, habitual, particular form of life have not yet parted ways; morality has not become autonomous *as* morality. Duties are interwoven with habitual concrete life practice in such a way that they derive self-evidence from background certitudes. At this stage, issues of justice are posed within the framework of questions of the good life, questions which have *always already been answered*. This is also true of religious and classical-philosophical ethics that take ethical life as their theme. They too understand and justify the moral not in its own terms but within the horizon of a larger soteriological or cosmological whole.

As we have seen, this syndrome disintegrates when a hypothetical attitude is introduced. Before the reflective gaze of a participant in discourse the social world dissolves into so many conventions in need of justification. The empirical store of traditional norms is split into social facts and norms. The latter have lost their backing in the certainties of the lifeworld and must now be justified in the light of principles. Thus the *orientation to principles of justice* and ultimately to the *procedure of norm-justifying discourse* is the outcome of the inevitable moralization of a social world become problematic. Such are the ideas of justice that, at the postconventional stage, take the place of conformity to roles and norms.

At the preconventional stage we cannot speak of conceptions of justice in the same sense as at later stages of interaction. Here no social world in my sense of the term has yet been constituted. The sociocognitive concepts available to the child lack a clear-cut dimension of deontological validity. For perspectives with socially binding force, the child must look to an inventory that interprets reciprocally interlocking action perspectives in terms of authority relations or external influence. Hence, *preconventional notions of bonds and loyalties* are based either on the complementarity of command and obedience or on the symmetry of compensation. These two types of reciprocity represent the natural embryonic form of justice conceptions inherent in the structure of action as such. Only at the conventional stage, however, are conceptions of justice conceived *as* conceptions of justice. And only at the postconventional stage is the truth about the world of preconventional conceptions revealed, namely that the idea of justice can be gleaned only from the idealized form of reciprocity that underlies discourse.

For now these few remarks will have to suffice to give plausibility to my thesis that there are structural relationships be-

Moral Consciousness and Communicative Action

Table 4
Stages of interaction, social pespectives, and moral stages

| Types of action | Cognitive structures | | |
	Perspective structure	Structure of behavioral expectations	Concept of authority
Preconventional Interaction controlled by authority ——— Cooperation based on self-interest	Reciprocal interlocking of action perspectives	Particular behavior pattern	Authority of reference persons: externally sanctioned will
Conventional Role behavior ——— Normatively governed interaction	Coordination of observer and participant perspectives	Group-wide generalization of behavior patterns: social roles ——— Group-wide generalization of roles: system of norms	Internalized authority of supraindividual will (*Willkür*): loyalty ——— Internalized authority of an impersonal collective will (*Wille*): legitimacy
Postconventional Discourse	Integration of speaker and world perspectives	Rules for testing norms: principles ——— Rules for testing principles: a procedure for justifying norms	Ideal vs. social validity

Concept of motivation	Social perspectives		State of moral judgment
	Perspective	Justice concept	
Loyalty to reference persons; orientation toward rewards and punishments	Egocentric perspective	Complementarity of order and obedience	1
		Symmetry of compensation	2
Duty vs. inclination	Primary-group perspective	Conformity to roles	3
	Perspective of a collectivity (the system's point of view)	Conformity to the existing system of norms	4
Autonomy vs. heteronomy	Principled perspective (prior to society)	Orientation toward principles of justice	5
	Procedural perspective (ideal role taking)	Orientation toward procedures for justifying norms	6

tween moral stages and social perspectives on the one hand
and stages of interaction on the other, relationships that justify
the parallels I drew in table 4. These parallels can sustain the
burden of a justification in terms of a logic of development,
however, only if what I have thus far merely tacitly anticipated
by using the term "stages" can in fact be demonstrated for
stages of interaction, namely that the proposed *hierarchy of
action types* reflects a *logic of development*. I have tried to make
this anticipatory theoretical characterization clear in my presentation of how stages of interaction are introduced and how
the transitions between them can be reconstructed. I began by
showing that the I-thou perspectives and the observer perspective serve as building blocks for an increasingly complex
perspective structure that culminates in the decentered understanding of the world displayed by subjects who act with an
orientation toward reaching understanding. Viewed in terms
of a *progressively decentered understanding of the world*, the stages
of interaction express a development that is directed and cu-
mulative. Second, I distinguished stages of interaction in terms
of different achievements of coordination. At the preconventional stage the action perspectives of different participants are
reciprocally related to one another. At the conventional stage
the observer perspective is added to these participant perspectives. In the end the separately formed systems of speaker
perspectives and world perspectives that have been developed
on the basis of these earlier achievements are integrated. The
existence of these *breaks* supports the view that successive perspective structures are in fact *discrete totalities*. Third, we saw
that in normatively regulated action the opposition between
authority-governed complementarity and interest-governed
symmetry characteristic of preconventional action types is overcome, just as the opposition between a consensual orientation
and a success orientation, which emerges in the relationship
between normatively regulated and strategic action, is overcome in argumentation. This seems to confirm the assumption
that higher-level cognitive structures replace the lower ones
while preserving them in reorganized form. This *dialectical
sublation of structures that have been superseded*—a relationship that

is difficult to analyze—would need to be demonstrated in detail in the restructuring of the sociocognitive inventory.

We can, however, identify a few trends in specific dimensions. For instance, it is possible to derive the more complex structures of *behavioral expectations* from the relatively simple ones through generalization and self-application: the generalized social expectation of reciprocally linked behavioral expectations gives rise to norms, and the generalized self-application of norms gives rise to principles by which other norms can be normatively assessed. Similarly, the more complex concepts of *normative validity* and *autonomy* emerge from the simpler concepts of an imperative will (*Willkür*) and personal loyalty, or pleasure-pain orientation. What happens in each of these cases is that the central semantic component of the more elementary concept is decontextualized and thus thrown into sharper relief, which allows the higher-level concept to stylize the superseded concept as a *counterconcept*. From the perspective of the next-higher stage, for instance, the exercise of authority by reference persons becomes *mere* arbitrary will, which is then explicitly contrasted with legitimate expressions of will. To cite another example, personal loyalties or pleasure-pain orientations become *mere* inclinations sharply set off from duties. Correspondingly, the legitimacy of action norms is viewed at the next stage as their *mere* social acceptance, which is contrasted with ideal validity, while action based on concrete duties is now contrasted with autonomy as something *merely* heteronomous.

A similar process of dichotomization and devaluation takes place with the transition from a concept of externally imposed punishment to the concepts of shame and guilt and with the transition from the concept of natural identity to the concepts of role identity and ego identity.[43] These comments are programmatic in nature. One would need a more precise concept of developmental logic to carry out this kind of analysis rigorously and to show how the sociocognitive inventory of the elementary stage is subjected to the reconstructive operations of self-application (reflexivity), generalization, and idealizing abstraction.

To review what has been said above, it is clear that placing moral development within the framework of a theory of communicative action has advantages for interpretation, both for a clearer understanding of the connections between moral judgment and social cognition and for grounding moral stages in a logic of development.

First, we saw that the same perspective structures are variously embodied in a whole range of types of interaction. A completely decentered understanding of the world develops only in the domains of behavior unaffected by competition. This decentered understanding becomes reflective with the transition from conventional action to discourse. The continuation of communicative action with argumentative means marks a stage of interaction that necessitates our going beyond Selman's stage of perspective taking. The integration of world perspectives and speaker perspectives achieved in argumentation represents the interface between social cognition and postconventional morality.

These clarifications proved helpful in the attempt to ground moral stages in a logic of development. Kohlberg's social perspectives are intended to have this function. As we saw, they can be correlated with stages of interaction that are ordered hierarchically according to perspective structures and basic concepts. This allows us to see how notions of justice are derived from the forms of reciprocity available at the various stages of interaction. With the transition from normatively regulated action to practical discourse, the basic concepts of principled morality spring directly from the reorganization of the available sociocognitive inventory, a reorganization that occurs with the necessity of developmental logic. This step marks the moralization of the social world, with forms of reciprocity that are built into social interaction and become increasingly abstract forming the naturalistic core, so to speak, of moral consciousness.

Whether the interpretive advantages I have tried to demonstrate here will prove fruitful in terms of research strategies as well is a question to be answered at another level. For the time being, I will use the reconstruction proposed here only to illuminate some of the difficulties Kohlberg's theory has had to contend with in recent years.[44]

V Anomalies and Problems: A Contribution to Theory Construction

At present the debates surrounding Kohlberg's approach revolve primarily around four problems. First, given that it has not yet been possible to prove experimentally the existence of a hypothetical stage 6 of moral judgment, the question arises whether and in what sense, if at all, we can speak of *natural* stages at the level of postconventional morality. Second, the cases of regression that occur in the postadolescent period, that is, in the third decade of life, raise doubts about whether the *normative point of reference of moral development* has been correctly chosen and especially about whether the morally mature adult's capacity for judgment and action can be adequately defined in terms of cognitivist and formalist theories. Third, the question of accommodating *relativists* or *value skeptics* as a group in Kohlberg's stage model remains problematic. Fourth, the question of whether structuralist theory can be combined with the findings of ego psychology in a way that would do justice to the *psychodynamic aspects of the formation of judgments* remains an open one.

The nature of these problems will become clearer if we can clarify some important issues: first, the degrees of freedom the adolescent attains when he makes the transition from normatively regulated action to discourse and achieves detachment from the social world of quasi-natural embeddedness (section 1), second, the problems of mediating between morality and ethical life that arise when the social world is moralized and cut off from the certainties that the lifeworld provides (section 2), third, the escape route that the adolescent takes when he distances himself from the devalued traditional world of norms but stops there without taking the further step of reorganizing the sociocognitive inventory of the conventional stage as a whole (section 3), and fourth, the discrepancies between moral judgment and moral action that result from a failure to separate the attitude oriented toward success from the attitude oriented to reaching understanding (section 4).

1

In recent decades Kohlberg has repeatedly revised his scoring schema [for assigning subjects' responses to a stage level—trans.]. I would not necessarily say that the most recent scoring method, on which the *Standard Form Scoring Manual* is based,[45] represents an improvement. In the coding of responses, theories in the Piagetian tradition require a theoretically based hermeneutic interpretation, a type of interpretation that is certainly not susceptible of being operationalized in a foolproof way, that is, in such a way as to neutralize highly complex preunderstandings. Be that as it may, the present methods of scoring interview material have forced Kohlberg to delete stage 6 because longitudinal studies in the United States, Israel, and Turkey no longer provide evidence for its existence. Today Kohlberg is reluctant to answer the question of whether stage 6 is a psychologically distinct natural stage or a philosophical construct.[46] A revision (if it were not based solely on problems of measurement) would necessarily affect the status of stage 5 along with that of stage 6. As soon as we give up the attempt to differentiate stages at the postconventional level, we face the question of whether principled moral judgments represent a natural stage *in the same sense* as judgments assigned to the preconventional and conventional levels.

From the standpoint of discourse ethics, I have already tacitly suggested a *different* interpretation of stages 5 and 6 by distinguishing the orientation toward general principles from the orientation toward procedures for the justification of possible principles (table 4). In this interpretation there is no differentiation of stages according to the kind of principles involved (utilitarian versus natural-right versus Kantian). The relevant distinction is conceived solely in terms of two *stages of reflection*. At stage 5, principles are viewed as being ultimate and beyond the need for justification. At stage 6 they are not only handled more flexibly but also explicitly made relative to procedures of justification. Differentiating stages of reflection in this way is intimately tied up with the larger framework of a specific normative theory and has to prove its mettle there. One must be able to show that a person relying not on the self-evident nature

of universal principles but on the legitimating power of procedures for justification is in fact better equipped to oppose
skeptical objections and thus also better able to judge consis-
tently. On the other hand, there are ethical positions that reject
proceduralism and insist that a procedure for moral justification in no way differs from, and is unable to achieve more
than, a universal moral principle. As long as this philosophical
controversy is not settled, the fundamental assumptions of discourse ethics should be defended in the arena where they clash
directly with other philosophical views rather than understood
naturalistically as propositions about natural stages of moral
consciousness. Discourse ethics itself certainly offers no
grounds for a (reifying?) interpretation that claims that *stages
of reflection* have the same status as natural intrapsychic *stages
of development.*

If there is no empirical evidence to suggest that we are
dealing with more than one postconventional stage, Kohlberg's
description of stage 5 also becomes problematic. We may at
least suspect that the ideas of the social contract and the greatest good for the greatest number are confined to traditions
that hold sway primarily in England and America and that they
represent a particular culturally specific substantive manifestation of principled moral judgment.

Taking up certain misgivings of John Gibbs, Thomas Mc-
Carthy points out that the relation between a psychologist
knowledgeable about moral theory and his experimental subject changes in a way that is methodologically significant as the
subject reaches the postconventional level and takes a hypothetical attitude to his social world:

The suggestion I should like to advance is that Kohlberg's account
places the higher-stage moral subject, at least in point of competence,
at the same reflective or discursive level as the moral psychologist.
The subject's thought is now marked by the decentration, differentiation and reflexivity which are the conditions of entrance into the
moral theorist's sphere of argumentation. Thus the asymmetry between the prereflective and the reflective, between theories-in-action
and explication, which underlies the model of reconstruction begins
to break down. The subject is now in a position to argue with the
theorist about questions of morality.[47]

In the same essay McCarthy draws a useful parallel between sociomoral and cognitive development:

Piaget views the underlying functioning of intelligence as unknown to the individual at lower stages of cognition. At superior levels, however, the subject may reflect on previously tacit thought operations and the implicit cognitive achievements of earlier stages, that is, he or she may engage in epistemological reflection. And this places the subject, at least in point of competence, at the same discursive level as the cognitive psychologist. Here, too, asymmetry between the subject's prereflective know-how and the investigator's reflective know-that begins to break down. The subject is now in a position to argue with the theorist about the structure and conditions of knowledge.[48]

At the level of formal operations the adult has reflectively appropriated the intuitive knowledge he used in successful problem solving. This means that he has acquired the ability to continue constructive learning processes by means of reconstruction. In principle, he has now broadened his competence to include the reconstructive sciences.

This acquisition has an implication for the methodology of the reconstructive sciences. A psychologist trying to test his hypotheses about the stage of formal operations is dependent on his experimental subjects, whom he must treat as partners *equal* in principle in the business of scientific reconstruction. His own theory will convince him that at this stage the asymmetry that existed on previous levels between prereflective mental functioning and the attempt to grasp that functioning reflectively disappears. To the extent to which the reconstructive scientist views himself as standing within the open horizon of a research process whose results he cannot foresee, he must accord that *same standpoint* to experimental subjects who have reached the highest stage of competence.

The same holds for respondents who handle moral dilemmas from the standpoint of a postconventional participant in discourse. Insofar as they essentially share the perspective of the moral psychologist who interviews them, their moral judgments no longer have the form of utterances that are naively generated with the help of an intuitive understanding of rules. Postconventional experimental subjects are drawn into the business of moral psychology—the reconstruction of moral intuitions underlying everyday life—in that their moral reasoning no longer *mirrors*, that is, prereflexively expresses, a pretheoretical knowledge but rather *explicates* potentially theoretical knowledge. Principled moral judgments are not possible without the first step in the reconstruction of underlying moral intuitions. Thus principled moral judgments already represent moral-theoretical judgments *in nuce*. As postconventional thought leaves the world of traditional norms behind, it operates in the same arena in which moral theorists debate their issues. This debate is fuelled by historical experience, and for the time being it is decided on the basis of philosophical arguments and not by developmental paths identified by psychology.

2

A second cluster of problems has sparked a wide-ranging discussion in the past few years. This cluster is difficult to disentangle. Studies by Norma Haan[49] and Carol Gilligan[50] marked the beginning of this particular debate. Its immediate occasion was the suspicion that in certain critical instances the stage level assigned in accordance with Kohlberg's schema might deviate too far from the intuitive understanding of a morally sensitive scorer. The two instances in question are, first, female respondents whose utterances have to be scored at stage 3 despite a presumption of greater moral maturity on their part and, second, experimental subjects classified as relativistic value skeptics at stage 4½ (see section 3 below) despite the fact that their utterances seem more mature than the usual postconventional judgments. Gilligan and Murphy make the point that Kohlberg's criteria would put more than half of the population of the United States at some level below the postconventional in terms of their moral consciousness. In addition, they show that in a sample of 26 subjects most of the subjects who were at first classified as postconventional in terms of the revised scoring procedure later regressed to relativistic positions (stage 4½).[51] Although Kohlberg disputes the facts on which his critics rely—the disproportionate numbers of female subjects at lower stages and instances of regressions that the theory cannot explain[52]—the controversy has drawn attention to problems that, in the language of the philosophical tradition, pertain to the relation of morality to ethical life (*Sittlichkeit*).

Gilligan and Murphy envisage a postconventional path of development leading from Kohlberg's stages 5 and 6 (the post-conventional formal stage) to a stage they call "contextual relativism" (the postconventional contextual stage). This notion is based on W. B. Perry's work on the overcoming of absolutist thought in late adolescence[53] and K. Riegel's hypotheses about postformal operations.[54] At the postconventional contextual stage, we are told, the adult who has become morally mature through conflicts and experiences learns to overcome the abstractions of a strict deontological morality of justice along Kantian lines, a morality that absolutizes the aspect of normative rightness. This *relativistic ethics of responsibility* deals with real moral dilemmas, not merely hypothetical ones, it takes the complexity of lived situations into account, it joins justice with caring and with responsibility for those under one's care, and it presupposes a more inclusive concept of a mature personality that goes beyond the abstract notion of autonomy:

While the logical concepts of equality and reciprocity can support a principled morality of universal rights and respect, experiences of moral conflict and choice seem to point rather to special obligations and responsibility for consequences that can be anticipated and understood only within a more contextual frame of reference. The balancing of these two points of view appeared to us to be the key to understanding adult moral development. In our view, this would require a restructuring of moral thought which would include but supersede the principled understanding of Kohlberg's highest stages.[55]

The position of an ethics of responsibility is thereby distinguished from that of value skepticism in the transitional stage 4½. While both are relativistic, only contextual relativism is based on ethical formalism while at the same time superseding it.

From the standpoint of discourse ethics, things look somewhat different. Gilligan and Murphy do zero in on the problems resulting from a successful transition to principled morality. Principled morality, as we have seen, emerges out of a peculiar abstractive achievement that robs the social world, with its legitimately ordered interpersonal relations, of its natural stability and compels it to justify itself. Initially the social world owes its unshakable facticity to its embeddedness in naively habituated concrete forms of life, which form an unquestioned prereflexively given background against which subjects act. By contrast, communicative actors have an explicit knowledge of the given institutional orders to which their speech acts refer. At the conventional stage, however, this explicit knowledge is so intimately tied up with the implicit background certainties of a particular form of life that the intersubjectively accepted norms are accorded absolute validity. As the social world becomes increasingly moralized in the hypothetical attitude of a participant in discourse and thus begins to stand over against the totality of the lifeworld, the erstwhile fusion of validity and what is merely accepted in society is dissolved. At the same time the unity of the practice of everyday communication splits into two parts: norms and values. The first part of the domain of the practical, which consists of norms, is susceptible to the requirement of moral justification in terms of its deontological validity; the second part, which consists of particular value configurations belonging to collective and individual modes of life, is not.

Cultural values embodied and fused in the totalities of life forms and life histories permeate the fabric of the communicative practice of everyday life through which the individual's life is shaped and his identity secured. It is impossible for the individual as an acting subject to distance himself from this life practice as he can distance himself from the institutions of his social world. Cultural values too transcend actual courses of action. They congeal into historical and biographical syndromes of value orientations, enabling individuals to distinguish the reproduction of mere life from ideas of the good life. But ideas of the good life are not notions that simply occur to individuals as abstract imperatives; they shape the identity of groups and individuals in such a way that they form an integral part of culture and personality. A person who questions the forms of life in which his identity has been shaped questions his very existence. The distancing produced by life crises of that kind is of another sort than the distance of a norm-testing participant in discourse from the facticity of existing institutions.

Thus the formation of the moral point of view goes hand in hand with a differentiation within the sphere of the practical: *moral questions*, which can in principle be decided rationally in terms of criteria of *justice* or the universalizability of interests are now distinguished from *evaluative questions*, which fall into the general category of issues of the *good life* and are accessible to rational discussion only *within* the horizon of a concrete historical form of life or an individual life style. The concrete ethical life of a naively habituated lifeworld is characterized by the fusion of moral and evaluative issues. Only in a rationalized lifeworld do moral issues become independent of issues of the good life. Only then do they have to be dealt with autonomously as issues of justice, at least initially. The word "initially" points to the problem dealt with under the rubric of an "ethics of responsibility."

For the increase in rationality brought about by isolating questions of justice has its price. Questions of the good life have the advantage of being answerable within the horizon of lifeworld certainties. They are posed as contextual and hence *concrete* questions from the outset. The answers to these questions retain the *action-motivating* potential of the forms of life that are presupposed in the contexts. In the framework of concrete ethical life within which conventional morality operates, moral judgments derive both their concreteness and their action-motivating potential from the intrinsic connection to ideas of the good life and institutionalized ethical life. At this level, problematization has not gone so deep as to jeopardize the advantages of an existing form of ethical life. This, however, is exactly what does occur with the transition to postconventional morality, when the social world becomes moralized and thus divorced from its background in the lifeworld. This abstractive achievement has a double effect: under a strict deontological point of view, moral questions are taken out of their contexts in such a way that moral solutions retain only the rationally motivating force of insights.

Moral issues are never raised for their own sake; people raise them seeking a guide for action. For this reason the *demotivated solutions that postconventional morality finds for decontextualized issues must be reinserted into practical life*. If it is to become effective in practice, morality has to make up for the loss of concrete ethical life that it incurred when it pursued a cognitive advantage. Demotivated solutions to decontextualized issues can achieve practical efficacy only if two resulting problems are solved: the abstraction from contexts of action and the separation of rationally motivated insights from empirical attitudes must both be undone. Every cognitivist morality will confront the actor with questions both of the situation-specific application and of the motivational anchoring of moral insights.[56] And these two problems can be solved only when moral judgment is supplemented by something else: hermeneutic effort and the internalization of authority.

The notion of a "stage" of contextual relativism rests on a misconception of the basic problem of how ethical life and morality are to be mediated. Carol Gilligan fails to make an adequate distinction between the *cognitive problem* of application and the *motivational problem* of the anchoring of moral insights. Accordingly, she tends to make the distinction between postconventional formalism and postconventional contextualism in terms of the distinction between hypothetical and actual situations. She ignores the fact that the question of whether what I ought to do is the same as what I would do concerns only the motivational side of the problem of mediation. The other side of the problem is cognitive in nature: In a given situation, how is one to interpret a universal command, which says merely what one ought to do, in such a way that one can then act in accordance with the command within the context of the situation?

Second, Gilligan fails to see that the two problems arise only after morality has been abstracted from ethical life and the basic moral-philosophical question of the justifiability of norms has been answered in terms of a cognitivist ethics. The question of the context-specific application of universal norms should not be confused with the question of their justification. Since moral norms do not contain their own rules of application, acting on the basis of moral insight requires the additional competence of hermeneutic prudence, or in Kantian terminology, reflective judgment. But this in no way puts into question the prior decision in favor of a universalistic position.[57]

Third, Gilligan's contextual relativism is designed to offset certain deficiencies that emerge at the postconventional level of moral judgment when the two resulting problems mentioned above are not dealt with. I speak of *moral rigorism*, one such deficiency, when hermeneutic sensitivity to the problem of application is lacking and when abstract moral insights are mechanically applied to concrete situations in line with the adage *Fiat justitia, preat mundus*. Max Weber's dichotomy between an ethics of conviction and an ethics of responsibility is based largely on this popular critique of Kant. I speak of *intellectualization*, another such deficiency, when moral abstractions serve as defenses. Gilligan tends to misconstrue these *deficiencies* as characteristic of a *normal* stage of postconventional formalism.

Finally, Gilligan sets up parallels between postconventional formalism and justice on the one hand and postconventional contextualism and caring and responsibility for a specific circle of people on the other, hypothesizing that the two orientations are unequally distributed between the two sexes.

Yet strictly speaking, the moral point of view is constituted only with the transition from the second to the third stage of interaction. This moral point of view comes about when the social world is moralized from the hypothetical attitude of a participant in argumentation and split off from the world of life. This deontological abstraction separates issues of justice from issues of the good life. Moral questions are thereby dissociated from their contexts and moral answers are dissociated from empirical motives. These dissociations make contextual application and a specific kind of motivational anchoring of moral insights necessary. If one keeps these facts in mind, the solution to these problems requires a mediation between morality and ethical life that goes beyond what can be accomplished by moral judgments as defined by deontological ethics. That is why it does not make sense to try to supplement or revise the stages of moral judgment. The two problems discussed above are on a different level than the capacity for moral judgment. They require a different order of achievement, to wit, contextual sensitivity and prudence on the one hand and autonomy and self-governance on the other. The critical contributions to the discussion touched off by Gilligan's work can be summarized under these headings.[58]

The cognitive problem of application
Those who seek to supplement Kohlberg's moral stages, whether by adding another postconventional stage (Carol Gilligan) or by introducing a parallel stage hierarchy (Norma Haan), fail to distinguish sufficiently between moral and evaluative issues, between issues of justice and issues of the good life. In terms of the conduct of an individual life, this corresponds to the distinction between self-determination and self-realization.[59] Typically, questions of preferences as to forms of life or life goals (ego ideals) and questions of the evaluation of personality types and modes of action arise only after moral issues, narrowly understood, have been resolved.[60] Furthermore, a definition of the moral point of view in terms of discourse ethics rules out the possibility of competing points of view with a status equal to that of justice or normative rightness. Since valid norms cannot but embody generalizable interests, it follows that the principle of the general welfare (Frankena's principle of beneficence, for example)[61] or the principle of care and responsibility—insofar as these expressions designate *moral* principles—are already contained in the meaning of the term normative validity.

The discourse-ethical conception of the moral principle also rules out any narrowing of moral judgment through considerations of an ethics of conviction. Again, consideration of the consequences and indirect effects which are expected to follow from the general application of a contested norm to specific contexts does not need to be *supplemented* by an ethics of responsibility. Interpreted from the perspective of discourse ethics, practical reason does indeed require practical prudence in the application of rules. But use of this capacity does not restrict practical reason to the parameters of a specific culture or historical period. Learning processes governed by the universalistic substance of the norm being applied are possible even in the dimension of application.

Ideal role taking has come to signify a procedural type of justification. The cognitive operations it requires are demanding. Those operations in turn are internally linked with motives and emotional dispositions and attitudes like empathy. Where sociocultural distance is a factor, concern for the fate of one's neighbor—who more often than not is anything but close by— is a necessary emotional prerequisite for the cognitive operations expected of participants in discourse. Similar connections among cognition, empathy, and *agape* can be shown to hold for the hermeneutic activity of applying universal norms in a context-sensitive manner. This integration of cognitive operations and emotional dispositions and attitudes in justifying and applying norms characterizes the *mature* capacity for moral judgment. It is only when we conceptualize maturity in this way that we can see moral rigorism for what it is: an impairment of the faculty of judgment. This concept of maturity, however, should not be applied *externally* to postconventional thought in the form of an opposition between an ethics of love and an ethics of law and justice. Rather, it should flow from an adequate description of the highest stage of morality itself.[62]

The motivational problem of anchorage

Those who would supplement Kohlberg's moral stages in one of the ways noted above fail to distinguish clearly between moral development and ego development. What corresponds in the personality system to moral judgment are behavioral controls, or superego structures. At higher stages these are formed only in a process of distancing oneself from and conflict with the social world understood as a matrix of relations in the social environment integrated through norms; superego structures can be analyzed in terms of the basic sociocognitive concepts of normatively regulated action. The formation of ego identity, on the other hand, takes place in the more complex contexts of communicative action, more specifically, in the interplay between an individual and the structures of the objective, social, and subjective worlds that gradually become differentiated from the contexts of the lifeworld.[63]

The postconventional disengagement of morality from ethical life signifies a loss of congruence between fundamental moral conceptions and what is taken for granted as part of a culture, or the certainties of the lifeworld in general. Moral insights and culturally habituated empirical motives are no longer one and the same. The resulting gap between moral judgments and moral actions needs to be compensated for by a system of internal behavior controls that is triggered by principled moral judgments (convictions that form the basis for motivations) and that makes *self-governance* possible. This system must function autonomously. It must be independent of the external pressure of an existing recognized legitimate order, no matter how small that pressure may be. These conditions are satisfied only by the complete internalization of a few highly abstract and universal principles that, as discourse ethics shows, follow logically from the procedure of norm justification. One way of *testing* postconventional superego structures is by checking responses to questions of the form "What should I do?" against responses to questions of the form "What would I do?" Responses to the latter Kohlberg calls responsibility judgments. They are indicators of the respondent's *intention* to act, or his *confidence* that he will act, in accordance with his moral judgments. Such responsibility judgments are at the same cognitive level as moral judgments. Even if we can interpret them as expressing a conviction (*Gesinnung*), as judgments they cannot in any way guarantee a correspondence between judgments and actions. We may be able to derive the *kind* of motivational anchoring without which a postconventional morality cannot be translated into action from the structure of our capacity to act, that is, from the sociocognitive inventory as restructured at the postconventional stage. But whether the psychodynamic processes will in fact meet the requirements of that structure is not something we can learn from *answers* to questions of the form "Why me?" Only actual practice can tell us that.[64]

Even if the passage to the postconventional level of moral judgment has been successful, an inadequate motivational anchoring can restrict one's ability to act autonomously. One especially striking manifestation of such a discrepancy between judgment and action is intellectualization, which uses an elaborate process of making moral judgments about action conflicts as a defense against latent instinctual conflicts.

3

Let me turn now to the complications Kohlberg faced when he dealt with the group of moral judgments that forced him to introduce the intermediate stage 4½. At issue are relativistic statements that tend to be made from a strategic rather than a moral point of view. Initially Kohlberg and his coworkers were tempted to stress the affinities of relativistic statements with the instrumental hedonism of stage 2. They could not classify these judgments as preconventional, however, because the general level of argumentation among respondents of this type was too high. The hypothetical attitude with which they judged the social world without moralizing it also spoke for an affinity of their statements with judgments on the postconventional level. For these reasons Kohlberg has placed these relativistic judgments between the conventional and the postconventional levels, assigning them to a transitional stage of their own, a stage that calls less for structural description than for psychodynamic explanation and is the expression of an unresolved crisis of adolescence.[65] This interpretation leaves something to be desired, since it cannot explain the possibility of this level of judgment becoming stabilized. That such stabilization is indeed possible is indicated, among other things, by the fact that a philosophical version of the value skepticism of stage 4½ has been developed and defended as a position to be taken seriously by thinkers in a line that starts with Weber and extends to Popper.

Common to subjectivist approaches in ethics is a value skepticism grounded in empiricist assumptions. Such value skepticism calls into question the rationalistic assumptions underlying Kohlberg's theory of moral development. Modern value skepticism disputes the contention that moral issues can be settled on the basis of valid (i.e., intersubjectively binding) reasons.

Instead, it conducts metaethical investigations designed to explain how the rationalistic illusions of everyday moral intuitions are rooted in our language. Psychology is certainly not the right forum for the dispute between the cognitivists and the skeptics.[66] The cognitivists will have to prevail on the basis of philosophical arguments—this is the premise of the theory of the development of moral consciousness. But psychology must be able to explain why value skepticism, for all its incongruence with the logic of moral development, seems to be a natural stage in that development. Kohlberg should not rest content with inserting a transitional stage into his overall scheme that can be explained only on a psychodynamic basis. By opting for classification as a solution to the problem, he commits himself to indicating the place of the transitional stage in the logic of development and thus to giving a structural description of stage 4½, as he has done with the other stages. The description he currently offers does not satisfy this demand. It reads as follows:

Level B/C, transitional level
This level is postconventional but not yet principled.
Content of transition: At Stage 4½, choice is personal and subjective. It is based on emotions, conscience is seen as arbitrary and relative, as are ideas such as "duty" and "morally right."
Transitional social perspective: At this stage, the perspective is that of an individual standing outside of his own society and considering himself an individual making decisions without a generalized commitment or contract with society. One can pick and choose obligations, which are defined by particular societies, but one has no principles for such choice.[67]

My own explanation for the troubling phenomenon of a transitional stage is that the group of respondents in question have only partially completed the transition to the postconventional level. If the integration of speaker perspectives with world perspectives has not been fully achieved and does not take in the social world and the norm-conformative attitude corresponding to it, there will fail to occur the coordination of the success-oriented attitude of the subject who acts strategically with the attitude oriented toward reaching understanding of the person who continues to communicate through argument—a coordination that discourse ethics presupposes. Moreover, it will fail to occur in precisely those cases in which problematic *normative claims to validity* are thematized. In such cases the sociocognitive inventory of the conventional stage of interaction can be said to have been only partly reorganized in the sense that while the adolescent has learned how to reason theoretically, he stops short of moral argumentation. In another context I formulated this hypothesis in the following way: by acquiring the ability to think hypothetically about moral-practical issues, the adolescent fulfills the necessary and sufficient condition for *dissociating himself from the conventional mode of thought.*[68]

But taking this step does not predetermine his decision between two alternative developmental paths. There are different ways in which the adolescent can use this newly acquired detachment from a world of conventions that have lost the naive force of social acceptance by being hypothetically relegated to a horizon of possibilities and have thereby become reflexively devalued. One alternative is that on his new level of reflection he can try to preserve something from that lost world of factually accepted conventions, namely what it *means* for norms and prescriptive statements to have validity. If he does that, he must reconstruct the basic concepts of morality without giving up the ethical perspective. He must relativize the de facto social currency of existing norms in terms of a normative validity that satisfies the criteria of rational justification. Maintaining a sense of normative validity reconstructed in this way is a necessary condition for the transition to the postconventional mode of thought. This is one path the adolescent can take.

Alternatively, the adolescent can dissociate himself from the conventional mode of thought without making the transition to the postconventional one. In this case he views the collapse of the world of conventions as a debunking of false cognitive claims with which conventional norms and prescriptive statements have hitherto been linked. The basic moral concepts in their cognitively devalued conventional form then appear retrospectively as requiring explanation. The adolescent's task is to come to terms with the dissonance between his moral intuitions, which continue to determine his unreflective everyday knowledge and actions, and his (presumed) insight into the illusory nature of this conventional moral consciousness, which reflection has discredited but which has not ceased to function in daily life. For the second developmental path, metaethical explanation of moral illusions takes the place of a postconventional renewal of ethical consciousness. The more successfully theoretical skepticism has been reconciled with the intuitions that go unchallenged in practice, the more easily such explanation can handle the dissonances. In this regard Weber's ethical skepticism, for example, has greater efficacy than Stevenson's emotivism. The former leaves untouched the existential nature of value bonds, whereas the latter explains moral intuitions away by reducing them to emotional dispositions and attitudes. From the viewpoint of Kohlberg's theory these metaethical versions must submit to being classified in terms of a logic of development and being subordinated to cognitivist ethics.

4

The last problem is one that Kohlberg's theory shares with any approach that distinguishes competence from performance. Such theoretical approaches face specific measurement problems because competence can be captured only in its concrete manifestations, that is, only in performance. Only insofar as these measurement problems have been solved can we isolate factors determining performance from theoretically postulated competences. It may be helpful to distinguish factors determining performance that, as *stimulators* or *accelerators*, must *supplement* or can accompany an acquired competence from the *braking* and *inhibiting* factors that act as filters.

To consider moral judgment as an indicator of competence and moral action or behavior as an indicator of performance is of course a crude simplification. On the other hand, the motivational anchoring of the capacity for postconventional judgment in homologous superego structures does represent an example of *supplementary* performance-determining factors without which moral judgments at this level could not become effective in practice.[69] As a rule, discrepancies between judgment and action can be accounted for in terms of the selective effect of *inhibiting* factors. A number of interesting studies point in this direction.[70] Among the performance-determining factors that act as inhibitors are some that explain motivational deficits. Of these the defense mechanisms first systematically studied by Anna Freud are of particular interest because they interfere with a process of motive formation that is structurally necessary. Accordingly, they can be analyzed from a *structural perspective*.

Identification and projection are the two fundamental mechanisms of defense against conflict. The individual acquires them in early childhood. Only later, at the conventional stage of interaction, do they seem to develop into the familiar system of defense mechanisms.[71] Defense mechanisms differ in terms of the ways in which they undermine the differentiation between action oriented toward success and action oriented toward reaching understanding that emerges at this level. Generally, the way defense works is that barriers to communication are set up in the psyche, separating the (unconscious) strategic aspect of action (which serves the gratification of unconscious desires) from the manifest intentional action that aims at reaching understanding. This explains why the subject can deceive himself about the fact that he is objectively violating the shared presuppositions of action oriented toward reaching understanding. Unconsciously motivated actions can be explained as a latent reversal of the differentiation between strategic and communicative action, a dedifferentiation that is hidden from the actor and others. The self-deceptive effect of the defense can be interpreted as an intrapsychic disturbance of communication. This interpretation makes use of the conception of systematically distorted communication that can manifest itself in similar ways on two different levels: the interpersonal and the intrapsychic. But this concept requires independent discussion in the framework of communication theory.[72]

Notes

1. See my "Discourse Ethics," in this volume.

2. On the methodology of the reconstructive sciences, see D. Garz, "Zur Bedeutung rekonstruktiver Sozialisationstheorien in der Erziehungswissenschaft unter besonderer Berücksichtigung der Arbeiten von L. Kohlberg," unpubl. diss. (Hamburg, 1982).

3. See the bibliography of Kohlberg's writings in L. Kohlberg, *Essays on Moral Development* (San Francisco, 1981), vol. 1, pp. 423–428.

4. T. Kesselring, *Entwicklung und Widerspruch* (Frankfurt, 1981).

5. See section 5 of my essay "Reconstruction and Interpretation in the Social Sciences," in this volume.

6. R. Bubner, "Selbstbezüglichkeit als Struktur transzendentaler Argumente," in W. Kuhlmann and D. Böhler, eds., *Kommunikation und Reflexion* (Frankfurt, 1982), pp. 304ff. Bubner is referring to the discussion in Bieri, Horstmann, and Krüger, eds., *Transcendental Arguments and Science* (Dordrecht, 1979).

7. See my "Philosophy as Stand-In and Interpreter," in this volume.

8. A good example is the study of M. Keller and S. Reuss, "Der Prozess der moralischen Entscheidungsfindung," unpubl. ms., *International Symposium on Moral Education* (Fribourg, 1982).

9. On the reception in Germany, see L. H. Eckensberger, ed., *Entwicklung des moralischen Urteilens* (Saarbrücken, 1978), and the recent G. Lind, H. Hartmann, and R. Wakenhut, eds., *Moralisches Urteilen und soziale Umwelt* (Weinheim, 1983).

10. L. Kohlberg, "A Reply to Owen Flanagan," *Ethics* 92 (1982), and "Justice as Reversibility," in *Essays on Moral Development*, vol. 1, pp. 190ff.

11. On this emotivist position, see G. Hartmann, *Das Wesen der Moral* (Frankfurt, 1981), pp. 38ff.

12. The ideal observer is replaced by the ideal speech situation. In the latter it is postulated that the exacting pragmatic presuppositions of argumentation as such are fulfilled. See P. Alexy, "Eine Theorie des praktischen Diskurses," in W. Oelmüller, ed., *Transzendentalphilosophische Normenbegründung* (Paderborn, 1978).

13. Kohlberg (1981), pp. 409ff.

14. Kohlberg (1981), pp. 409ff.

15. R. L. Selman, *The Growth of Interpersonal Understanding* (New York, 1980).

16. H. Lenk, "Philosophische Logikbegründung und rationaler Kritizismus," in *Zeitschrift für philosophische Forschung* 24 (1970): 183ff.

17. J. Habermas, *Theorie des kommunikativen Handelns*, (Frankfurt, 1981), 2 vols.; English translation as *Theory of Communicative Action*, 2 vols., (Boston 1984 and 1987). J. Habermas, "Erläuterungen zum Begriff des kommunikativen Handelns," in J. Habermas, *Vorstudien und Ergänzungen zur Theorie des kommunkativen Handelns* (Frankfurt, 1984).

Moral Consciousness and Communicative Action

18. J. Habermas, *Theory of Communicative Action*, vol. 1, pp. 88ff.

19. See K.-O. Apel, "Intentions, Conventions, and Reference to Things," in H. Parret and J. Vouveresse, eds., *Meaning and Understanding* (Berlin, 1981), pp. 79ff, and "Lässt sich ethische Vernunft von Rationalität unterscheiden?" ms. (Frankfurt, 1983).

20. J. Habermas, *Theory of Communicative Action*, vol. 1, pp. 286ff.

21. J. Habermas, *Theory of Communicative Action*, vol. 2, pp. 119ff.

22. This oversimplified opposition disregards the differences between those parts of the lifeworld that have *never* been dissociated from intuitive background knowledge and thematized, and those that have been focused upon at least *once* only to sink back into the lifeworld, there to be reabsorbed once more. The latter sort of taken-for-grantedness is a *second-order* immediacy. I owe this insight to U. Matthiesen.

23. A corresponding hypothesis concerning the construction of an inner world and how it is delimited from the objective and social worlds need not concern us here except insofar as the subjective world and its thematizable experiences represent a further basic attitude and perspective, *rounding out the system of world perspectives*.

24. I am ignoring stage 0, where the child does not differentiate in a way that would be relevant for us. I am also ignoring stage 4. Stage 4 already presupposes the concept of an action norm. I will argue below that this concept defies reconstruction in terms of perspective taking *alone* and requires instead sociocognitive concepts of a *different* provenance. Selman is unable to differentiate stages 3 and 4 solely in terms of perspective taking.

25. R. Selman, *The Growth of Interpersonal Understanding*, pp. 38ff. M. Keller, *Kognitive Entwicklung und soziale Kompetenz* (Stuttgart, 1976). D. Geulen, *Perspektivenübernahme und soziales Handeln* (Frankfurt, 1982).

26. Age indicators vary with the situation being investigated. Placed in their natural environment, children in Western societies today turn out to acquire the corresponding competences earlier.

27. The link between possessive-pronoun use and action perspectives is discussed by K. Böhme, *Children's Understanding and Awareness of German Possessive Pronouns* (Nijmegen, 1983), pp. 156ff.

28. R. L. Selman, "Stufen der Rollenübernahme in der mittleren Kindheit," in R. Döbert, J. Habermas, and G. Nunner-Winkler, eds., *Entwicklung des Ichs*, (Cologne, 1977), p. 111.

29. W. Damon has investigated the increasing depersonalization of authority in "Zur Entwicklung der sozialen Kognition des Kindes," in W. Edelstein, and M. Kellner, eds., *Perspektivität und Interpretation* (Frankfurt, 1982), pp. 110ff. See especially p. 121f.

30. M. Auwärter and E. Kirsch, "Zur Interdependenz von kommunikativen und interaktiven Fähigkeiten," in K. Martens, ed., *Kindliche Kommunikation* (Frankfurt, 1979), pp. 243ff. Auwärter and Kirsch, "Katja, spielst Du mal mit Andrea?" in R. Mackensen and F. Sagebiel, eds., *Soziologische Analysen* (Berlin, 1979), pp. 473ff. Auwärter and Kirsch, "Zur Ontogenese der sozialen Interaktion," ms. (Munich, 1983).

31. "Holly is an 8-year-old girl who likes to climb trees. She is the best tree climber in the neighborhood. One day while climbing down from a tall tree she falls off the

bottom branch but does not hurt herself. Her father sees her fall. He is upset and asks her to promise not to climb trees any more. Holly promises. Later that day, Holly and her friends meet Sean. Sean's kitten is caught up in a tree and cannot get down. Something has to be done right away or the kitten may fall. Holly is the only one who climbs trees well enough to reach the kitten and get it down, but she remembers her promise to her father." (R. Selman, "Stufen de Rollenübernahme," p. 112)

32. J. Youniss, "Die Entwicklung von Freundschaftsbeziehungen," in Edelstein and Keller (1982), pp. 78ff.

33. J. H. Flavell et al., *The Development of Role-Taking and Communication Skills in Children* (New York, 1968).

34. Flavell (1968) pp. 45ff. Compare Selman's (1981) comments on the relation between his levels of perspective taking and Flavell's strategies: "Level 2 (B) is assigned to the responses of children who indicate an awareness that the *other* child knows that the *subject* knows: (a) One choice has certain advantages (monetary) over the other; (b) this might influence that other child's choice; and (c) this in turn has implications for the choice that the subject is to make. It should be stressed that success at this level implies the child has an understanding of the reciprocal functioning of the social-awareness process; as the child makes a decision on the basis of his attributing thoughts and actions to other, the child also sees that other is capable of similarly attributing thoughts and actions to the self. . . . Level 3 (C) thinking goes beyond the child's realization that the self must take into consideration that one's opponent can take into consideration the self's motives and strategies. It is a level of understanding at which the child is able to abstractly step outside the dyad and see that each player can simultaneously consider the self's and other's perspectives on each other, a level of abstraction which we now call *mutual* perspectivism." (pp. 26–27).

35. W. Damon, *The Social World of the Child* (San Francisco, 1977).

36. H. R. Schaffer, "Acquiring the Concept of the Dialogue," in M. H. Bornstein and W. Kessen, eds., *Psychological Development from Infancy* (Hillsdale, 1979), pp. 279ff. B. Sylvester-Bradley, "Negativity in Early Infant-Adult Exchanges," in W. P. Robinson, ed., *Communication in Development* (New York, 1981), p. 1ff. C. Trevarthen, "The Foundations of Intersubjectivity," in D. R. Olsen, *The Social Foundations of Language and Thought* (New York, 1980), pp. 316ff. A synopsis of the current state of research can be found in M. Auwärter and E. Kirsch, ms. (Munich, 1983).

37. Selman (1980), pp. 131ff.

38. M. Miller, "Moral Argumentations among Children," *Linguistische Berichte* 74 (1981): 1ff. M. Miller, "Argumentationen als moralische Lernprozesse," in *Zeitschrift für Pädagogik* 28 (1982): 299ff.

39. This becomes evident when one tries to describe the conventional stage of the interaction in terms of exchange. Compare Damon in Edelstein and Keller (1982), pp. 121ff., especially the third level of social regulation, p. 128.

40. The simplest case is the one where *B*'s expectation that *A* will obey his imperative that *q* and *A*'s reciprocal expectation that his wish that *r* will be fulfilled by *B* are conjoined in pairs. This conjunction occurs in the framework of the socializing interaction between parent and child. As far as *B* is concerned, this relation is based on norms that govern the parent-child relationship. However, in the context of this parental care *A* experiences the same normative nexus of behavioral expectations as nothing but an empirical regularity. In uttering *r, A* anticipates that *B* will fulfill his

wish in the expectation that *A* for his part will obey *B*'s imperative that *q*. By taking over *B*'s expectation of how *A* will behave, *A* acquires the concept of a *pattern of behavior*. This concept conditionally joins the particular interlocking and complementary behavioral expectations of *A* and *B*.

41. On what follows, see Habermas (1987), vol. 2, pp. 31ff.

42. Habermas (1984), vol. 1, pp. 326ff.

43. J. Habermas, "Moral Development and Ego-Identity," in Habermas, *Communication and the Evolution of Society* (Boston, 1979), p. 78ff.

44. I will not deal with the methodological criticisms that have been made by W. Kurtines and E. Greif in "The Development of Moral Thought," *Psychological Bulletin* 81 (1974): 453ff. See F. Oser, "Die Theorie von L. Kohlberg im Kreuzfeuer der Kritik—eine Verteidigung," in *Bildungsforschung und Bildungspraxis* 3 (1981): 51ff. Nor can I take up the equally valid issue of whether the stage model is cross-culturally valid. See J. C. Gibbs, "Kohlberg's Stages of Moral Judgment," *Harvard Educational Review* 47 (1977): 5ff.

45. A. Colby, "Evolution of a Moral-Developmental Theory," in W. Damon, ed., *Moral Development* (San Francisco, 1978), pp. 89ff.

46. Kohlberg has emphasized that the construction of stage 6 resulted from material obtained from a small elite sample (it included statements by Martin Luther King). "Such elite figures do not establish stage 6 as a natural stage of development." L. Kohlberg, "Philosophic Issues in the Study of Moral Development," ms. (Cambridge, 1980).

47. T. McCarthy, "Rationality and Relativism," in J. B. Thompson and D. Held, eds., *Habermas: Critical Debates* (London, 1982), p. 74.

48. T. McCarthy, "Rationality and Relativism," p. 74.

49. N. Haan, "Two Moralities in Action Context," *Journal of Personality and Social Psychology* 36 (1978): 286ff.

50. C. Gilligan, "In a Different Voice: Women's Conceptions of Self and Morality," *Harvard Educational Review* 47 (1977): 481ff.

51. C. Gilligan and J. M. Murphy, "The Philosopher and the Dilemma of the Fact," in D. Kuhn, ed., *Intellectual Development beyond Childhood* (San Francisco, 1980). C. Gilligan's *In a Different Voice* (Cambridge, 1982) came out in book form after I had completed this manuscript.

52. L. Kohlberg, "A Reply to Owen Flanagan," *Ethics* 92 (1982): 513ff.

53. W. B. Perry, *Forms of Intellectual and Ethical Development in the College Years* (New York, 1968).

54. K. Riegel, "Dialectical Operations," *Human Development* 16 (1973): 345ff and his *Zur Ontogenese dialektischer Operationen* (Frankfurt, 1978).

55. C. Gilligan and J. M. Murphy, "Moral Development in Late Adolescence and Adulthood: A Critique and Reconstruction of Kohlberg's Theory," *Human Development* 23 (1980): 159ff.

56. The general problem of applying norms to situations of action is already posed at the conventional stage of moral judgment and interaction. In this context the focus is on the particular aggravation this problem undergoes when the links are severed through which norms and situations of action, as parts of one and the same unproblematic form of life, *refer to each other* through their prior coordination. See H. G. Gadamer, *Truth and Method* (New York, 1975).

57. W. Kuhlmann, *Reflexion und kommunikative Erfahrung* (Frankfurt, 1975). D. Böhler, "Philosophische Hermeneutik und hermeneutische Methode," in M. Fuhrmann, H. R. Jauss, and W. Pannenberg, eds., *Text und Applikation* (Munich, 1981), pp. 483ff. J. Habermas, *Theory of Communicative Action* (Boston, 1984), vol. 1, pp. 134ff.

58. Some of the more important sources are L. Kohlberg and C. Candee, "The Relationship between Moral Judgment and Moral Action," in J. Gewirtz and W. Kurtines, eds., *Morality, Moral Behavior, and Moral Development* (New York, 1983); J. Habermas, "Responsibility and Its Role in the Relationship between Moral Judgement and Action," ms. (Cambridge, 1981); G. Nunner-Winkler, "Two Moralities? A Critical Discussion of an Ethic of Care and Responsibility versus an Ethic of Rights and Justice," in Gewirtz and Kurtines (1983).

59. J. Habermas, *Theory of Communicative Action*, vol. 2 (Boston, 1987), pp. 96ff.

60. This is the case with the decisions about abortion studied by Gilligan. Possible repercussions for one's relation to friend or husband, for the occupational careers of man and woman, for family life can be considered important only when abortion itself has been accepted as morally licit. The same goes for problems of divorce and adultery. This is confirmed by the two cases that Gilligan and Murphy (1981) refer to. Only when sexual infidelity is morally unobjectionable can the problem arise of under what conditions concealment of the facts is less harmful to or more considerate of the party directly or indirectly concerned than immediate disclosure.

61. W. K. Frankena, *Ethics* (Englewood Cliffs, N.J., 1973), pp. 45ff.

62. In terms of his moral theory the young Hegel was still a Kantian when he worked out the historical dichotomy between a Christian ethics of love and a Jewish ethics of law and justice.

63. On the concepts of ego identity and ego development, see J. Habermas, "Moral Development and Ego Identity," in Habermas, *Communication and the Evolution of Society* (Boston, 1979), pp. 69ff; R. Döbert, J. Habermas, and G. Nunner-Winkler, eds., *Entwicklung des Ichs* (Cologne, 1977), pp. 9ff.; and G. Noam and R. Kegan, "Soziale Kognition und Psychodynamik," in Edelstein and Keller (1982), pp. 422ff.

64. To that extent Kohlberg and Candee (1983) assign too great a burden of proof to "responsibility judgments."

65. R. Döbert and G. Nunner-Winkler, *Adoleszenzkrise und Identitätsbildung* (Frankfurt, 1975).

66. See pp. 36–41 in this volume.

67. Kohlberg (1981), p. 411.

68. Habermas, "Reply to my Critics," in Thompson and Held, eds., *Habermas: Critical Debates*, pp. 260ff.

Moral Consciousness and Communicative Action

69. R. Döbert and G. Nunner-Winkler, "Performanzbestimmende Aspekte des moralischen Bewusstseins," in G. Portele, eds., *Sozialisation und Moral* (Weinheim, 1978).

70. W. Edelstein and M. Keller, "Perspektivität und Interpretation," in Edelstein und Keller, eds., *Perspektivität und Interpretation* (Frankfurt, 1982), pp. 22ff. R. Döbert and G. Nunner-Winkler, "Abwehr- und Bewältigungsprozesse in normalen und kritischen Lebenssituationen," ms. (Munich, 1983).

71. N. Haan, "A Tripartite Model of Ego Functioning," in *Journal of Neurological and Mental Disease* 1 (1969): 14–29.

72. An interesting model of false self-understanding has been proposed by Martin Löw-Beer, "Selbsttäuschung," diss., University of Frankfurt, 1982.

Morality and Ethical Life: Does Hegel's Critique of Kant Apply to Discourse Ethics?

In recent years Karl-Otto Apel and I have begun to reformulate Kant's ethics by grounding moral norms in communication, a venture to which I refer as "discourse ethics."[1] In this paper I hope to accomplish two things: first, to sketch the basic idea of discourse ethics and then to examine Hegel's critique of Kantian moral philosophy. In part I, I will deal with two questions: What is discourse ethics? and What moral intuitions does discourse ethics conceptualize? I will address the complicated matter of how to justify discourse ethics only in passing.

In part II, I will turn to the question of whether Hegel's critique of Kantian ethics applies to discourse ethics as well. The criticisms Hegel leveled against Kant as a moral philosopher are many. From among them I will single out four which strike me as the most trenchant. These are as follows:

• Hegel's objection to the *formalism* of Kantian ethics. Since the moral principle of the categorical imperative requires that the moral agent abstract from the concrete content of duties and maxims, its application necessarily leads to tautological judgments.[2]

• Hegel's objection to the *abstract universalism* of Kantian ethics. Since the categorical imperative enjoins separating the universal from the particular, a judgment considered valid in terms of that principle necessarily remains external to individual cases and insensitive to the particular context of a problem in need of solution.[3]

• Hegel's attack on the *impotence of the mere ought*. Since the categorical imperative enjoins a strict separation of "is" from "ought," it necessarily fails to answer the question of how moral insight can be realized in practice.[4]

• Hegel's objection to the terrorism of *pure conviction (Gesinnung)*. Since the categorical imperative severs the pure postulates of practical reason from the formative process of spirit and its concrete historical manifestations, it necessarily recommends to the advocates of the moral worldview a policy that aims at the actualization of reason and sanctions even immoral deeds if they serve higher ends.[5]

I

1   What is Discourse Ethics?

First I want to comment briefly on the general nature of Kantian moral philosophy. It has all of the following attributes: it is deontological, cognitivist, formalist, and universalist. Wanting to limit himself strictly to the class of justifiable normative judgments, Kant was forced to choose a narrow concept of morality. Classical moral philosophies had dealt with *all* the issues of the "good life." Kant's deals only with problems of right or just action. To him, moral judgments serve to explain how conflicts of action can be settled on the basis of rationally motivated agreement. Broadly, they serve to justify actions in terms of valid norms and to justify the validity of norms in terms of principles worthy of recognition. In short, the basic phenomenon that moral philosophy must explain is the normative validity (*Sollgeltung*) of commands and norms of action. This is what is meant by saying that a moral philosophy is *deontological*. A deontological ethics conceives the rightness of norms and commands on analogy with the truth of an assertoric statement. It would be erroneous, though, to equate the moral "truth" of normative statements with the assertoric validity of propositional statements, a mistake made by intuitionism and value ethics. Kant does not make this mistake. He does not confuse theoretical with practical reason. As for myself, I hold the view that normative rightness must be regarded as a claim to validity that is analogous to a truth claim. This notion is captured by the term "*cognitivist* ethics." A cognitivist ethics must answer the question of how to justify normative statements. Although Kant opts for the grammatical form of an imperative ("Act only according to that maxim by which you can at the same time will that it should become a universal law"), his categorical imperative in fact plays the part of a principle of justification that discriminates between valid and invalid norms in terms of their universalizability: what every rational being must be able to will is justified in a moral sense. This is what one means when one speaks of an ethics as being *formalist*. Discourse ethics replaces the Kantian categorical imperative by a procedure of moral argumentation. Its principle postulates,

Only those norms may claim to be valid that could meet with the consent of all affected in their role as participants in a practical discourse.[6]

While retaining the categorical imperative after a fashion, discourse ethics scales it down to a principle of universalization (U). In practical discourses (U) plays the part of a rule of argumentation:

(U) For a norm to be valid, the consequences and side effects of its general observance for the satisfaction of each person's particular interests must be acceptable to all.

Finally, an ethics is termed *universalist* when it alleges that this (or a similar) moral principle, far from reflecting the intuitions of a particular culture or epoch, is valid universally. As long as the moral principle is not justified—and justifying it involves more than simply pointing to Kant's "fact of pure reason"— the ethnocentric fallacy looms large. I must prove that my moral principle is not just a reflection of the prejudices of adult, white, well-educated, Western males of today. This is the most difficult part of ethics, a part that I cannot expound in this paper. Briefly, the thesis that discourse ethics puts forth on this subject is that anyone who seriously undertakes to participate in argumentation implicitly accepts by that very undertaking general pragmatic presuppositions that have a normative content. The moral principle can then be derived from the content of these presuppositions of argumentation if one knows at least what it means to justify a norm of action.[7] These, then, are the deontological, cognitivist, formalist and universalist assumptions that all moral philosophies of the Kantian type have in common. Let me make one more remark concerning the procedure I call practical discourse.

The viewpoint from which moral questions can be judged *impartially* is called the moral point of view. Formalist ethical theories furnish a rule explaining how something is looked at from the moral point of view. John Rawls, for example, recommends an original position, where those concerned meet as rational and equal partners who decide upon a contract, not knowing their own or each other's actual social positions.[8] G. H. Mead for his part recommends a procedure that he calls ideal role taking. It requires that any morally judging subject put itself in the position of all who would be affected if a problematic plan of action were carried out or if a controversial norm were to take effect.[9] As a procedure, practical discourse is different from these two constructs, the Rawlsian and the Meadian. Argumentation insures that all concerned in principle take part, freely and equally, in a cooperative search for truth, where nothing coerces anyone except the force of the better argument. Practical discourse is an exacting form of argumentative decision making. Like Rawls's original position, it is a warrant of the rightness (or fairness) of any conceivable normative agreement that is reached under these conditions. Discourse can play this role because its idealized, partly counterfactual presuppositions are precisely those that participants in argumentation do in fact make. That is why I think it unnecessary to resort to Rawls's fictitious original position with its "veil of ignorance." Practical discourse can also be viewed as a communicative process *simultaneously* exhorting *all* participants to ideal role taking. Thus practical discourse transforms what Mead viewed as *individual, privately enacted* role taking into a *public* affair, practiced intersubjectively by all involved.[10]

2 What Moral Intuitions Does Discourse Ethics Conceptualize?

How can it be argued that the *procedural* explanation discourse ethics gives of the moral point of view—in other words, of the impartiality of moral judgment—constitutes an adequate account of moral intuitions, which are after all *substantive* in kind? This is an open question that needs to be addressed.

Moral intuitions are intuitions that instruct us on how best to behave in situations where it is in our power to counteract the extreme vulnerability of others by being thoughtful and considerate. In anthropological terms, morality is a safety device compensating for a vulnerability built into the sociocultural form of life. The basic facts are the following: Creatures that are individuated only through socialization are vulnerable and morally in need of considerateness. Linguistically and behaviorally competent subjects are constituted as individuals by growing into an intersubjectively shared lifeworld, and the lifeworld of a language community is reproduced in turn through the communicative actions of its members. This explains why the identity of the individual and that of the collective are interdependent; they form and maintain themselves together. Built into the consensus-oriented language use of social interaction is an inconspicuous necessity for participants to become more and more individuated. Conversely, everyday language is also the medium by which the intersubjectivity of a shared world is maintained.[11] Thus, the more differentiated the structures of the lifeworld become, the easier it is to discern the simultaneous growth of the autonomous individual subject and his dependence on interpersonal relationships and social ties. The more the subject becomes individuated, the more he becomes entangled in a densely woven fabric of mutual recognition, that is, of reciprocal exposedness and vulnerability. Unless the subject externalizes himself by participating in interpersonal relations through language, he is unable to form that inner center that is his personal identity. This explains the almost constitutional insecurity and chronic fragility of personal identity—an insecurity that is antecedent to cruder threats to the integrity of life and limb.

Moral philosophies of sympathy and compassion (Schopenhauer) have discovered that this profound vulnerability calls for some guarantee of mutual consideration.[12] This considerateness has the twofold objective of defending the integrity of the individual and of preserving the vital fabric of ties of mutual recognition through which individuals *reciprocally* stabilize their fragile identities. No one can maintain his identity by himself. Consider suicide, for example. Notwithstanding the Stoic view that held that this final, desperate act reflects the imperious self-determination of the lone individual, the responsibility for suicide can never be attributed to the individual alone. This seemingly loneliest of deeds actually enacts a fate for which others collectively must take some of the blame, the fate of ostracism from an intersubjectively shared lifeworld.

Since moralities are tailored to suit the fragility of human beings individuated through socialization, they must always solve *two* tasks at *once*. They must emphasize the inviolability of the individual by postulating equal respect for the dignity of each individual. But they must also protect the web of intersubjective relations of mutual recognition by which these individuals survive as members of a community. To these two complementary aspects correspond the principles of justice and solidarity respectively. The first postulates equal respect and equal rights for the individual, whereas the second postulates empathy and concern for the well-being of one's neighbor. Justice in the modern sense of the term refers to the subjective freedom of inalienable individuality. Solidarity refers to the well-being of associated members of a community who intersubjectively share the same lifeworld. Frankena distinguishes a principle of justice or equal treatment from a principle of beneficence, which commands us to advance the common weal, to avert harm and to do good.[13] In my view, it is important to see that both principles have one and the same root: the specific vulnerability of the human species, which individuates itself through sociation. Morality thus cannot protect the one without the other. It cannot protect the rights of the individual without also protecting the well-being of the community to which he belongs.

The fundamental motif of an ethics of compassion can be pushed to the point where the link between the two moral principles becomes clear. In the past these principles have served as core elements of two contrary traditions in moral philosophy. Theories of duty have always centered on the principle of justice, whereas theories of the good have always emphasized the common weal. Hegel was the first to argue that we misperceive the basic moral phenomenon if we isolate the two aspects, assigning opposite principles to each. His concept of ethical life (*Sittlichkeit*) is an implicit criticism of two kinds of one-sidedness, one the mirror image of the other. Hegel opposes the abstract universality of justice manifesting itself in the individualist approaches of the modern age, in rational natural right theory and in Kantian moral philosophy. No less vigorous is his opposition to the concrete particularism of the common good that pervades Aristotle and Thomas Aquinas. The ethics of discouse picks up this basic Hegelian aspiration to redeem it with Kantian means.

This idea is not so remarkable if one keeps in mind that discourses, treating as they do problematic validity claims as hypotheses, represent a reflective form of communicative action. To put it another way, the normative content of the pragmatic presuppositions of argumentation is borrowed from that of communicative action, onto which discourses are superimposed. This is why all moralities coincide in one respect: the same medium, linguistically mediated interaction, is both the reason for the vulnerability of socialized individuals and the key resource they possess to compensate for that vulnerability. Every morality revolves around equality of respect, solidarity, and the common good. Fundamental ideas like these can be reduced to the relations of symmetry and reciprocity presupposed in communicative action. In other words, the common core of all kinds of morality can be traced back to the reciprocal imputations and shared presuppositions actors make when they seek understanding in everyday situations.[14] Admittedly, their range in everyday practice is limited. While equal respect and solidarity are present in the mutual recognition of subjects who orient their actions to validity claims, normative obligations usually do not transcend the boundaries of a concrete lifeworld, be it that of a family, a neighborhood, a city, or a state. There is only one reason why discourse ethics, which presumes to derive the substance of a universalistic morality from the general presuppositions of argumentation, is a promising strategy: discourse or argumentation is a more exacting type of communication, going beyond any particular form of life. Discourse generalizes, abstracts, and stretches the presuppositions of context-bound communicative actions by extending their range to include competent subjects beyond the provincial limits of their own particular form of life.

These considerations address the issues of whether and why discourse ethics, though organized around a concept of procedure, can be expected to say something relevant about substance as well and, more important perhaps, about the hidden link between justice and the common good, which have traditionally been divorced, giving rise to separate ethics of duty and the good. On the strength of its improbable pragmatic features, practical discourse, or moral argumentation, serves as a warrant of insightful will formation, insuring that the interests of individuals are given their due without cutting the social bonds that intersubjectively unite them.[15]

In his capacity as a participant in argumentation, everyone is on his own and yet embedded in a communication context. This is what Apel means by an "ideal community of communication." In discourse the social bond of belonging is left intact despite the fact that the consensus required of all concerned transcends the limits of any actual community. The agreement made possible by discourse depends on two things: the individual's inalienable right to say yes or no and his overcoming of his egocentric viewpoint. Without the individual's uninfringeable freedom to respond with a "yes" or "no" to criticizable validity claims, consent is merely factual rather than truly universal. Conversely, without empathetic sensitivity by each person to everyone else, no solution deserving universal consent will result from the deliberation. These two aspects—the autonomy of inalienable individuals and their embeddedness in an intersubjectively shared web of relations—are internally connected, and it is this link that the procedure of discursive decision making takes into account. The equal rights of individuals and the equal respect for the personal dignity of each depend upon a network of interpersonal relations and a system of mutual recognition. On the other hand, while the degree of solidarity and the growth of welfare are indicators of the quality of communal life, they are not the only ones. Just as important is that *equal* consideration be given to the interests of every individual in defining the general interest. Going beyond Kant, discourse ethics extends the deontological concept of justice by including in it those structural aspects of the good life that can be distinguished from the concrete totality of specific forms of life.

II

For all its affinities with Kant's moral theory, discourse ethics is rather different. Before going on to consider Hegel's objections to Kant's ethics, I want to focus briefly on three differences that strike me as important. First, discourse ethics gives up Kant's dichotomy between an *intelligible* realm comprising 1) duty and free will and a *phenomenal* realm comprising inclinations, subjective motives, political and social institutions, etc.[16] The quasi-transcendental necessity with which subjects involved in communicative interaction orient themselves to validity claims is reflected only in their being *constrained* to speak and act under idealized conditions. The unbridgeable gap Kant saw between the intelligible and the empirical becomes, in discourse ethics, a mere tension manifesting itself in *everyday communication* as the factual force of counterfactual presuppositions. Second, discourse ethics rejects the monological ap- 2) proach of Kant, who assumed that the individual tests his maxims of action *foro interno* or, as Husserl put it, in the loneliness of his soul. The singularity of Kant's transcendental consciousness simply takes for granted a prior understanding among a plurality of empirical egos; their harmony is preestablished. In discourse ethics it is not. Discourse ethics prefers to view shared understanding about the generalizability of interests as the *result* of an intersubjectively mounted *public discourse*. There are no shared structures preceding the individual except the universals of language use. Third, discourse ethics 3) improves upon Kant's unsatisfactory handling of a specific problem of justification when he evasively points to the alleged "fact of pure reason" and argues that the effectiveness of the "ought" is simply a matter of experience. Discourse ethics solves this problem by deriving (U) from the universal presuppositions of argumentation.

2.
examples
given by
Kant?.

1   On the Formalism of the Moral Principle

Neither Kantian ethics nor discourse ethics lays itself open to the charge that since it defines the moral principle in formal or procedural terms, it can make only tautological statements about morality. Hegel was wrong to imply that these principles postulate logical and semantic consistency and nothing else. In fact, they postulate the employment of a substantive moral point of view. The issue is not whether normative statements must have the grammatical form of universal sentences. The issue is whether we can *all* will that a contested norm gain binding force under given conditions.[17] The content that is tested by a moral principle is generated not by the philosopher but by real life. The conflicts of action that come to be morally judged and consensually resolved grow out of everyday life. Reason as a tester of maxims (Kant) or actors as participants in argumentation (discourse ethics) *find* these conflicts. They do not create them.[18]

There is a somewhat different sense in which Hegel's charge of formalism does ring true. Any procedural ethics must distinguish between the structure and the content of moral judgment. Its deontological abstraction segregates from among the general mass of practical issues precisely those that lend themselves to rational debate. They alone are subjected to a justificatory test. In short, this procedure differentiates *normative* statements about the hypothetical justice of actions and norms from *evaluative* statements about subjective preferences that we articulate in reference to what our notion of the good life happens to be, which in turn is a function of our cultural heritage. Hegel believed it was this tendency to abstract from the good life that made it impossible for morality to claim jurisdiction over the substantive problems of daily life. He has

that's too
simple

a point, but his criticism overshoots its aim. To cite an example, *problem of* human rights obviously embody generalizable interests. As *universality* such they can be morally grounded in terms of what all could *and* will. And yet nobody would argue that these rights, which *particularity* represent the moral substance of our legal system, are irrelevant for the ethics (*Sittlichkeit*) of modern life.

In the back of Hegel's mind was a theoretical question that is rather more difficult to answer: Can one formulate concepts like universal justice, normative rightness, the moral point of view, and the like independently of any vision of the good life, i.e., independently of an intuitive project of some privileged but concrete form of life? <u>Noncontextual definitions of a moral principle</u>, I admit, have not been satisfactory up to now. Negative versions of the moral principle seem to be a step in the right direction. They heed the prohibition of graven images, refrain from positive depiction, and as in the case of discourse ethics, refer negatively to the damaged life instead of pointing affirmatively to the good life.[19]

2 On the Abstract Universalism of Morally Justified Judgment

Neither Kantian ethics nor discourse ethics lays itself open to the objection that a moral point of view based on the generalizability of norms necessarily leads to the neglect, if not the repression, of existing conditions and interests in a pluralist society. As interests and value orientations become more differentiated in modern societies, the morally justified norms that control the individual's scope of action in the interest of the whole become ever more general and abstract. Modern societies are also characterized by the need for regulations that impinge *only* on particular interests. While these matters do require regulation, a discursive consensus is not needed; compromise is quite sufficient in this area. Let us keep in mind, though, that fair compromise calls for morally justified procedures of compromising.

Hegel's objection sometimes takes the form of an attack on rigorism. A rigid procedural ethics, especially one that is monologically practiced, fails to take account, so the argument goes, of the consequences and side effects that may flow from the generalized observance of a justified norm. Max Weber was prompted by this objection to counterpose an ethics of responsibility to what he termed Kant's ethics of conviction. The charge of rigorism applies to Kant. It does not apply to discourse ethics, since the latter breaks with Kant's idealism and monologism. Discourse ethics has a built-in procedure that insures awareness of consequences. This comes out clearly in the formulation of the principle of universalization (U), which requires sensitivity to the results and consequences of the general observance of a norm for every individual.

Hegel is right in another respect too. Moral theories of the Kantian type are specialized. They focus on questions of *justification*, leaving questions of *application* unanswered. An additional effort is needed to *undo* the abstraction (from particular situations and individual cases) that is, initially at least, an inevitable part of justification. No norm contains within itself the rules for its application. Yet moral justifications are pointless unless the decontextualization of the general norms used in justification is compensated for in the process of application. Like any moral theory, discourse ethics cannot evade the difficult problem of whether the application of rules to particular cases necessitates a separate and distinct faculty of *prudence* or judgment that would tend to undercut the universalistic claim of justificatory reason because it is tied to the parochial context of some hermeneutic starting point? The neo-Aristotelian way out of this dilemma is to argue that practical reason should forswear its universalistic intent in favor of a more contextual faculty of judgment.[20] Since judgment always moves within the ambit of a more or less accepted form of life, it finds support in an evaluative context that engenders *continuity* among questions of motivation, empirical issues, evaluative issues, and normative issues.

In contrast to the neo-Aristotelian position, discourse ethics is emphatically opposed to going back to a stage of philosophical thought prior to Kant. Kant's achievement was precisely to dissociate the problem of justification from the application and implementation of moral insights. I argue that even in the prudent application of norms, principles of practical reason take effect. Suggestive evidence is provided by classical *topoi*, for instance, the principles that all relevant aspects of a case must be considered and that means should be proportionate to ends. Such principles as these promote the idea of *impartial* application, which is not a prudent but a moral point of view.

3   On the Impotence of the "Ought"

Kant is vulnerable to the objection that his ethics lacks practical impact because it dichotomizes duty and inclination, reason and sense experience. The same cannot be said of discourse ethics, for it discards the Kantian theory of the two realms. The concept of practical discourse postulates the inclusion of all interests that may be affected; it even covers the critical testing of interpretations through which we come to recognize certain needs as in our own interests. Discourse ethics also reformulates the concept of autonomy. In Kant, autonomy was conceived as freedom under self-given laws, which involves an element of coercive subordination of subjective nature. In discourse ethics the idea of autonomy is intersubjective. It takes into account that the free actualization of the personality of one individual depends on the actualization of freedom for all.

In another respect Hegel is right. Practical discourse does disengage problematic actions and norms from the substantive ethics (*Sittlichkeit*) of their lived contexts, subjecting them to hypothetical reasoning without regard to existing motives and institutions. This causes norms to become removed from the world (*entweltlicht*)—an unavoidable step in the process of justification but also one for which discourse ethics might consider making amends. For unless discourse ethics is undergirded by the thrust of motives and by socially accepted institutions, the moral insights it offers remain ineffective in practice. Insights, Hegel rightly demands, should be transformable into the concrete duties of everyday life. This much is true: any universalistic morality is dependent upon a form of life that *meets it halfway*. There has to be a modicum of congruence between morality and the practices of socialization and education. The latter must promote the requisite internalization of superego controls and the abstractness of ego identities. In addition, there must be a modicum of fit between morality and socio-political institutions. Not just any institutions will do. Morality thrives only in an environment in which postconventional ideas about law and morality have already been institutionalized to a certain extent. *postconventional = reflective, non-intuitive*

Moral universalism is a *historical result*. It arose, with Rousseau and Kant, in the midst of a specific society that possessed corresponding features. The last two or three centuries have witnessed the emergence, after a long seesawing struggle, of a *directed* trend toward the realization of basic rights. This process has led to, shall we cautiously say, a less and less selective reading and utilization of the universalistic meaning that fundamental-rights norms have; it testifies to the "existence of reason," if only in bits and pieces. Without these fragmentary realizations, the moral intuitions that discourse ethics conceptualizes would never have proliferated the way they did. To be sure, the gradual embodiment of moral principles in concrete forms of life is not something that can safely be left to Hegel's absolute spirit. Rather, it is chiefly a function of collective efforts and sacrifices made by sociopolitical movements. Philosophy would do well to avoid haughtily dismissing these movements and the larger historical dimension from which they spring.

4   On the Subject of "Virtue and the Way of the World"

Neither Kantian ethics nor discourse ethics exposes itself to the charge of abetting, let alone justifying, totalitarian ways of doing things. This charge has recently been taken up by neo-conservatives. The maxim that the end justifies the means is utterly incompatible with both the letter and the spirit of moral universalism, even when it is a question of politically implementing universalistic legal and constitutional principles. A problematic role is played in this connection by certain notions held by philosophers of history, Marxists, and others. Realizing that the political practice of their chosen macrosubject of society is sputtering, if not paralyzed, they delegate revolutionary action to an avant-garde with proxy functions. The error of this view is to conceive of society as a subject writ large and then to pretend that the actions of the avant-garde need not be held any more accountable than those of the higher-level subject of history. In contrast to any philosophy of history, the intersubjectivist approach of discourse ethics breaks with the premises of the philosophy of consciousness. The only higher-level intersubjectivity it acknowledges is that of public spheres.

Hegel rightly sets off action *under* moral laws from political practice that aims to bring about, or at least to promote, the institutional prerequisites for general participation in moral reasoning of a posttraditional type. Can the realization of reason in history be a meaningful objective of intentional action? As I argued earlier, the discursive justification of norms is no guarantee of the actualization of moral insight. This problem, the disjunction between judgment and action on the output side, to use computer jargon, has its counterpart on the input side: discourse cannot by itself insure that the conditions necessary for the actual participation of all concerned are met. Often lacking are crucial institutions that would faciliate discursive decision making. Often lacking are crucial socialization processes, so that the dispositions and abilities necessary for taking part in moral argumentation cannot be learned. Even more frequent is the case where material living conditions and social structures are such that moral-practical implications spring immediately to the eye and moral questions are answered, without further reflection, by the bare facts of poverty, abuse, and degradation. Wherever this is the case, wherever existing conditions make a mockery of the demands of universalist morality, moral issues turn into issues of political ethics. How can a political practice designed to realize the conditions necessary for a dignified human existence be morally justified?[21] The kind of politics at issue is one that aims at changing a form of life from moral points of view, though it is not reformist and therefore cannot operate in accordance with existing laws and institutions. The issue of revolutionary morality (which incidentally has never been satisfactorily discussed by Marxists, Eastern or Western) is fortunately not an urgent one in our type of society. Not so moot are cognate issues like civil disobedience, which I have discussed elsewhere.[22]

III

In sum, I argue that Hegel's objections apply less to the reformulation of Kantian ethics itself than to a number of resulting problems that discourse ethics cannot be expected to resolve with a single stroke. Any ethics that is at once deontological, cognitivist, formalist, and universalist ends up with a relatively narrow conception of morality that is uncompromisingly abstract. This raises the problem of whether issues of justice can be isolated from particular contexts of the good life. This problem, I believe, can be solved. But a second difficulty makes its appearance, namely whether practical reason may be forced to abdicate in favor of a faculty of judgment when it comes to applying justified norms to specific cases. Discourse ethics, I think, can handle this difficulty too. A third problem is whether it is reasonable to hope that the insights of a universalist morality are susceptible to translation into practice. Surely the incidence of such a morality is contingent upon a complementary form of life. This by no means exhausts the list of consequent problems. I mention only one more: How can political action be morally justified when the social conditions in which practical discourses can be carried on and moral insight can be generated and transformed do not exist but have to be created? I have so far not addressed two other problems that flow from the self-limitation of every nonmetaphysical point of view.

Discourse ethics does not see fit to resort to an objective teleology, least of all to a countervailing force that tries to negate dialectically the irreversible succession of historical events—as was the case, for instance, with the redeeming judgment of the Christian God on the last day. But how can we live up to the principle of discourse ethics, which postulates the consent of *all*, if we cannot make restitution for the injustice and pain suffered by previous generations or if we cannot at least promise an equivalent to the day of judgment and its power of redemption? Is it not obscene for present-day beneficiaries of past injustices to expect the posthumous consent of slain and degraded victims to norms that appear justified to us in light of our own expectations regarding the future?[23] It is just as difficult to answer the basic objection of ecological ethics:

How does discourse ethics, which is limited to subjects capable of speech and action, respond to the fact that mute creatures are also vulnerable? Compassion for tortured animals and the pain caused by the destruction of biotopes are surely manifestations of moral intuitions that cannot be fully satisfied by the collective narcissism of what in the final analysis is an anthropocentric way of looking at things.

At this point I want to draw only one conclusion from these skeptical considerations. Since the concept of morality is limited, the self-perception of moral theory should be correspondingly modest. It is incumbent on moral theory to explain and ground the moral point of view. What moral *theory* can do and should be trusted to do is to clarify the universal core of our moral intuitions and thereby to refute value skepticism. What it cannot do is make any kind of substantive contribution. By singling out a procedure of decision making, it seeks to make room for those involved, who must then find answers on their own to the moral-practical issues that come at them, or are imposed upon them, with objective historical force. Moral philosophy does not have privileged access to particular moral truths. In view of the four big moral-political liabilities of our time—hunger and poverty in the third world, torture and continuous violations of human dignity in autocratic regimes, increasing unemployment and disparities of social wealth in Western industrial nations, and finally the self-destructive risks of the nuclear arms race—my modest opinion about what philosophy can and cannot accomplish may come as a disappointment. Be that as it may, philosophy cannot absolve anyone of moral responsibility. And that includes philosophers, for like everyone else, they face moral-practical issues of great complexity, and the first thing they might profitably do is to get a clearer view of the situation they find themselves in. The historical and social sciences can be of greater help in this endeavor than philosophy. On this note I want to end with a quote from Max Horkheimer from the year 1933: "What is needed to get beyond the utopian character of Kant's idea of a perfect constitution of humankind, is a materialist theory of society."[24]

Notes

1. See the essays by K.-O. Apel in K.-O. Apel, D. Böhler, and G. Kadelbach, eds., *Praktische Philosophie/Ethik* (Frankfurt, 1984), and J. Habermas, "Discourse Ethics," in this volume.

2. "But the content of the maxim remains what it is, a specification or singularity, and the universality conferred on it by its reception into the form is thus a merely analytic unity. And when the unity conferred on it is expressed in a sentence purely as it is, that sentence is analytic and tautological." G. W. F. Hegel, *Natural Law*, trans. T. M. Knox (Philadelphia: University of Pennsylvania Press, 1975), p. 76. The same formalism manifests itself in the fact that any maxim at all can take the form of a universal law. "There is nothing whatever which cannot in this way be made into a moral law." Hegel, *Natural Law*, p. 77.

3. "The moral consciousness as the simple knowing and willing of pure duty is . . . brought into relation with the object which stands in contrast to its simplicity, into relation with the actuality of the complex case, and thereby has a complex moral relationship with it. . . . As regards the many duties, the moral consciousness heeds only the pure duty in them; the many duties qua manifold are specific and therefore as such have nothing sacred about them for the moral consciousness." G. W. F. Hegel, *Phenomenology of Spirit*, trans. A. V. Miller (Oxford: Oxford University Press, 1977), pp. 369–370. The counterpart to abstracting from the particular is hypostatizing the particular, for it becomes unrecognizable in the form of the universal: "By confusing absolute form with conditioned matter, the absoluteness of the form is imperceptibly smuggled into the unreal and conditioned character of the content; and in this perversion and trickery lies the nerve of pure reason's practical legislation." *Natural Law*, p. 79.

4. "The moral consciousness . . . learns from experience that Nature is not concerned with giving it a sense of the unity of its reality with that of Nature. . . . The nonmoral consciousness . . . finds, perhaps by chance, its realization where the moral consciousness sees only an occasion for acting, but does not see itself obtaining, through its action, the happiness of performance and the enjoyment of achievement. Therefore it finds rather cause for complaint about such a state of incompatibility between itself and existence, and about the injustice which restricts it to having its object merely as pure duty, but refuses to let it see the object and itself realized." *Phenomenology*, p. 366.

5. In the *Phenomenology of Spirit* Hegel devotes a famous section entitled "Virtue and the Way of the World" to a discussion of Jacobin moral zeal (*Gesinnungsterror*). In it he shows how morality can be turned into a means to bring "the good into actual existence by the sacrifice of individuality." P. 233.

6. K. H. Ilting seems to have missed the fact that the notion of what can be consented to merely operationalizes what he himself calls the "imposability" of norms. Only those norms are imposable for which a discursive agreement among those concerned can be reached. See K. H. Ilting, "Der Geltungsgrund moralischer Normen," in W. Kuhlmann and D. Böhler, eds., *Kommunikation und Reflexion* (Frankfurt, 1982), pp. 629ff.

7. The concept of the justification of norms must not be too strong, otherwise the conclusion that justified norms must have the assent of all affected will already be contained in the premise. I committed such a *petitio principii* in the essay on "Discourse Ethics" cited in note 1 above. [Habermas is referring here to the first edition of *Moralbewusstsein und kommunikatives Handeln*. In the second edition, on which this

translation was based, the appropriate changes were made. They occur at the bottom of p. 92 of this volume.—Trans.]

8. "The idea of the original position is to set up a fair procedure so that any principles agreed to will be just." J. Rawls, *A Theory of Justice* (Cambridge, Mass., 1971), p. 136.

9. G. H. Mead, *Mind, Self and Society* (Chicago: Chicago University Press, 1934), "Fragments on Ethics," pp. 379–389. The concept of ideal role taking also underlies Kohlberg's theory of moral development. Also see H. Joas, *G. H. Mead: A Contemporary Re-examination of His Thought* (Cambridge, Mass., 1985), chapter 6, pp. 121ff.

10. Practical discourse can fulfill functions other than critical ones only when the subject matter to be regulated touches on generalizable interests. Whenever exclusively particular interests are at stake, practical decision making necessarily takes the form of compromise. See J. Habermas, *Legitimation Problems in Late Capitalism* (Boston, 1975), pp. 111ff.

11. J. Habermas, *The Theory of Communicative Action*, vol. 2, *Lifeworld and System* (Boston, 1987), pp. 58ff.

12. Compare my critique of Arnold Gehlen: "The profound vulnerability that makes necessary an ethical regulation of behavior as its counterpoise is rooted, not in the biological weaknesses of humans, not in the newborn infant's lack of organic faculties and not in the risks of a disproportionately long rearing period, but in the cultural systems that are constructed as compensation. The fundamental problem of ethics is guaranteeing mutual consideration and respect in a way that is effective in actual conduct. That is the core of truth in any ethics of compassion." J. Habermas, "Imitation Substantiality," in J. Habermas, *Philosophical-Political Profiles* (Cambridge, Mass., 1983), p. 120.

13. W. Frankena, *Ethics* (Englewood Cliffs, N.J., 1973), pp. 45ff.

14. This is an old topic of action theory. See A. Gouldner, "The Norm of Reciprocity," *American Sociological Review* 25 (1960): 161–178.

15. Michael Sandel has justly criticized Rawls for saddling his construct of an original position with the atomistic legacy of contract theory. Rawls envisions isolated, independent individuals who, prior to any sociation, possess the ability to pursue their interests rationally and to posit their objectives monologically. Accordingly, Rawls views the basic covenant not so much in terms of an agreement based on argumentation as in terms of an act of free will. His vision of a just society boils down to a solution of the Kantian problem of how the individual will can be free in the presence of other individual wills. Sandel's own anti-individualist conception is not without problems either, in that it further deepens the separation between an ethics of duty and an ethics of the good. Over against Rawls's presocial individual, he posits an individual who is the product of his community; over against the rational covenant of autonomous individuals, he posits a reflective awareness of prior social bonds; over against Rawls's idea of equal rights, he posits the ideal of mutual solidarity; over against equal respect for the dignity of the individual, he posits the advancement of the common good. With these traditional juxtapositions Sandel blocks the way to an intersubjectivist extension of Rawls's ethics of justice. He roundly rejects the deontological approach and instead returns to a teleological conception that presupposes an objective notion of community. "For a society to be a community in the strong sense, community must be constitutive of the shared self-understandings of the participants and embodied in their institutional arrangements, not simply an attribute of certain of the participants'

plans of life." M. J. Sandel, *Liberalism and the Limits of Justice* (Cambridge, 1982), p. 173. Clearly, totalitarian (i.e., forcibly integrated) societies do not fit this description, which is why Sandel would have to explicate carefully the normative content of such key notions as community, embodied, and shared self-understanding. He does not do so. If he did, he would realize just how onerous the burden of proof is that neo-Aristotelian approaches must bear, as in the case of A. MacIntyre in *After Virtue*, (London, 1981). They must demonstrate how an objective moral order can be grounded without recourse to metaphysical premises.

16. K.-O. Apel, "Kant, Hegel und das aktuelle Problem der normativen Grundlagen von Moral und Recht," in D. Henrich, ed., *Kant oder Hegel* (Stuttgart, 1983), pp. 597ff.

17. G. Patzig, "Der Kategorische Imperativ in der Ethikdiskussion der Gegenwart," in G. Patzig, *Tatsachen, Normen, Sätze* (Stuttgart, 1980), pp. 155ff.

18. The controversial subjects Kant focused upon, the stratum-specific "maxims of action" in early bourgeois society, were not produced by law-giving reason but simply taken up by law-testing reason as empirical givens. Thus Hegel's attack on Kant's deposit example (*Critique of Practical Reason*, section 4, "Remark") becomes groundless.

19. Conversely, one might critically ask what evidence there is for the suspicion that universal and particular are always *inextricably* interlocked. We saw earlier that practical discourses are not only embedded in complexes of action but also represent, at a higher plane of reflection, continuations of action oriented toward reaching understanding. Both have the same structural properties. But in the case of communicative action there is no need to extend the presuppositions about symmetry and reciprocity to actors *not* belonging to the particular collectivity or lifeworld. By contrast, this extension into universality does become necessary, indeed forced, when argumentation is at issue. It is no wonder that ethical positions starting from the ethics (*Sittlichkeit*) of such concrete forms of life as the polis, the state, or a religious community have trouble generating a universal principle of justice. This problem is less troublesome for discourse ethics, for the latter presumes to justify the universal validity of its moral principle in terms of the normative content of communicative presuppositions of *argumentation* as such.

20. E. Vollrath, *Die Rekonstruktion der politischen Urteilskraft* (Stuttgart, 1977).

21. Compare J. Habermas, *Theory and Practice*, trans. J. Viertel (Boston, 1973), pp. 32ff.

22. J. Habermas, *Die neue Unübersichtlichkeit* (Frankfurt, 1985), and *The New Conservatism*, trans. Shierry Weber Nicholsen (Cambridge, Mass., 1989). The only comment I want to make on this subject here is that problems of this kind do not lie on the same plane of complexity as the objections discussed earlier. First, the relation of morality, law, and politics has to be clarified. While these universes of discourse may overlap, they are by no means identical. In terms of justification, posttraditional ideas about law and morality are structurally similar. At the heart of modern legal systems are basic moral norms which have attained the force of law. On the other hand, law differs from morality, *inter alia*, in that the target group of a law—those who are expected to comply with a legal norm—are relieved of the burdens of justifying, applying, and implementing it. These chores are left to public bodies. Politics too has an intimate relation to morality and law. Basic political issues are moral issues. And exercising political power is tantamount to making legally binding decisions. Also, the legal system is for its part tied up with politics via the legislative process. As far as the field of public will formation is concerned, the main thrust of politics is to pursue collective

ends in an agreed-upon framework of rules rather than to redefine this framework of law and morality.

23. See H. Peukert, *Science, Action, and Fundamental Theology* (Cambridge, Mass., 1984), and C. Lenhardt, "Anamnestic Solidarity," *Telos*, no. 25, 1975.

24. M. Horkheimer, "Materialismus und Moral," *Zeitschrift für Sozialforschung* 2 (1933): 175. English translation, "Materialism and Morality," *Telos*, no. 69 (1986): 85–118.

Index

Studies in Contemporary German Social Thought
Thomas McCarthy, General Editor

Joachim Ritter, *Hegel and the French Revolution: Essays on the* Philosophy of Right

Alfred Schmidt, *History and Structure: An Essay on Hegelian-Marxist and Structuralist Theories of History*

Dennis Schmidt, *The Ubiquity of the Finite: Hegel, Heidegger, and the Entitlements of Philosophy*

Carl Schmitt, *The Crisis of Parliamentary Democracy*

Carl Schmitt, *Political Romanticism*

Carl Schmitt, *Political Theology: Four Chapters on the Concept of Sovereignty*

Gary Smith, editor, *On Walter Benjamin: Critical Essays and Recollections*

Michael Theunissen, *The Other: Studies in the Social Ontology of Husserl, Heidegger, Sartre, and Buber*

Ernst Tugendhat, *Self-Consciousness and Self-Determination*

Mark Warren, *Nietzsche and Political Thought*

Thomas E. Wren, editor, *The Moral Domain: Essays in the Ongoing Discussion between Philosophy and the Social Sciences*